# TAKING SOAPS SERIOUSLY

# TAKING SOAPS SERIOUSLY:

## The World
## of
## *GUIDING LIGHT*

*by*
### Michael James Intintoli

## PRAEGER SPECIAL STUDIES • PRAEGER SCIENTIFIC

New York • Philadelphia • Eastbourne, UK
Toronto • Hong Kong • Tokyo • Sydney

**Library of Congress Cataloging in Publication Data**

Intintoli, Michael James.
    Taking soaps seriously.

    Bibliography: p.
    Includes index.
    1. Guiding light (Television program) I. Title.
PN1992.77.G83I57          1984          791.45'72          83-27232
ISBN 0-03-070554-1 (alk. paper)

Published in 1984 by Praeger Publishers
CBS Educational and Professional Publishing
a Division of CBS Inc.
521 Fifth Avenue, New York, NY 10175 USA

© 1984 by Praeger Publishers

456789 052 987654321

Printed in the United States of America
on acid-free paper

# Acknowledgments

The cooperation and work of many people made this book possible. I would like to thank the people I learned from at Edge of Night, Guiding Light, CBS and ABC. The members of my Ph.D. committee, Jay Ruby, Richard Chalfen and Dan Schiller contributed in many ways, as did my colleagues at Burlington County College. The sabbatical I received from the college enabled me to carry out the initial research. Several individuals were very helpful and I want to thank them for their assistance: Charles Perrone, Judy Poinsett, Alana Karnarek, Holli Weller, Tim Tracz, Glenn Malsbury, and Frank Nappo. My wife Joann and son Christian were supportive of the work, reminded me me of other worlds and were patient with the conceits this kind of work fosters.

Finally, I would like to recognize my debt to the work of the late Philip Elliot and have this book seen as a part of an on-going conversation over how and why we tell ourselves the stories that we do.

# Contents

Acknowledgments      v

**1**
TAKING SOAP OPERA SERIOUSLY: The World of Guiding Light      1

**2**
CONSTRUCTING AN UNDERSTANDING      20

**3**
THE WORLD THROUGH A SOAP FRAME:
Guiding Light as a Symbolic Community      34

**4**
THE ECONOMIC CONTEXT      62

**5**
SOAP STORYTELLING AS CORPORATE ENTERPRISE      82

**6**
SOAP AS INDUSTRIALIZED CULTURAL PRODUCTION:
Authority and Work      121

**7**
CONVENTIONS FOR EXPRESSION AND EXPERIENCE:
Visual, Audio, and Musical      158

**8**
THE AUDIENCE AS VIEWER, STATISTIC, AND SOCIAL BEING:
Letters and Ratings      181

**9**
GUIDING LIGHT AS A SOCIALLY CONSTRUCTED REALITY      226

Notes      237

References      240

Index      249

About the Author      261

# TAKING SOAPS
# SERIOUSLY

# 1

# Taking Soap Opera Seriously: The World of *Guiding Light*

The . . . true human genius and necessity is
to build up models of reality by the agency
of differing types of symbols--verbal, written, mathematical, gestural, kinesthetic--and
by differing symbolic forms--art, science,
journalism, ideology, ordinary speech, religion, mythology. . . . In trying to understand the meanings persons place on experience, then, it is necessary to work through a
theory of fictions: a theory explaining how
these forms operate, the semantic devices
they employ, the meanings they sustain, the
particular glow they cast over experience.
  This is a processs of making large claims
from small matters: studying particular
rituals, poems, plays, conversations, songs,
dances, theories, and myths and generally
reaching out to the full relations within a
culture or a total way of life. For the student of communication, other matters press
in: how do changes in forms of communication
technology affect the constructions placed on
experience? How does the technology change
the forms of community in which the experience is apprehended and expressed? What
under the force of history, technology and
society, is thought about, thought with, and
to whom is it expressed. (Carey 1975:190)
[Emphasis mine]


SOAP OPERA AND SOCIETY

This study explores how and why the soap opera Guiding Light
provides its particular potential for experience. I studied
the production process for the program to determine the actual

1

practices, conventions, and legitimations employed by people making them. In abstract terms, my aim was to explore the relationship between expressive mediated culture and society. In more concrete terms, I wanted to discover how a soap opera reflects the society and the process that generates it.

Conventionally, scholars in both the social sciences and humanities, as well as "culture"[1] critics tend to focus on the symbolic form--a novel or a television program--as a finished product and to analyze its form and content. As a result, a "text" is studied independently of its context of production and use. Inferences are then made about cultural themes or trends, the social sources of such content, and/or the impact of the content. I argue instead that the connections between society and symbolic forms as sources of potential experience can be best identified empirically through a study of the production process in context. I look at the context of production and examine the product as part of an event. As Raymond Williams says, "we have to break from the notion of isolating the object and then discovering its components. On the contrary, we have to discover the nature of a practice and then its conditions" (1973:16). Given the objective of determining the actual processes involved, I primarily employed participant observation to construct this account.

This study poses and answers the following questions:

1. What is the nature of the symbolic world in soap[2] performances generated by the production process?
2. How and why are organizationally controlled resources made available for the production and distribution of soap operas?
3. How do the goals of organizations affect the kinds of performances (soaps) made available, particularly in terms of story creation, selection, and realization?
4. How is the work process organized, hierarchically and as a form of collective action involving an elaborate division of labor?
5. How do people in various roles, particularly producers, directors, and actors, adapt to the pressures, risks, and conflicts between personal or occupational goals or skills and the requirements of work on a soap?
6. What are the major visual, audio, and musical conventions that are embodied in soaps that structure and influence the potential experience of performances?
7. How have technological developments affected or been incorporated into the work process?

8. How do people who work in soap production perceive the viewing audience, and how do they arrive at those perceptions? What are the patterns of interaction between the audience and the producers?

The specific questions and overall study take soap opera seriously. I see televised soap operas as one aspect of the transformation in social conditions and human experience that has been part of the spread of urban-industrial society following the development of mass media and popular culture. We typically distinguish popular or mass culture from elite, folk, or traditional expressive culture or distinguish electronic culture from print and oral cultures. From another perspective, there has been a change from ceremony and ritual to performances and fictions as representations of popular experience (Turner 1977a; Chaney 1979). Major contemporary examples of this development are televised dramatic performances.

In most parts of the world, since the spread of television, there has been a scale and intensity of dramatic performance which is without precedent in the history of human culture.
Many, though not all, societies have a long history of dramatic performances of some kind; but characteristically, in most societies, it has been occasional or seasonal. . . . It is clearly one of the unique characteristics of advanced industrial societies that drama as an experience is not an intrinsic part of everyday life, at a quantitative level which is so very much greater than precedent as to seem a fundamental qualitative change . . . it is clear that watching dramatic simulation is now an essential part of our modern cultural pattern. (Williams 1975:59)

The creation of the potential for experience through the deliberate restoration or simulation of behavior in myriad forms appears to be one of the characteristics of modernity (MacCannell 1976; Schechner 1981). Victor Turner notes the change from ritual to performance and notes "its conversion into a multiplicity of performative arts gives us a hall of mirrors, each reflecting the reflections of the others" as they systematically magnify and distort reality (1977b:73). The extent of this "hall of mirrors" is enlarged and its nature changed and complicated by the proliferation of media constructing and reflecting reality.

The growth in the number of sources of mediated performance or expressive culture and information has created a complex situation. This is particularly true because media organizations draw upon the constructions of other media and organizations. The creation, use, and reuse of mediated constructions and resources suggest a social process underlying the realities constructed or reflected. This social process has been labelled a "media culture" (Elliott 1972; Chaney 1972) or the product of Enzensberger's "consciousness industry" (1979).

The existence and pervasiveness of so many mediated performances, images, and information make separating mediated from nonmediated experience in our continuing personal and social constructions of reality and behavior extremely problematic. Each draws from the other. With so many sources of experience, identifying the origins of our conceptions of self and, particularly, our conceptions of society "out there" becomes exceptionally difficult.

Television, as a source of mediated experience, has received the most attention, both popular and academic. As with other areas of study of mass communication and popular culture--which I will refer to as mediated communication or mediated expressive culture--much more attention, by far, has been paid to television's content and purported effects than has been paid to the forces that shape television programming.

[But] as more and more people look to television for information and entertainment, it becomes increasingly important to ask not only what effect does it have on them, what do they make of it, what do they get out of it; but also how is it that these are the programs made available, how is the material selected and created . . . ? (Elliott 1972:6)

In the case of media content, we conventionally tend to make a distinction between fictional and nonfictional accounts or constructions. In the case of a number of media, particularly television, our culture has taught us to identify news or documentaries as informative, more or less truthful accounts reflecting reality. These are distinguished from a range of fictional (created) genres such as westerns, detective stories, situation comedies, and soap operas. Both types of programming have been the focus of an on-going concern about their effects, but much more attention has been given to fictional programming. This attention is often expressed in terms of its potentially harmful consequences for children or society in general, particularly because of a reliance upon violence and sex in such programming.

Network television is dominated by entertainment programming. Bogart surveyed network television programming for the 1976-77 season and determined that "86% of the network programs were devoted to fictional drama of one kind or another" (1980:209). Only 5% was devoted to nonfiction programming. Ironically, fictional drama has received the least attention in terms of how such programming is produced, while it has also occasioned the most alarm.

Over the last decade, a number of production studies have appeared, but the number of empirical studies is still limited and largely concentrated on nonfictional programming.[3]

Although the last five or six years have seen a revival of interest in questions of production among researchers on both sides of the Atlantic, most of the resulting studies have concentrated on actuality television—on news, current affairs and documentaries. This work is certainly overdue and has added considerably to our knowledge, but unfortunately it has not so far been matched by a comparable series of studies of fiction and entertainment production. <u>Paradoxically, then, we know the least about the production of the very programs that are the most popular with the viewers.</u> (Murdock and Halloran 1979:274) [Emphasis mine]

I have chosen to study soap opera as a form of fictional programming. The mere mention of soap operas tends to elicit strong opinions. For some people they are the epitome of television's penchant for the unrealistic and fantastic, a waste of time, a sop for the lonely and bored housewife, a manipulative commercial vehicle to sell soap. With the recent increase in younger viewers, familiar warnings are issued about their impact on youngsters who cannot separate the programming from reality. For others, soaps are engaging dramatic fare, programming that deals with real life problems in a way that prime-time television does not, a web of social relationships and significance they participate in, an exciting, and ultimately pleasurable, experience that complements or compensates for the experience of other portions of the day.

That people react strongly to soaps is an indication of their seriousness. The traditional justification for studying forms of mediated expressive culture, such as a soap, is that they are extremely popular. Their longevity, the size and demographic characteristics of the audiences they reach, and their economic importance for the networks and advertisers can all be cited to justify their study. Approximately 50 million women a week watch soaps, with approximately one-quarter of all women in America between the ages of 18 and 49 watching on any one day. The networks make about 1.5 billion dollars a year on soaps (Steinberg 1980; Brown 1982a). Yet, despite their evident significance, there are no in-depth academic studies of the production of an afternoon television serial.[4]

In addition to these more traditional and apparent economic and social considerations (and justifications), the issue of the construction of fictions that are taken as realistic and that resonate with conceptions of everyday reality is extremely important. News, textbooks, and documentaries all play a part in our conceptions (constructions) of what society is like or should be like. Along with a range of fictions or performances in various mediated or nonmediated forms, soaps also play a role in the development of our notions of what society "out there" is like, should be like, or could be like. The experience and participation in the could be, or "as if," when we are engaged by a performance have implications for other orientations, or other frames for experience.

One way of understanding what is going on in popular fiction is to look at different types of story-telling as different ways of thinking about what the collectivity we share is. In other words, what are the implications of discussing social experience for the nature of the experience that is being discussed, the reflexivity of self-consciousness. (Chaney 1979:29)

The characterizations of society that people develop, the distinctions they make between private and public realms, and the conceptions they have of what the collectivity we all share is like or should be like derive from the basic capacities and qualities of human consciousness. Similarly, the quest to document (capture) behavior in ethnographic form itself is related to the production of fictions and theater, and to the symbolic and reflexive character of human consciousness (Ruby 1982). Both this ethnographic account and

Guiding Light "show society in process." Both present and explain the character of experience, each for a time claiming to convey what is really important. Guiding Light, of course, does not overtly and consistently claim such a stance. The common general argument that the program is about everyday life and that it reflects society supports this contention. Guiding Light and this account are both reflections of and reflections on social process.

It is only logical to argue that an ethnography, as a symbolic form, itself can be and should be understood and assessed as a product of social practice. While taking different stances, both soaps and ethnographies provide accounts of society in process, and thus provide occasion for forms of communal self-reflection (Turner 1977a; Chaney 1979).

Placing soaps and enthnographic accounts in the same frame may be disturbing to some readers. While anthropological ethnographic accounts are serious and privileged as forms of knowledge and experience, soaps are not. But lumping them together forces us to recognize that the social conditions and processes of making sense of the world, and of constructing the world, apply to both soaps and ethnographic accounts.

This ethnography is interpretive in that it deals with meaning in relation to social conditions, empirical in that it is rooted in self-conscious observation of specific practices, and critical in its description and analysis of communicative and sociocultural processes (Bernstein 1978). It is critical in two interrelated ways: it challenges our conventional frames for experience by focusing on the socially constitutive nature of expression and experience; it lays bare dynamics and relationships that may have been unrecognized and thereby contributes to the formation of practical options for people. Put differently, this ethnography plays a role in our social self-understanding through its exploration of how and why we tell ourselves the stories that we do.

SOAP OPERA AS A CONSTRUCTED REALITY

In the development of the social scientific study of the media, neither "administrative" research nor the critical tradition of the Frankfurt school paid much attention to the way cultural products are actually created. Research focused on the content of the cultural product, on its homologous connection to broadly characterized political and social forces or on the response to the product among audiences. But what concrete social structures shaped the product itself?

This question has come to be a centre of
research interest in the sociology of culture
in the past decade. (Curran and Schudson
1982:1)

This study is part of an emerging tradition of production studies that focus precisely on how the product is
shaped. I approach the soap opera as part of a communicative
process that is both socially structured and culturally patterned. I have drawn upon two major research traditions.
One is American and anthropological, the other British and
part of what has been termed "cultural studies" (Carey 1975;
Hall 1981).

One important body of recent anthropological research
has its foundation in the effort to broaden the anthropological study of communication. Research from the perspectives
of sociolinguistics and "sociovidistics"[5] has sought to
explore communication events and symbolic forms as socially
structured and culturally patterned. This ethnography follows in that quest.

A major foundation for my research is the work of Dell
Hymes, Sol Worth, and Richard Chalfen. Hymes, a linguist
interested primarily in speech, has argued for the compila-
tion of ethnographies of speaking (1964) and more recently
has broadened his conception to include the study of all
modes, media, and codes (1974). Sol Worth (1966) and Richard
Chalfen have examined visual communication as a culturally
patterned and socially structured activity, applying Hymes's
suggestions to different codes and contexts. Worth's major
empirical study, written with John Adair, explored the cultural patterning of film communication among the Navajo after
they had introduced film media to the Navajo (1972). Chalfen
has explored visual communication by nonprofessionals, again
approaching communication as a socially structured and culturally patterned activity or process. In one study, he
observed how teenagers differing in sex, race, and class went
about making first films. He noted how the films differed as
products and, to a lesser degree, observed the films as part
of exhibition events (1974). One important result has been
the development of a sociovidistic framework for the study of
visual communication. This study is a further development of
the perspective and in Chalfen's language can be considered
"an ethnography of mass communication."

Another important source and resource is British cultural studies. A number of scholars, including Raymond Williams (1961, 1974), David Chaney (1972, 1979), Phillip Elliott (1972, 1979, 1982) and Stuart Hall (1981), have explored

the relationships between expressive forms and social order. They begin from the premise that reality and meaning are socially created. On the one hand, they explore the character of the experience various symbolic forms make possible, often by intensively and extensively examining particular products or cultural artifacts, as Williams calls them, much as an art critic or historian might do, whether the product be a ballet, a comic strip, a film, or a classroom lecture. On the other hand, they view the particular product as part of an event or process and relate the character of the experience made possible or embodied in the form to the conditions and practices that generated it and to the conventions relied upon for both construction and interpretation.

A major concern is that the study of symbolic forms not be limited to elite notions of what is valuable or creative, nor should such a study be limited to the theoretical and methodological approaches built upon those premises. In Williams's view, art entails the creative description and interpretation of experience in the context of changing organizational patterns of society, thus rendering the patterns of personal experience significant. Given that all reality is a creative and social construction, and that the meanings of art are intimately associated with the meanings of other domains of experience, the study of communicative behavior is broadened to include all forms of discourse, whether conversational or mediated, mass produced or specialized, formal or informal, elite or popular (1961, 1974).

Chaney suggests, and I agree, that we treat popular culture and expressive culture seriously as a way of exploring social consciousness (1979). Clear-cut distinctions between fiction and nonfictions, serious and popular, superior and inferior, reflect an epistemological and social stance that precludes seeing all experience of reality as a construction or fiction, related to social negotiation, and embedded in a number of contexts. Instead of accepting a priori distinctions between fiction versus fact, popular and elite, serious and worthwhile versus frivolous and inferior (and prejudging the worth of the audience through those categorizations), we can view symbolic forms as realized in and through various social practices and relationships, and as having implications for other realms of experience and activity. Chaney emphasizes the "constitutive social relations of production" (1979) for the understanding of expressive or popular culture. His insights and suggestions are an important basis for this ethnography.

The growing importance of production studies and the focus on symbolic forms are reactions to the many limitations of previous mass communication research. James Carey provides a useful overview of conventional American and European research:

American studies are grounded in a transmission or transportation view of communication. They view communication, therefore, as a process of transmitting messages at a distance for the purpose of control. The archetypal case of communication, then, is persuasion, attitude change, behavior modification, socialization through the transmission of information, influence or conditioning. . . . By contrast, the preponderant view of communication in European studies is a ritual view of communication: communication is viewed as a process through which a shared culture is created, magnified and transformed. The archetypal case of communication is ritual and mythology, for those who come to the problem from anthropology; art and literature, for those who come at the problem from literary criticism and history. (Carey 1975:177)

The major American research tradition can be labelled scientistic or positivistic, with all the pejorative connotations those terms imply. The dominant European tradition, conversely, has primarily concerned itself with complex and elite systems of thought and experience from the standpoint of the sociology of knowledge and aesthetic inquiry, and often in less than empirically satisfying ways (Merton 1968).

The major corpus of the American research tradition makes use of a stimulus-response (S-R) model of communication as part of the dominant paradigm and has been labelled "administrative research" (Gitlin 1981; Curran and Schudson 1982; Thomas 1982). Halloran characterizes the research as "having a mainly value-free, positivistic, empiricist, behavioristic, psychological emphasis" (1981:23).

As a consequence, many of the difficult questions never get asked: questions about the nature of media as institutions as part of a larger sociocultural context, as agencies of socialization that define social reality, legitimate social arrangements and changes and that set the public agenda (Gitlin 1981; Halloran 1981).

By its methodology, media sociology has highlighted the recalcitrance of audiences, their

resistance to media generated images, and not
their dependency, their acquiesence, their
gullibility. It has looked to "effects" of
broadcast programming in a specifically behaviorist fashion, defining "effects" so narrowly, microscopically as to make it very likely
that survey studies could show only slight effects. . . . It has tended to seek "hard
data," often enough with results so mixed as
to satisfy anyone and no one, when it might
have more fruitfully sought hard questions.
By studying only the "effects" that could be
measured" experimentally or in surveys, it has
put the methodological cart ahead of the theoretical horse. (Gitlin 1981: 73-74)

The European tradition, however, while asking hard questions, has often done so in less than empirically adequate
ways. Instead of focusing on opinion and effects, the European tradition has focused on knowledge, its production by
experts, and what happens to knowledge and elite culture when
it is reshaped and largely distorted as part of popular culture. The Frankfurt school, for example, has discussed popular culture and mass communication often critically, but from
an elitist bias and with little empirical support to its
assertions (Gans 1974).

The dominant view in European studies is a ritual view,
in which "communication is viewed as a process through which
a shared culture is created, magnified and transformed" (Carey
1975:177). Much of the research, however, is limited by its
reliance on what might be termed literary or formal approaches. The productive emphasis on myth, ritual, and social experience has been undercut by an emphasis on texts or codes as
a result of the influence of structuralism and semiotics on
European researchers and theorists.

The text, in the content analysis of tele-visual communication, is analyzed as if it exists independently of maker,
user, and analyst. The idealist emphasis is connected with
the complex associations and assumptions characteristic of
print.

The durability of the printed word seemed to
give the written tradition an independence
from any particular social or cultural locale,
any discrete age or place. Paul Ricoeur suggests that writing lends discourse a peculiar

autonomy and it is by analogy with the "autonomy of texts" that intellectuals begin to
talk of the "autonomy" of superstructures and
cultural traditions in general. In the mass
of inscriptions a world of meaning is created
which is parallel to, but nowhere wholly coin-
cident with social and cultural realities....
Because of the autonomy of texts and the much
more obvious autonomy of the entire tradition
from any particular social context, writing
and print were seen as media of transcen-
dence, a means by which individuals could
remove themselves in mind from their social
place.
This severance of superstructures, of the
world dependent upon documents, duplicable
texts, and visual representations, from infra-
structures, from the activities in which men
reproduce the material conditions of their
lives, is generally thought to be one of the
characteristic marks of modern societies.
(Leed 1980:55-56)

    Conventionally, a performance is viewed as a product or
thing that can be discussed independently of the constitutive
relationships and capacities rendering the product meaningful.
We often speak as if symbolic forms are miraculously snatched
out of the air and given concrete form by a writer. At other
times we proceed as if an analyst's reading of a performance
is in the performance and that the meaning is the real meaning.
    Typically, an analyst examines how codes and subcodes
are deployed within the text and then makes statements about
the meaning of the text in terms of the social context that
generated it or in terms of the cultural themes it reflects.

However well conceived and executed, textual
readings remain a variety of content analysis
and as such suffer from the intractable problems of inference. It is one thing to argue
that all cultural forms contain traces of the
relations of production underlying their construction, and of the structural relations
which surround them. It is quite another to
go on and argue that analysis of form can
deliver an adequate and satisfactory account

of these sets of relations and of the deter-
minations they exert on the production process. They can't. In our view, the sociology of culture and communication has been
seriously incapacitated by the tendency to
overprivilege texts as objects of analysis.
(Golding and Murdock, 1979:206-07)

For people interested in the social and cultural character of performances, structuralist interpretations are particularly unconvincing. They often seem to reflect the categories of the analyst who is eager to illustrate the universal
principles of ordering in the human mind. The categories,
however, seem more often to be in the mind of the analyst.
Even the work of Roland Barthes (1973), while critical and
insightful, suffers from this characteristic.

One final major criticism is that studies of mass communication and popular culture have generally been pursued
without an explicit or developed conception of society and
culture. Research that does not take into account social and
cultural processes, that deals solely with "communication,"
is necessarily limited and misleading. Golding and Murdock
suggest we need ethnographic studies of mass media that view
the communicative process as a social process and that consider both production and use:

In our view, the primary task of mass communications research is not to explore the meanings of media messages, but to analyze the
social processes through which they are constructed and interpreted and the contexts and
pressures that shape and constrain the constructions. To accomplish this, we certainly
require more adequate theories and conceptual
schemes, but they need to be themes of social
structure and social process, not themes of
communication. (1980:72)

Given these insights, I have focused on the actual
production process and described and analyzed the way the
performances are shaped by the production process. This
meant relating the performances and practices that generated
them to the larger society in terms of organizational relationships, market competition, the hierarchical and collective nature of the work process, and the interaction with
the audience.

FICTIONS AS FRAMES

The fundamental premise of the study is that reality is a social construction that partakes of both social conditions and patterns of meaning or symbolic codes. I find it useful to employ the concept of framing as a way of discussing how experience is organized. Frames are fictions or symbolic forms that people use to make sense of the world and organize experience.

I assume that definitions of a situation are built up in accordance with principles of organization which govern events--at least social ones--and our subjective involvement in them; frame is the word I use to refer to such of these basic elements as I am able to identify. (Goffman 1974:10-11)

Goffman argues that humans have the ability to transform, that is, shift everyday, conventional activity to another context through keying and rekeying:

[We] have the capacity and inclination to use concrete, actual activity--activity that is meaningful in its own right--as a model upon which to work transformations for fun, deception, experiment, rehearsal, dream, fantasy, ritual, demonstration, analysis, and charity. These lively shadows of events are geared into the on-going world but not in quite the close way that is true of ordinary, literal reality. (1974:560)

The concept of key refers to the process of switching or transforming what is experienced and how it is identified and interpreted. A key is a "set of conventions by which a given activity, one already meaningful in terms of some primary framework, is transformed into something patterned on this activity but seen by the participants as something quite else" (Goffman 1974:44).

While all human communicative interaction and experience involves makings or fictions, at times the boundaries between the fictions as frames become problematic and confusing. Play can stop being play, or what was considered a utilitarian, everyday article becomes a "work of art." Categories get crossed, genres become blurred (Geertz 1980); real life seems to be confused with a dramatic performance. People take a soap as real life, confuse the performers with the characters they play.

Again, while all communicative expressions are fictions, we have been led to make fundamental distinctions between fictional and nonfictional constructions or creations. Some fictions, such as televised domestic comedies or soap operas, are generally clearly identifiable as such whereas other fictions such as news and documentary films are not. They are, in fact, labelled as nonfictional in nature. As Chaney says, "They are fictions that deny their authorship."

The distinction between fiction and nonfiction provides a different grounding or persuasive basis for our assent, with implications for how we relate the experience to other frames for experience. At times, however, the boundaries are unclear and problematic. Historical fiction, docudramas, and the new journalism render the strength of our distinctions and convictions about categories suspect and, perhaps, frighteningly or amusingly arbitrary.

The strength of the common-sense distinction between fiction and nonfiction is reflected in the concentration on elitest or nonfictional knowledge in the sociology of knowledge and mass communication. As I noted earlier, European studies have traditionally dealt with specialized, intellectual, elitest knowledge whereas American research has dealt with opinions, attitudes, and so on, particularly as related to political decision making (Merton 1968). Only forms of consciousness or knowledge that are serious and real have been considered worthy of study.

Another consequence of this distinction is that content is largely considered as information, as either true, false, or harmful in its effect on behavior. This has prompted much discussion of the accuracy of news and documentaries as well as of fictional presentations. Truthfulness is assessed by the correspondence between a media event or product such as news and the real event. Fictional content is also assessed as information that is accurate or inaccurate and that is potentially effective in stimulating behavior.

The positivist bias and the desire to avoid subjectivity has had other consequences for the study of mediated communication. What people experience clearly depends upon their engagement or involvement in a performance, a point that applies to an academic analyst as well as to viewers in their home. Given this realization, we understand that the conventional reliance on coding categories of the analyst may not uncover what people actually experience (Gans 1980). Similarly, the tendency to view content as discrete bits of information that fit the analyst's categories and facilitate the "quantification of the data" ignores the narrative frameworks, in and through which the content is meaningful (Peacock 1975:132).

Whereas products/performances have an objective existence, the meaning/experience of them is a result of subjective engagement. But it is easier to focus on a product than on its meaning. That focus in turn makes it easier to proceed as if one were discussing a world independent of engagement and subjectivity. Just as we often proceed as if there were a world of facts that can be gathered like eggs in a basket, so we tend to ignore the constitutive nature of experience.

As a symbolic form the soap opera is potentially part of our experience. As part of a communication process, it is related to a range of social contexts, relationships, and patterns of meaning. The form is not reducible to a statement describing its content but is part of a participatory process. The traditional distinctions (both popular <u>and</u> scholarly) between producers-content-audience, with a message produced that is transmitted to the audience, can be replaced by a more wholistic and processual understanding.

Symbolic form is based on the cultural and social experience of the people who participate, whether they are producers, performers or audience. It breaks down these distinctions. Content analysis on the other hand suggests the creation of content by producers in terms set out by the traditional mass communication triad. (Elliott 1982:589)

Studying a performance entails linking all participants and considering how a performance or symbolic form articulates with associative patterns of meanings. Whereas a soap, for example, might be considered entertainment and escapism, as a form of expressive (mediated) culture, it can be linked to patterns of meanings as values, beliefs, and norms and as affording kinds of participation. Questions can be raised about the social relationships, values, beliefs, and norms expressed through soaps and about how they articulate with other realms of experience. Do they challenge or reaffirm particular patterns of meaning? Do they stimulate, resolve, and restimulate ideal expectations and related frustrations? Content, then, is not reducible to a summary descriptive statement of information in a program.

Similarly, if a symbolic form is part of a socially structured process, it can be related to a number of contexts and relationships, particularly contexts of production and use. Elliott (1972) proposes a useful way to explore these issues by relating various types of programming to society as source and to society as audience. Whereas he studied non-fictional production largely in terms of the content as in-formation, his general approach is applicable to fictional productions because it facilitates the exploration of the way the soap frame is made available to be experienced as a per-formance.

By looking at society as composed of different and potentially contending groups whose interests and values may vary, we can examine the realm of public fictions for evi-dence of these points of contention or agreement. Given the heterogeneity of groups and viewpoints in American society, it is clear that the world in a soap frame provides a very restricted and repetitive frame for experience and a very narrow view of social life. A crucial question is: why are some views ignored while others are incorporated or changed to fit within the frame of a soap? How soap production reflects or furthers contending forms and beliefs and/or encompasses such differences within the dominant frame is best understood by examining the actual production process and observing how and why the world in the frame takes on its characteristics.

Elliott (1972) developed a useful typology for examining how society is incorporated into a program and, thus, how the program provides a conception of society that ultimately is a resource through which people interpret and construct their world (see Table 1-1).

In the documentary Elliott observed being made, the pro-duction organization relied on personal contacts, legitimated organizations and representatives, and previously produced material in such a way that the production organization could get the job done easily but could also claim to have been unbiased and objective. They filtered what came from, or was constructed during, the production process.

I have studied soap production in an analogous manner by looking at the practices that not only constrain what becomes part of a performance but are themselves resources through which they are generated. Soaps are fictional dramatic pre-sentations that are created, but they must appeal to audi-ences and be believable and authoritative. Even though they are fictions, they must draw upon widely shared resources, including notions of what society is like or should be like embodied in nonfictional accounts such as news and documen-taries.

Whereas a soap may be considered entertainment, it is also a form of public entertainment and thus open to the potential criticisms and attacks of competing characteriza-tions of life, or better competing life forms or cultural

TABLE 1-1
A TYPOLOGY OF MASS COMMUNICATION

| Production Function | Example Programme Type | Access of Society as Source | Audience Relationship |
|---|---|---|---|
| **Scope of Production: Limited** | | | |
| Technical facilitation | Party political | Direct | Persuasive-effectiveness |
| Facilitation, selection | Adult education | Modified direct | Informative-effectiveness |
| Selection, presentation | News bulletin | Filtered | Information-satisfaction |
| Selection, compilation | Documentary | Remade | Satisfaction, informative |
| Realization, creation | 'Realistic' Serial | Advisory | Satisfaction, entertainment |
| **Scope of Production: Extensive** | | | |
| Creation, origination | 'One Shot' Plays | Uncontrolled | Artistic satisfaction |

Source: Elliott 1972:155

worlds.   The world in the soap frame enters into public consciousness and self-consciousness, becomes both a window on
and a mirror of experience, and, as such, a resource for constructing experience.

# 2
# Constructing an Understanding

[We] have to break from the notion of isolating the object and then discovering its components. On the contrary, we have to discover the nature of a practice and then its
conditions. (Williams 1973:16)

The way I went about carrying out the study followed from an
emphasis on the actual practices and conditions involved. I
used participant observation as a way of developing a firsthand understanding. The method is particularly suited for
the study of behavior in natural settings and for capturing
both subjective and objective processes. Put differently,
meanings, social conditions, and behavior can all be studied
and interrelated.

For the case study, I largely focused on one soap opera,
although I did observe the making of Edge of Night and, to a
lesser extent, All My Children. I embodied the results of
my research in an ethnographic account that relays data but
also ideally communicates a sense of what it means to participate in the production process on a number of levels. I
hope the detail, concreteness, and thoroughness make the
argument persuasive and contribute to the reader's grasp of
the experience of making a soap.

In this brief account of how I went about doing the
research and how and why I arrived at some of my conclu-
sions, my aim is to aid the reader in assessing the study.
I do not pretend to completeness, and my understanding of
the research process has been constructed in retrospect.
But I share in the growing interest in the understanding of
the research process (Ruby 1982). A danger in my account is
that I personalize what is actually a social process. My
role as a scientific investigator gathering information for
a dissertation was a powerful and important factor in virtually every area of the research. While my skills and manner
of self-presentation affected what I learned, the way people
in media organizations perceive academic research strongly
influenced what I was able to learn.

20

My interest in the social shaping of consciousness underlies my interest in reflexivity as a part of ethnographic practice as well as the topic and approach of my research. My initial research choices reflected the common prejudice that only nonfictional production was to be taken seriously; I planned to study how television news was constructed or how television documentaries were made. However, there were a number of good ethnographic accounts of news production (Tuchman 1969; Gans 1979). I also determined it was very doubtful I could do a study of local documentary production because few are made, their production schedule might not correspond to when I was free to carry out the research, and such projects might entail great expense for me and perhaps be shelved at any time.

Surveying the literature, I found few lengthy, detailed studies of fictional production, particularly television production. Soaps suggested themselves because they are very popular and long-lived, and many are made five days a week, 52 weeks a year, in New York. Daytime television has largely been ignored by academics, and the scholarly research I was able to find concentrated on effects and content.

Soap production intrigued me. Soaps seemed to be exotic, perhaps even glamorous, since they involved show business. Ideally I would gain some added social stature as one who knows about them firsthand, from the inside or backstage. But I also knew that they were very popular and seemed to have such a strong hold on some viewers that soap fans were often labelled hopeless addicts. Also, there were, and are, anecdotes about fans confronting or attacking performers whom they identify with the parts they play and stories that some audience members do not distinguish the show from reality. The issue of soaps' realism and the relationships between realism in fictional and nonfictional constructions of reality is a major theme of this study.

In part, I saw my production study as perhaps demystifying the process and the performances. Just as studies of news production showed it to be a limited construction or account of the world and very much a product of work routines and organizational pressures, so I hope to reveal what was really behind or involved in soaps' construction.

During a sabbatical from teaching duties, I spent an average of four days a week at Edge of Night, January through March of 1981. In April, I began observing how Guiding Light was made. Later I could spend only two or three days a week because I had to resume teaching. I could spend only two days a month from October 1981 to October 1982 when I was writing up the research. The opportunity to go back to the field situation while I wrote this dissertation was extremely helpful. It was this effort to make sense of what I had seen that led to a clear focus on what to look for.

My ability to gain entry clearly had to do with my doing dissertation research. Also, I was a professor as well as a Ph.D. candidate, and I used both identities as a way to gain access to information. People are willing, if not eager, to offer help and teach students. As a professor, I had established credentials already. The people I observed saw themselves as participating in my work, aiding me and contributing to science. People wanted to contribute to a deeper understanding of soaps than the one they knew society had, given the popular press about soaps. Many people felt I appreciated their work because of the depth of my study and the long time I spent in the studio.

In my initial contacts, I emphasized that I wanted to understand how soaps were made and not judge them. Much of the early literature on soaps, both popular and elite, has been critical of soaps and their audiences.[6] As a form of popular culture, soaps have been subjected to a great deal of criticism, compounded by the fact that their audience is largely composed of housewives. Only recently have they been viewed as legitimate, and I suspect my research itself is part of that trend. I stressed that I was there to study the way work was accomplished and that I would largely be writing down what they took for granted.

That I was not there for commercial purposes was very important. Soap production is extremely competitive and relatively secretive. Budget and future story are strategic resources that are part of a competitive process with large financial and personal stakes. I emphasized I was not gathering information for personal profit, and I stressed that my interests were academic.

When I began observing I wasn't sure of what I was gaining or learning from my observations, and there was a great deal of self-doubt. Would I be able to write a meaningful account—would it be valid and reliable, and was I letting things pass unnoticed that really were significant? In a sense, because everything might be important, nothing was, and the continual preoccupation with the meaning of virtually everything made it seem meaningless.

While in the studio, I recorded my observations on a legal pad, began using a tape recorder after three weeks at Edge of Night, and a camera three or four weeks after that. I transcribed the tapes as soon as possible and found it consumed many hours. I then decided it would be best to spend three or four days observing and then a few days, including weekends, transcribing interviews and working with the information I had gathered--or created.

The atmosphere in the studios was contradictory. Camerapersons, prop persons, and stage crews, for example, were frequently bored, yet there was an intensity and air of excitement as the program or a scene grew closer and closer to the time when it was to be taped. The overall schedule, the work routines, and the formulaic nature of soaps generated boredom and disinterest on the set, but the necessity to stage and block each scene, capture all nuances of interpretation, camera shots, lighting, and other technical concerns, demanded complete attention to the work at hand.

The reactions to my presence on the set varied. (At Guiding Light a memo was circulated saying I would be doing dissertation research.) Some people were flattered and seemed eager to talk of their work experiences, frustrations, and goals. Like most people, they enjoyed the attention. Others quickly told me that there wasn't anything to observe, it was all routine. Some people, particularly camerapersons, compared the routine of current production to earlier days when shows were aired live and to the golden age of television when workers felt a sense of importance from having worked televising relatively prestigious material live. After I had been around for a month or two, workers would express surprise I was still there, wondering what there was to see that would take so long.

It was easier than might be imagined to fit into the production situation. I started by carrying a clipboard with a yellow legal pad, looking, I guess, like a staff member who might be keeping a record of time or noting factors important for continuity. Several people are on set with notebooks or scripts. Actors, the director, the sound technicians, the associate director and the production assistant make reference to scripts or take notes. (The production assistant's role includes keeping track of the time required or expected for the program or scenes and recording the producer's comments to the director in the control room. The director then relies on the production assistant for those comments or notes when on the set.) Another basis for my rapid acceptance was the occasional presence of journalists on the set interviewing principals for magazines and newspapers. Also, much of the work is oriented to an audience, and I was an audience member in the studio.

The physical settings and production schedule of both shows varied, in part, because Edge of Night is 30 minutes long whereas Guiding Light is one hour long. At Edge of Night fewer people were involved, the rehearsal schedule permitted regular break periods, and work order was more predictable. Scenes were typically rehearsed in their order of appearance. There was an overall sequence of dry rehearsal, a "no fax" (with no technical facilities), a "fax," a dress rehearsal, and then the final taping. At <u>Guiding Light</u>, the day was broken up into two segments. One grouping of scenes would be rehearsed and shot in one studio from early morning until mid-afternoon. A similar routine would be followed in another studio later in the day into early evening. The scheduling might vary considerably if there was a need to pretape or posttape material; that is, to tape material produced earlier or later than the taping of the bulk of the material for a particular episode. Because of the different methods of taping the shows, it was much easier for me to become involved and enjoy <u>Edge of Night</u> as a program. It was impossible to get the same feeling of fulfillment from <u>Guiding Light</u>. At the end of the day, there was no final product that was experienced as a meaningful performance, whereas the result of the day's work at <u>Edge of Night</u> was a coherent dramatic production. At <u>Guiding Light</u> it was a series of isolated scenes, taped out of sequence, and never shown as a final performance. The episodes were edited the day after taping; it was only then that the episode took its final shape, without the commercials, however, which are added later.

At <u>Edge of Night</u> there were regular periods when everyone took breaks. There was also a coffee room where actors, technicians, office workers, or other members of the production company would join together. This made it easy to fit in and overhear conversations, or even conduct an impromptu interview. Actors, for example, would come there when they weren't needed for rehearsal. At <u>Guiding Light</u> there was no one place where people from various areas of production came together.

Another reason I found it relatively easy to observe much of the production process is that people come and go, with varying numbers of people on the set at any one time. In fact, it was easier to observe in the studio, where I could be relatively unobtrusive, than in the office areas, where I felt conspicuous. Not wanting to infringe on privacy, I tended to avoid going into the producers' offices at <u>Guiding Light</u>, even though they were next to the production office. At <u>Edge of Night</u> the producer's office was on another floor and was much less accessible.

The research at <u>Edge of Night</u> was limited by this factor. Not only was I apprehensive about offending people, and less sure of what I needed to find out, but the show had only one producer/executive producer and an associate producer whose involvement in the work process was limited. The executive producer was always extremely busy, and I found it difficult to interview him. At Guiding Light there was an executive producer, but there were also two producers, one of whom did more of the line producing, or actual overseeing of the taping process. In addition, there was an associate producer who also was available. Their offices were near the production office and were connected--I had to walk through the associate producer's office to get to the office of the two producers, and through their office, in turn, to get to the executive producer. People at every level were willing to help me, as long as they had time. The only exception was the former supervising producer for Guiding Light. I guaranteed that all informants would be anonymous.

Initally, I observed the more accessible routines and interviewed the more immediately available people. I was in either the control room or the studio, interviewing technicians, actors, or production personnel. Camerapersons or prop persons enjoyed talking, partly as a way of breaking the daily routine. It is difficult to imagine just how routine the work is. The limited settings, movements, and ways they are shot, repeated daily, guaranteed boredom. Humor was the major means of alleviating it. At Guiding Light the personnel are largely CBS staff people, some of whom have worked for CBS for thirty years. Many compared the work, as I said earlier, to the golden years or to other forms of work in television.

I interviewed some people, particularly the headwriters, directors, and producers, in their homes or over lunch. Some people were extremely busy during the production process and often did not have time to talk. It was easier and more successful to schedule interviews. In addition to interviewing the headwriters of Guiding Light and Edge of Night, I also interviewed two other headwriters. Finally, as I explored the organizational relationships later in the study, I interviewed CBS and advertising executives.

Two important areas that shape the performances--budget and future story--were largely inaccessible to me. At Guiding Light I could ask about anything except for budget. It was surprising how few people had an overall knowledge of the bottom line figures and, in general, how much of a secret budget is. I was told that Procter and Gamble tends to keep a low profile and that figures were not available on production costs because the shows did not want competitors to know what their dollars produced. One employee suggested that public knowledge of salaries of performers, for example, would be divisive and lead performers to compare salaries and make greater demands. This problem, in fact, had recently occurred.

Individuals having some responsibility for budget spoke of the difficulties of answering Procter and Gamble's questions about costs. Procter and Gamble often wanted to know what an average scene cost, but producers found it impossible to define the average scene. I did gain some information about the budgets or costs for stage crews and technicians. The individuals responsible for this information at Edge of Night and Guiding Light were not employees of Procter and Gamble.

The secretiveness about production cost had to do with the competitive environment in which the soaps are made. Procter and Gamble shows (then) aired on CBS (As the World turns, Guiding Light, Search for Tomorrow), NBC (Another World, Texas), and ABC (Edge of Night), and Procter and Gamble attempted to make the best deal they could with each network, not letting any of the competing networks know what their agreements were. The agency of production (an advertising agency) handles the payments for Procter and Gamble so that the costs for the agency of production are not known to the individuals responsible for budget at Guiding Light. This adds to the mystery of the budget process.

One assistant to the producer summarized the complexity and difficulty of understanding budget:

Obviously you have gleaned that money goes from one pocket to the other--between CBS, Compton and Procter and Gamble. It's a mire. It's half barter, it's half money set on historical precedent. . . . We get some things as part of a package. . . .

I can be sticking my nose in as much as I can and you can't get to the bottom of it. If you have ever talked to sales, they are the biggest bunch of double talkers. They wouldn't tell you what was going on if your life depended on it.

P & G sells their show to CBS; CBS in turn gives them the commercial minutes--there's a certain amount of barter in there, but then the facilities are paid for by P & G to CBS. Most of it is computer money--debit, credit --at some point there is a reckoning at the end of the year. That's when we get hysterical when actual dollars have to be exchanged.

People handling budget matters for the program had difficulty in determining costs themselves.

The other major area that I found difficult to study
was future story. Put simply, the future story is what they
want to use to hook the audience. Suspense and anticipation
are two of the major components that are counted on to capture and hold the audience. Knowledge of future story was
restricted, in a sense, to those who have a need to know. I
was not allowed to participate in story conferences but was
able to discuss the story projection with producers.

At Edge of Night, which is a mystery melodrama, the
very nature of the storytelling depends on mystery. At
Guiding Light there was more openness about future story,
except again, when a mystery was involved or an important
character was in jeopardy. Once a number of alternative
endings to a mystery story were taped so that the production
staff itself would not know who was responsible for a series
of murders in the story.

I experienced several problems utilizing an ethnographic approach to study behavior in an organizational
setting. Some of the difficulties have to do with the highly competitive, high stakes nature of the business. One's
attention tends to be focused on the creative or dramatic
character of the production process or on the work routines
and roles, but there is a larger organizational and market
context underlying the process, and that context provides
the resources through which performances are created. At
one point, it struck me that news production was probably
easier to study than soap production. It was the larger
(economic) setting that I initially had difficulty linking
to the work process in a meaningful way.

In the studio, however, money is not forgotten about,
ratings are not ignored, and corporate interests are not
overlooked. Economic considerations surface in a number of
ways. When I asked one technician about his work, he
laughed and said, "They bribe us. They pay us lots of
money, lots of it!" Actors were aware of the commercial
pressures. They recognized that the pace of production and
the content of the scripts were strongly influenced by commercial considerations. Directors often remarked that producers suggested that they keep requests for extras down and
explained this was due to pressure from the production hierarchy. Directors would then cite decisions they felt reflected a misuse of money. They complained that the tardiness of actors for rehearsal, and their failure to know
their lines, often led to a longer production day, which
translated into significantly increased production costs.
And for everyone there was the pressure and awareness of the

production schedule. A major referent was the lunch break. Contractually, the technicians were entitled to an hour for lunch after five hours of work. At both shows, the lunch hour was a basic indicator of how well the production was going. Finally, a writers' strike during the spring of 1981 was also a clear indicator of the economic stakes involved. The strike was difficult to settle, in part, because the potential income from cable, video discs and tapes, and syndication for all involved was unclear.

Some of my näiveté was related to the traditional anthropological study of groups with less power or whose financial stakes are smaller. Anthropologists have tended to focus on the exotic or the marginal, have tended to study down as opposed to up. Reading about people's lives, even in a book like Tally's Corner (Liebow 1967), in which the Negro males and their ways of living are clearly structured by the larger political economy, is to focus on people made marginal by the class structure and racism of American society.

Millions of dollars are at stake in the competitive world of soaps. Budgets and story are used to create potential markets and are at the heart of the "business behind the box." Perhaps the most unsettling quality of the research experience had to do with the discrepancy between the content of the shows—the symbolic world that is created—and the world which leads to the manufacture of that world. While the world of Guiding Light is largely upper and upper-middle class, full of things appropriate to a way of life based on consumption and ease, and about the powerful and the pursuit of power, the nature of the political economy of the real world is so far removed it doesn't exist. We don't see the workings of our society directly because the impersonal forces of the political economy—its embodiment in corporate decision making, routines on the assembly line or in a bureaucracy, and many of the frustrations of contemporary life—are absent. From one perspective, trying to understand soaps is to try to understand the world of corporate profit seeking, which the world of the soap denies. It was as if the harder I looked into the content of the program itself, the greater the potential mystification.

Also the way people at the corporate level go about doing what they do makes observation difficult. Conversations over the phone are difficult to observe. The executive producer and headwriter continually have telephone conversations covering all aspects of production. The decisions they make during these phone conversations are extremely important. This observation difficulty also holds true for decisions that are affected by written communications. Private meetings were inaccessible or unannounced. For example, the executive producer and a performer might confer over salary or story behind closed doors.

There was one other source of difficulty. I was initially mystified by a native's view of the world of soap opera as show business, as in some way more vital and sacred than other forms of work. There is an aura to the world of entertainment, even the most commercial aspects, that sets it apart. It took me a while to shake such a perspective.

The competitive profit seeking, the complex, continuous production process, a product that was a secret (and ephemeral to boot), along with the nature of communications in an organizational context made the research frustrating and difficult.

Another major difficulty, of course, was making sense of it all. There was a point when it was clear I was constructing an understanding or explanation of the production process, and not simply gathering data. At first I was observing, taking notes, and transcribing them. I was separate from and, in a sense, passively registering or collecting information. Then, after I began to organize and write up the data in the fall of 1981, the experience of the research and writing changed, and I became more active in the process of making sense of how and why others go about making sense that results in a soap opera. What became clear is largely reflected in the organization of the ethnography.

My first efforts in writing were directed toward describing the production process in terms of the visual conventions that are used. Then I began to write a description of the process in terms of the most important roles. I did this is such a way as to (1) check my generalizations with people involved in the production process by giving them the essay to read, (2) see some concrete results of the research, and (3) generate more areas of research. The concept of role was, however, very unsatisfying because I was suspicious of the ease with which I used the concept. It fit the ready-made typifications of people involved in the process itself, and it also seemed a very static way to apprehend a process.

One other major problem in the initial process of description and analysis had to do with seeing the organizational relationships in the studio where I could observe firsthand. I then developed a strategy of focused interviewing about the relationships and did more reading about industry trends and relationships. I was uncomfortable speaking about corporate policies because they were removed from the actual daily activities, yet they controlled and

made Guiding Light and Edge of Night available. I realized
that much of what occurred was the result of strategies to
reduce uncertainty and minimize risk. Economic factors also
affected the production process in terms of the procedures,
routines, and practices that were used to meet production
deadlines. Storytelling and its realizations became a hierarchically controlled corporate and collective activity in a
competitive market setting.

A major issue involved the relationship of the audience
to the show. I sensed that the audience varied depending on
where one was in the process, that the audience was an economic (viewer/consumer) being, as well as a social being
inhabiting different social worlds, and that the audience
out there obviously could not be known directly. The perceptions of the audience were a major factor in decision
making. I compiled a selection of letters to document the
types of letters Guiding Light received, but I also wanted
to create a more concrete sense of the variety of audience
members. Also, on-going interaction between program and
audience meant that ratings and letters could be used differently than in other forms of production. Research questions were then raised about this interactive process and
its implications for the performances that were generated.

The metaphor of domains helped me to grasp a number of
simultaneous and interactive relationships. I was particularly impressed by Eric Barnouw's (1979) analysis of the
commercial support for network and public television and his
use of the metaphor of domains. At the core of the system
lies the commercial and the entertainment programming surrounding it. Domains that are further removed, but that are
still affected by the commercial underpinnings of the
system, are public affairs programming and even public television itself. The image of various domains resonated with
my concern for identifying relationships on both a social
and cultural (symbolic) level. Placing the commercial at
the heart of the system of relationships, as Barnouw does,
became for me a key to constructing an understanding. While
I was aware from the start of the importance of economic
factors, the metaphor of domains provided a concrete and
persuasive means for identifying and communicating
relationships. To some degree that metaphor avoids the
danger of the base/superstructure metaphor, which dicho-
tomizes a process that can be, and often is, very complex and
interactive and which also often makes the symbolic seem as
if it is a form of epiphenomena. The metaphor also seems
fresh and free of the associations of base and superstructure
in much of the literature.

I did not do a study of commercial production or an elaborate, quantified content analysis of commercials aired with soaps. But my understanding, based as it is on a view of the communication process as involving a number of relationships, is supported by the patterns I observed in soaps and commercials. The audience member is both a viewer and consumer and can be understood in such a way as to link programming and commercial. Again, even though I did not study how people fit soaps into their lives--or how people build their lives around soaps--the fit between program and commercial content and the fact that they are viewed largely in the home by women was significant. Soaps and commercials, from the perspective I adopted, provide forms of participation that are experienced largely in the home, during the afternoon. It is difficult to avoid making sense of what soaps mean without some understanding of the participatory process. Careful ethnographic study of program use or participation is vitally needed.

I viewed the content of the programming as performances and as creating the possibility of participating in an alternative social world. This approach was consistent with an emphasis on the social and symbolic nature of the communication process. From my perspective, as a participant in the larger society, as a participant in the production process, and as a participant in the process of social self-understanding given my role as an anthropologist, my description of the performances relates them to an anthropological or sociological view of social life. At times my understanding and account reads as if I have discovered or revealed what the performances really mean. My account more accurately provides a way of reflecting on soaps in relation to social process and their implications for the kind of society we create and in which we are invited to participate.

I consciously attempted to assess the accuracy of my account and interpretation in several ways. I observed the production process for All My Children, an ABC soap, for two days in order to develop a comparative perspective. Ideally, I would have liked to study two soaps, one owned by Procter and Gamble and another owned by ABC. I chose to study two Procter and Gamble owned shows because I realized that task was large enough.

I asked various production personnel to read some of my work. The opportunity to do so partially reflected the educational level or general sophistication of people working on production and their interest in an academic account. I described my work as partially a matter of writing down the unwritten rules for what they did and as putting on paper what they largely took for granted. At times, they would reflect a "so what?" attitude, then elaborate on their reaction. My account was accurate, they would say, but it stated what they already knew to be the case. Others appreciated my overview of the process and often corrected minor errors. In some cases they ended questioning their work in what they were reminded was a highly commercial activity. When I had completed the study, a producer read several of the chapters and indicated they were fair and accurate. This affirmed the validity of the account.

One factor shaping my reading of the performances is a strong personal and professional view that is very much opposed to the understanding of the social world that soaps present—at least as I view them. Soaps either personalize social forces or completely deny them. If a sociological imagination entails the understanding of experience as the intersection of individual biography, social setting, and history, soap understanding is a matter of personal and interpersonal conflicts or factors in a small, bounded community. As an alternative reality, they are crafted to deal with conflicts in a way that prime-time television does not, yet, at the same time, conflict is handled in the most ahistorical and personalized individual manner.

Power is personalized and simultaneously glamorized and denigrated, particularly in characterizations of the super wealthy and powerful. The power inherent in the role of doctor and lawyer is largely ignored, while the people in such roles, and the roles as a result, are romanticized. Social mobility and the pursuit of money and social success are made appealing, while morality tales are told of their proper and inproper pursuit. Work is largely ignored, and many of the tensions of contemporary life are mystified as a result. And if work and leisure are chosen as dominant themes of contemporary life, leisure takes on the quality of a commodity, never calling into play the grounds for its existence.

Ultimately, I have used a conventional anthropological approach to study an unconventional topic. I relied primarily upon participant observation and formal interviews, complemented by library research and the use of trade journals and popular magazines to construct an understanding of soap performances in relation to the conditions and practices that generate them. The results of the research support Elliott's contention that a "phenomenological approach to social research . . . seems to offer a way of approaching 'socio-cultural wholes' from the bottom up" (1972:10). Beginning with the actual production process by working outward and upward, I identified the significant relationships and forces affecting the work process and the performances it generates.

An integral element of this account is this discussion of my major aims and practices.  As an ethnographic rendering of social process, this work itself is a product of specific social conditions and research practices.  This discussion of my aims and methods and of my theoretical, professional, and personal orientation ideally contributes to the reader's ability to assess the account.

# 3

# The World Through a Soap Frame: *Guiding Light* as a Symbolic Community

[Soap opera] . . . as we know it is costume
drama in a time-capsule, whose only time is
the suspended time of idyll and erotic day
dreams. That does not mean conflict is absent
and love is simple, since even in Arcadia the
existence of stories presupposes 'the crooked
path.' It does mean that neither work nor
history intervene to distract soap opera's
characters from the endless pursuit of personal emotional satisfaction. (Porter 1979:
92)

Initially a fifteen-minute radio program when it was first
broadcast in 1937, Guiding Light of the past would strike us
as extremely cliched and melodramatic.[7]

Originally, the Guiding Light was about the
life of Dr. Rutledge, pastor of a church in
the city of Five Points (Anywhere, U.S.A.) and
the lives of the members of his family and
parish. The show had a rather religious tone,
with a theme that faith brings happiness.
Whole episodes were frequently devoted to a
single sermon by Dr. Rutledge. (La Guardia
1977:34)

The setting of the program changed to increasingly larger urban settings, paralleling the changes of the program's
production sites. In the mid-1940s the Bauers replaced the
Rutledges as the central continuing characters.

The old inspirational theme persisted . . .
but Reverend Rutledge's spiritual lessons
were woven into the fabric of family life.

Instead of challenges to religious faith, the
story told of threats to the stability and
perserverance of family and home. Romance,
insanity, disease, and even murder tested the
strength of the Bauers. Each time they tri-
umphed, it proved the family of good will
could stay together. (Gilbert 1979:24)

The original Bauer clan was headed by Papa Bauer, a car-
penter, and Mama Bauer, both German immigrants. Their son
Bill married Bert, who is still a continuing character on the
program. Bert's children Mike, a lawyer, and Ed, a doctor,
are now both successful upper-middle class professionals,
with all traces of their German heritage gone from the program. The current programming now also includes their
children and grandchildren.

Basing their generalizations on a recent study of Guiding Light scripts from 1948, 1958, and 1968 and videotapes
of the March 1982 programming by Mies (1982), Cantor and
Pingree note a number of changes. The world of Guiding
Light 1982 differed from earlier years in that business settings were more common, more was discussed in business settings, and women and men discussed business in business settings (1983:97-112). Earlier programming tended to present
women almost exclusively in the home in a world where there
was more sex-role segregation.

The Guiding Light moved from an introspective
and inwardly oriented world in 1948, one
focusing on feelings and personalities, to a
sex-segregated world of business and home in
1958, to a world where both sexes were concerned with romantic relationships in their
separate settings in 1968, to one where women
and men both focus on business in a much more
open social environment. (Cantor and Pingree
1983:112)

The nature of the world that Guiding Light invites
viewers to participate in was changing when I carried out my
research. How and why that world was changing is explored
in virtually every chapter. In this chapter, I describe the
performances as creating the potential for participation in
an alternative community. What that community or world was
like from the spring of 1981 to the summer of 1982 is
sketched broadly in the following pages.

SETTINGS

Guiding Light takes place in the present in the fictional
city of Springfield, U.S.A.  Springfield is located in mid-
dle-America, a short plane ride away from New York and
Chicago.  According to members of the production staff, the
name is ideal because there is a Springfield in every state.
     The city is not small.  Spaulding Enterprises, one of
the world's largest corporations, is headquartered there.
Cedars Hospital, a large, wealthy, technically sophisticated
organization, is a major setting for much of the drama.  But
even though those are the two major work settings, the
viewer is given little sense of what each looks like.  There
are no concrete images, no panoramic views, to place the
organizations in a larger visual context.
     Almost all the action in Springfield occurs indoors.
This indoor world consists of domestic settings—living
rooms, bedrooms, kitchens; business settings, particularly
offices; and public settings—nurses' station, cafeteria,
restaurant, disco.  The wealthy are seen in their libraries,
dens, and studios; the working-class Reardons socialize in
their kitchen or on their porch.  In the domestic milieu,
much of the action takes place in bedrooms and living rooms,
whereas the world of work occurs primarily in the offices of
doctors, lawyers, and businessmen.
     The interiors of homes are clearly distinguishable.
Most interiors are upper-middle class.  The homes of both
the upper-class and working-class families are clearly differentiated from the dominant upper-middle pattern.  But
there is a sense of order in almost all settings.  Orderli-
ness, cleanliness, neatness are the normal state of affairs.
     The material culture of each setting is also distin-
guishable, again in a clearly representative way.  The homes
of the rich are spacious, wood panelled (particularly the
den and studio), the walls are hung with ornately framed
portraits and, in general filled with expensive objects.
The homes and rooms of the working class are smaller, com-
monplace, and often give the impression that they are not
planned or decorated in a coherent way.  There is an overall
sense of order in all the homes, appearances of disorder
signalling a dramatic rupture or a pathological state.
(Disorder even seems orderly, partially because too much
disorder creates problems for prop people responsible for
continuity.)
     Horace Newcomb's characterization of the interior world
still remains apt, despite today's larger production budgets.

Any departure from the norm of upper—middle
class stability results in . . . blatant re—
presentation in which richness is defined ex—
clusively by their extravagant homes, so is
the addict's room defined by its squalor.
(1974:167)

The greater production values of recent soaps have gone
in part toward making the homes of the rich more glamorous
and spectacular. At the other end of the class hierarchy,
the homes of the working class are functional, practical,
simple but adequate. In the working—class Reardon home, the
setting is clearly designed to embody a sense of home—of
warmth, caring, and closeness.

Recent storylines emphasizing gothic mystery and ro—
mance are set in the homes of the wealthy. Houses become
mansions; studies and dens take on a mysterious air as
strange and frightening things occur. In one storyline,
Amanda, hurt by her love, retreats to her bedroom, regress—
ing and becoming a child in a large, dark mansion. Simi—
larly, another character, Quint, a mysterious archaeologist—
anthropologist, makes his laboratory a forbidden place in his
mansion. Calling attention to the conventions of gothic
mysteries and films, the stories and settings contribute to
a fantastic and tongue—in—cheek quality to the programming,
a quality only recently introduced.

Work settings tend to be the corporate offices of the
upper class or offices of upper—middle class doctors and
lawyers. Doctors' and lawyers' offices are very functional
in design, orderly, and unobtrusive, whereas corporate board
rooms or executive offices are more elaborate. Doctors'
offices, many located in Cedars Hospital, tend to have an
impersonal air. They are aptly characterized by Newcomb's
description of place as

designed by function. A doctor's office is
so designated by the "whiteness" of tables
and pans, by diplomas on the walls, and by
the medical books on the shelves. . . . In
many ways the office is indistinguishable
from that of the lawyer, which also displays
books and diplomas. The lawyer's office is
likely to be more clearly adaptable to use by
clients. There are more chairs; there is a
richer look of mahogany and leather rather
than steel and plastic. (1974:164)

Depictions of public settings include restaurants, the nurses' station on the fourth floor of Cedars Hospital, and a hospital cafeteria. People continually meet or see each other in such settings. These seemingly public places are settings in which familiar characters interact in personal ways so that the settings lose their public nature. Strangers (extras) come and go fleetingly, but by no means dominate such settings as might be true in the real world.

When the action occurs outdoors, it is primarily for high romance and adventure. Examples include Jamaica, the Canary Islands, St. Croix, and Paris. Laurel Falls, an important setting for the romance and trials of Morgan and Kelly, even though close to Springfield, takes on the quality of an exotic and romantic setting. On other occasions, business, intrigue, or travel will take people to important business or financial centers such as San Francisco, New York, or London. The big city is also a place where anything can happen, as it does when Morgan is nearly raped in New York City.

Scenes shot on location (out of the studio), typically in romantic or spectacular settings, are combined with scenes shot in the studio, although they are contextualized as occurring on location. Romantic scenes of the beaches of Jamaica are combined with a studio interior of a villa bedroom. Similarly, a chase across mountains and deserts includes studio interiors of mountain caves. While a great deal is invested in creating relatively realistic studio sets, it is generally clear when a scene has been shot in a studio.

The world of Guiding Light is frequently an indoor world. It is largely an upper-middle-class domestic world, which is differentiated from the working-class and, to a lesser degree, upper-class domestic world. The exterior world is primarily romantic, spectacular, or starkly representative. Public and private realms, however, merge because they are people with familiar faces.


PARTICIPANTS

The continuing inhabitants of the world of Springfield number between 30 and 35. They are largely in their twenties, thirties, or forties, with an increase in the number of young (new) characters during the last two years. The largest percentage is upper-middle class, with both the upper class and lower-middle/working class represented in smaller numbers. All are white, seemingly Protestant, with no ethnic or religious differences represented, other than the

Reardon family, which was "Irish" in name only. They were more working class than Irish. The Bauer family, the central family on the program, was originally of German immigrant extraction, but it has lost any trace of its ethnic origin.

Occasionally minority group members appear on soaps, but their place in a storytelling strategy that involves romance and intertwined intimate relationships is problematic. On the one hand, it is difficult to "get as much mileage out of a character." On the other hand, placing minority group members in intimate and/or romantic relationships with whites might offend the audience and affect ratings.

The characters can be grouped together by class and as family groups, although class lines are blurred by marriage, and rapid changes in social position can occur. One can get a good sense of the density and complexity of the relationships from a brief description of the characters and their relationships. The various family groups are connected to other groups through ties of marriage and friendship. Overlapping these, of course, are the ties of past marriages and friendships and business. In the circumscribed world of Springfield, people continually meet, overhear each other, or hear of each other's behavior and intentions. The following descriptions of the characters are based on descriptions prepared by the production office of Guiding Light.

## UPPER CLASS

Alan Spaulding: Old-monied industrialist with unsavory past that he came to regret through his love for current wife, Hope. Sent to jail after confessing to conspiracies of past in order to make clean start in life. Was married to Elizabeth Marler and Jackie Marler. Is "father" of Philip Spaulding, who is actually Jackie and Justin Marler's biological son. Fathered Amanda in teenage affair with Jennifer Richard. Past affairs include Rita Stapleton Bauer. In his thirties, dashing.

Philip Spaulding: Son of Jackie and Justin, but thinks he is son of Alan and Elizabeth. Troubled and confused about where he belongs, with his "dad" or with his "Aunt Jackie and Uncle Justin." Teenager.

Hope Bauer Spaulding: Beautiful, charming, sweet, trusting. Talented interior decorator. Very in love with Alan Spaulding and their child Alan Michael. Daughter of Mike Bauer who was once Alan's sworn enemy. Granddaughter of Bert. Very supportive of Alan and intolerant of those who aren't. (Part of upper group by recent marriage.) In her twenties.

Henry Chamberlain: Corporate-wise, wealthy father of Vanessa. Once very unscrupulous, recent health problems and his search for his illegitimate son, Sean Ryan, have made him reexamine his values. He regrets the values he's instilled in Vanessa and devotes much of his thoughts and energies to her. In his sixties.

Vanessa Chamberlain: Dark, passionate, and old-money wealthy. Henry Chamberlain's daughter. Amoral and excellent businesswoman. Once in love with Ross Marler but married another to save father's business. Conniving and manipulative, with a sarcastic wit. Will cheat, lie, whatever to succeed in business or romance. Once involved with Ed Bauer and recently involved with Mark Evans. In her thirties.

Trish Lewis: In her mid-twenties, pretty sister to Josh. Once very insecure because of sheltered, unloving upbringing of her father, oil magnate H. B. Lewis. Once married to Andy Norris and now divorced. Co-owns Hideout and Wired for Sound with Vanessa Chamberlain. Trying to gain self-assurance and prove herself self-sufficient. Adores Josh and does not see his darker side.

Josh Lewis: Early twenties playboy, brother of Trish. Spoiled and egotistical. Eager to step out of his father's shadow and establish business on his own; he shows a dark side willing to do anything to accomplish this. Presently liaison for Lewis Oil at Spaulding, and helps Trish with Hideout/Wired for Sound. Manages Floyd Parker. Has designs on Morgan Nelson.

Quint McCord: Gothic, grim, and mysterious anthropologist-archaeologist. Nola's employer. Regrets not having family life during his childhood and shows much concern for Nola and her baby. Involved in quest for Golden Temple. Becomes romantically involved with Nola Reardon. In his twenties.

The upper-class groups include both old money and new money, equally concerned to retain power and wealth. Quint McCord (old money with English origins) is free largely to dedicate himself to a quest for a mysterious and valuable archaeological goal--the Golden Temple. Power and wealth are personalized and related to the psychological motivations of individual characters. Vanessa, for example, has been spoiled by her father's wealth, but Josh is motivated to escape from his father's domination. Corporate power is presented largely as an arena in which individuals compete with each other. The elite are also seen as mixing freely with individuals lower in the class hierarchy, linking all the participants in the same symbolic community.

UPPER-MIDDLE CLASS

Bauer Family - Historically the central family of Guiding Light.

Bert Bauer: Wise and strong leader of the Bauer family. Always helpful in personal crises and insightful. Mother of Mike and Ed Bauer. Grandmother of Hope Bauer Spaulding. In her fifties.

Ed Bauer: Honest, diligent, caring chief of staff at Cedars. Son of Bert and brother of Mike. Disillusioned by failed relationships with wives Holly and Rita and later romance with Vanessa. Father of Freddy (teenage son by first wife Leslie). Upstanding, godfather to Kelly. In his thirties.

Mike Bauer: Strong, masculine, honest lawyer. Moral to the point of self-righteousness in past. Once out to get Alan Spaulding; his opinion has changed since Alan's confession and an incident in which Alan saved Mike's life. Ed's brother. Bert's son. Hope's father. Frequently helps police in criminal cases. Presently single. "Mr. Right" type. In his forties.

Rita Bauer: Separated wife of Ed; sister of Eve Stapleton. Left Springfield after love affair with Alan Spaulding. Disappears in San Francisco. Mike tries to find her to get divorce for Ed. In her early thirties.

Hillary Bauer: Sensitive, witty young nurse. She was "illegitimate." Fights her love for Kelly Nelson to avoid jeopardizing friendship with Kelly and Morgan and her relationship with Derek Colby. In her twenties.

Kelly Nelson: Young, dedicated clerk at Cedars. Morgan's husband. Honest and upright, old-fashioned, and a tough male chauvinistic. Creeping jealousy for wife, Morgan. Once a target for Nola's wiles, his caution caused him to hesitate when Nola called for help during her delivery. He feels guilty but still distrusts Nola. In his mid-twenties.

Richards/Wexler Group

Jennifer Richards Evans: Warm, loving mother of Morgan and Amanda. Very protective; risked jail for murder rather than reveal Amanda was her daughter and shatter Amanda's then unstable sense of security with her "mother" Lucille Wexler. Marries Mark Evans in summer of 1982. In her early forties.

Morgan Richards Nelson: Eighteen-year-old, pretty daughter of Jennifer Richards and half-sister to Amanda. Married to Kelly Nelson and a fashion model. Highly emotional but gaining maturity after marrying Kelly.

Mark Evans: Successful young mid-thirties businessman having affair with Vanessa Chamberlain and Amanda. Marries Amanda's mother Jennifer. Behind plot placing Alan in jeopardy.

Amanda "Wexler" McFarren: Daughter of Jennifer Richards and Alan Spaulding. Wealthy from stocks in Spaulding left her by Alan's father before her true origin was publicly known. Once frigid and insecure because of overprotective "mother" Lucille Wexler, she still suffers residual unstableness. Professes distrust of men because of past failed relationships, particularly her marriage to Ben McFarren, and her trust in Alan shattered by revelation of his admitted crimes. Talented pianist and potentially warm but is distant and cold for fear of being hurt again. Becomes head of Spaulding Enterprises when father, Alan Spaulding, gives her his stock in company. In her late twenties/early thirties.

Lucille Wexler: (now dead) "Mother" of Amanda, rearing her from childhood at request of Brandon Spaulding, Alan's father (see Jennifer).

Ben McFarren: Mid-twenties, talented artist. Presently being divorced from Amanda. Still has strong feelings for first wife, Eve. Has gone to Europe to continue work.

Eve McFarren: Young, quiet, moral. Rita's younger, shyer sister. Once married to Ben and still in love with him.

Chet Stafford: (now dead) Jennifer's brother. Killed trying to get revenge on Eve for breaking up Amanda and Ben's marriage.

Marler Family

Dr. Justin Marler: Good, strong, masculine. Head of cardiology department at Cedars Hospital. Divorced from Elizabeth and remarried to Jackie. Biological father of Philip (see Philip Spaulding in upper-class group). Ross and Lainie's brother. In his late thirties.

Jackie Marler: Justin's wife. Ex-wife of Alan Spaulding. Biological mother of Philip.

Beautiful, sophisticated and warm (see Elizabeth Marler). Owns gift shop where Eve presently works. Died summer of 1982. In her early thirties.

Lainie Marler: Bright, pretty sister to Ross and Justin. Now married and living in Chicago. Was Mike's secretary, Eve's roommate. Doesn't appear on show.

Ross Marler: Bright, ambitious lawyer. Once was manipulative and willing to do anything to succeed. His love for Carrie now takes precedence and he regrets the deceptions and connivances of his past, though he never did anything strictly illegal. Justin and Lainie's brother. In his mid-thirties.

Carrie Todd Marler: Warm, honest, talented artist with a past history of psychological disorders caused by past traumas. Carrie Anderson MacKenzie took the name of her husband, Todd, after he killed himself because of a scandal engineered by Diane Ballard. Carrie later killed Diane accidentally in a blind rage when Diane threatened Ross and others with blackmail. Carrie confessed and was acquitted on grounds of temporary insanity. Married to Ross. Revealed to have a multiple personality. Leaves for treatment in England, summer of 1982.

Elizabeth Marler: (character now in Europe) Beautiful, frail ex-wife of Justin Marler and Alan Spaulding. Became "mother" of Philip when her unborn child died and Alan switched the dead infant with another child (not knowing it was Jackie's). This occurred at the break-up of Jackie and Justin's first marriage.

Thorpe Family

Adam Thorpe: Businessman husband to Sara McIntyre and adoptive father to Tim Werner. Character is unseen on show. In his fifties.

Barbara Thorpe:  Mother of Holly and Andy Norris.  Moved to Switzerland to be with Holly after Andy went to jail for blackmail. In her fifties.

Dr. Sara McIntyre:  Attractive, intelligent, sensitive, mature internist and psychiatric counselor specializing in sex therapy, relationship counseling.  Assistant to Dr. Ed Bauer.  Married to Adam Thorpe and adoptive mother of Tim Werner.  In her late forties.

Tim Werner:  College student.  Adopted son of Sara.  Alcoholic.  Once in love with Morgan Richards and petulantly jealous of Kelly. Currently resolving his overly emotional nature and selfish tendencies.  A good student and athletic scholar.

Andy Norris:  Son of Barbara; now in jail for blackmail.

Holly Norris:  (now in Switzerland) Ex-wife of Ed.  Mother of Freddy.  Andy's sister.

Individuals

Dr. Steve Jackson:  Energetic elderly doctor on Cedars staff.  Good friend of Bert's and mentor to Ed Bauer.  (Character unseen on show.)  In his late sixties.

Diane Ballard:  (now dead) Very bright, sexy, strong.  Alan Spaulding's unscrupulous assistant who was in love with him.  Killed by Carrie Todd while attempting to blackmail Ross, Jackie, and others.  In her late twenties.

Joe Bradley:  Private investigator, unscrupulous.  Killed by Carrie Todd in self defense after trying to blackmail Alan, others.  In his twenties.

Derek Colby:  Young, dedicated, honest lawyer.  Was reserved but has opened up since becoming romantically involved with Hillary Bauer.  Works with Mike Bauer.  In his twenties.

## MIDDLE CLASS/WORKING CLASS

### Reardon Family

<u>Bea Reardon</u>:  Strong, loving mother of Nola, Tony, Maureen, and four other Reardon children.  Reared her children alone after father left family.  Runs boarding house.

<u>Maureen Reardon</u>: Vibrant, straightforward sister of Nola, Tony.  Bea's daughter.  In her thirties.

<u>Nola Reardon</u>:  Bouncy early twenties daughter of Bea, sister of Tony.  Grew up fascinated with old romantic movies and fantasizes a better life based on them.  Gutsy, ambitious, and manipulative.  Bitter about her poor upbringing.  Wants a better life and will do almost anything to get it.  Became pregnant by Floyd Parker hoping to convince Kelly Nelson that the baby (Kelly Louise Reardon) was his.  Works for Quint McCord, who is teaching her to become more sophisticated.  She becomes romantically involved with him.

<u>Tony Reardon</u>:  Macho brother of Nola Reardon.  Son of Bea.  Former truck driver now developing ambitions as manager of Wired for South.  Rough-edged but with underlying sensitivity.  Expert in karate and once a neighborhood bully.  Secretly in love with Hillary Bauer.  In his twenties.

### Parker Family

<u>Katie Parker</u>:  Bubbly young nurse with a history of soured romances (Mark Hamilton, Andy Norris).  Floyd's sister.  In her twenties.

<u>Floyd Parker</u>:  Talented, naive, loving brother of Katie.  Good, honest, warm.  Once exceedingly in love with Nola and is father of her baby, Kelly Louise.  Did not know for over a year that she used him to try to trap Kelly.  Performed at Hideout/Wired for Sound and has become very successful musical performer--able to move into former Spaulding

home because of rapid success. Worked as
Cedars assistant maintenance head. Currently
getting over his feelings for Nola by falling
in love with Lesley Ann.

Mrs. Renfield: Housekeeper and confidant of
Quint McCord. Dour and reserved, mysterious.
In her fifties.

Characters at the upper and lower ends of the social
hierarchy tend to be most distinctive in their life styles.
At the upper end, the Chamberlains and Quint McCord are distinguished by their wealth and styles of dress and patterns
of speech. Individuals from the working class, particularly
Nola, Floyd, and Tony, dress and speak in ways that make
their class position clear to viewers. Most of the characters are upper-middle class. Each individual in this group
is unique but each displays the common characteristics of a
homogeneous upper-middle class. One such characteristic is
the sameness of their speech--although members of other
classes can sound the same.
The boundaries between classes are blurred, as I mentioned, by a number of factors. Class positions are changed
through marriage, as in Hope's marriage to Alan Spaulding.
There can be a very rapid change in status because of social
and financial success. Floyd Parker, originally a maintenance man at Cedars Hospital, earnest, sincere, hard-working
in his efforts at self-improvement, becomes a successful
musical star within a year. He is so successful that he is
able to buy the former Spaulding mansion. (Floyd lost his
fortune just as quickly as he made it after a new writer
joined the show in the fall of 1982.) Nola and Quint are
linked in a Pygmalion relationship, as he literally transforms her behavior. Also, members of various classes interact constantly and are tied together by kinship, friendship,
or romance. For example, Bea Reardon, Nola's mother, was
portrayed as a simple, honest, down-to-earth working-class
person who dated Henry Chamberlain, clearly a member of the
upper class.
Other participants appear less frequently and are less
central to the on-going relationships. Some characters,
such as a Detective Wyatt, may be involved in a series of
criminal cases. But they do not become involved in the on-
going relationships. Orderlies, nurses, and patients appear
only in the setting of the hospital, particularly at the
nurses' station (4-East) or in the cafeteria. Other typical
settings for strangers are the various restaurants and dance

places frequented (The Hideout and Wired for Sound, a disco).
Minority members, particularly racial minorities, appear
among these background figures.

There are few infants in the community, and they appear
infrequently. Hope and Alan's child, Alan Michael, and
Nola's baby, Kelly Louise, were the only infants. There
were no children who were not infants or teenagers. Philip
Spaulding, a teenager, appeared only occasionally. As part
of the change in the look of the show, older and long-lived
characters such as Barbara Norris and Dr. Steve Jackson no
longer appeared on the program. Henry Chamberlain and Bert
Bauer were perhaps the oldest major characters. Bert Bauer,
as the matriarch of the Bauer family, plays a key role in
aiding various family members and friends through times of
trouble and in celebrating their times of joy and success.
Henry Chamberlain was progresively limited by his heart conditions and eventually turned much of his wealth over to his
daughter, Vanessa. (However, he suddenly became very active
in a proxy fight in the fall of 1982, again after the new
writer took over.)

The characterizations of sex roles are interesting in
that women occupy important roles in business or the professions, but with less stability or continuity than the male
professionals, with the exception of Dr. Sara McIntyre.
Quests for power, wealth, and revenge occur largely in the
business arena. Doctors and lawyers are characterized in
largely positive terms. Some men, such as Josh Lewis or
Mark Evans, or women, such as Diane Ballard or Amanda Richards, are shown to be manipulative and greedy for power and
wealth for personal, often vindictive ends. At the other
extreme, doctors and most lawyers are shown to be selfless
and professional in the best senses of the word.

The main inhabitants of Springfield, U.S.A., are primarily white, Anglo-Saxon Protestants who are wealthy, talented, and/or ambitious. There are also working-class characters appropriately or inappropriately aspiring to the
life-styles of the successful and wealthy. Most individuals
introduced into the community are ultimately integrated into
family or friendship networks, usually through romantic
couplings and marriage. Isolated characters not essential
to the long-term dynamic of the story (Joe Bradley, Wyatt)
are killed off or fade away.


THE ALTERNATIVE COMMUNITY

[Realism] in popular art is less likely to be
an explicit engagement with the boundaries of

conventional forms of knowledge, than an exploration of romantic or exciting or spectacular or intriguing or sentimental, and so
on, alternatives to everyday experience. Such
utopias have to be comprehensible and possible, that is, they need a realism of detail
to sustain the narrative but they usually lack
a realism of structure--set in the terms of
genre forms which stereotype narrative resolution. Popular art tends to be naturalistic
except that its narratives are alternatives;
they postulate a world other than the everyday, which has been carefully constructed and
which is inherently extraordinary. The performance invites our wonder and admiration
because it spectacularly shows up the arbitrary basis of distinctions between the real
and the surreal. (Chaney 1979:77)

The alternative world of Guiding Light is centered on
the problematic fit between romance, sex, marriage, family
and friendship. It is a world of domestic romance made more
dramatic by elements of mystery, adventure, and intrigue.
More recently, it is a world changed and lightened by elements of fantasy, humor, and action. This alternative world,
whether viewed as resource and/or escape, seems ideally
crafted to connect with the working day or isolation in the
home and the frustrations and tensions of domestic life.
Guiding Light embodies society where home is no longer
a world of work and where the world of work is no longer
routine or threatening, largely because it does not exist.
Home as a place of work disappears, and the world outside
the home becomes an extension of domestic and personal relationships and conflicts. The line typically drawn between
private and public realms is erased with the entire community sharing one implicit or explicit set of values and
beliefs. Phrased differently, the world of the program is a
domesticated world. While the program stimulates and resolves familiar tensions, frustrations, and expectations, it
simultaneously provides an alternative handling of those conflicts in a more spectacular, glamorous, romanticized, controlled environment.
As a never-ending realistic melodrama set in the present that mirrors the everyday reality of supposedly ordinary people, Guiding Light presents itself as a parallel world
that resonates with the life of a viewer.

> Soap opera derives . . . from the tradition
> of realism in the theatre and cinema, but
> more than any other . . . genre, its interest
> resides in an implicit claim to portray a
> parallel life. It offers itself to its audi-
> ence as the representation of lives that are
> separate from but continuous with their own.
> (Porter 1979:88)

The program partakes of the reality outside the frame by articulating with the cycle of holidays and seasons of the year in real life. Contemporary public events, many of which are themselves mediated constructions, are drawn upon or alluded to. Nola Reardon has a dream of meeting Prince Charles and Lady Diana about the same time the couple is actually married. The characters of the program refer to "these difficult times" as they, too, find themselves without income, as are people in the real world. Characters change and grow older.

The realism of Guiding Light is often attributed to its focus on ordinary people. One producer spoke directly to the issue:

> [These] people could be your neighbors down
> the street that you know, and in many instan-
> ces audiences react to these characters as if
> they are indeed people that they recognize.
> As anybody watching a drama knows, it is a
> hyper world, a created compacted environment
> --therefore, dramatic. But the essence of
> what is going on is, for the most part, with
> the exception of on our show, the archaeolog-
> ical dig, is all in the context of "this
> could happen to me." It has happened to peo-
> ple I know--divorce, babies, jealous lovers,
> infidelity.

The "archaeological dig" referred to the story and relationships revolving around wealthy archaeologist Quint McCord, a mysterious figure in search of a mysterious golden temple, a quest filled with romance, danger, and adventure. Making Guiding Light more entertaining and successfully competitive with General Hospital led to the telling of more overtly fantastic stories not rooted in the same reality of daily life. General Hospital's story of a quest for an Ice Princess, part of a plot to freeze the world, combined adventure, romance, mystery, and comedy in the context of a sci-fi story. The McCord figure was also partially patterned after Indiana Jones, a mysterious, daring archaeologist in the highly successful film, <u>Raiders of the Lost Ark</u>. This story-line represented a breaking away from the conventional limits of realism in the program, as the pro- ducer noted, in part because it called attention to other media and performances.

Harding LeMay insightfully identifies some of the sources of the realism of soaps:

The immediacy of soap opera reality is magnified by its being seen in one's own living-room, which carries it beyond the realm of mere make-believe. Written in colloquial dialogue and acted in most cases by players skilled in projecting naturalistic realism, soap operas are paced in the rhythms of everyday life rather than those of theatrical urgency. The viewer is drawn closer to what is watched until the traditional distance between actor and audience is practically eliminated. (1981:115)

The visual, writing, and acting conventions conspire to create a sense of immediacy and accessibility. A viewer is seemingly a privileged spectator catching a glimpse of the ways things really are, the transparency reinforcing the sense that what is revealed is an objective rendering. The immediacy, actuality, transparency, and intimate quality of stories dealing with everyday life also draw from or build upon the repeated and continuing experience of the performances.

The daytime serial . . . benefits from a cumulative factor. With each episode watched, the viewer invests more deeply in the undertaking. The continuing characters, expanded by the illusion of reality that accompanies the extended action, become as real as neighbors. More real, perhaps, because the viewer knows every secret—the child a mother cannot acknowledge . . . the marriage that is in name only. This detailed knowledge adds nuance to each piece of action, and it adds meaning that critics (who watch only occasionally, and clinically) cannot detect or appraise. (Stedman 1977:490)

Repeated viewing of intimate relationships in the intimacy of one's living room contributes to the hold of the programming. Any dramatic sequence is informed by a viewer's past experiences, and since there is no sense of an ending, it is difficult to predict when resolutions to dramatic conflicts will occur. Since there are several interrelated stories, any resolution is only partial and temporary. What is in the frame takes on the problematic nature of real life.

The unpredictability of an expected resolution is an extremely important factor in the creation and uses of suspense and anticipation. A story or plot line can go through a number of stages, as happens when a mystery is partially solved and the audience is made aware of the identity of an evil character. But the audience then becomes involved in predicting and anticipating how and when the evildoer will be revealed to the characters on the show, who are unaware of his identity. Similarly, because audiences identify with characters and have access to information that characters are not privy to, viewers cannot be sure of an outcome or the well-being of any character during any particular program. An example of this dynamic was the kidnapping of Alan, in which the identity of the kidnapper was a mystery. Eventually Mark Evans was revealed as the kidnapper who was trying to destroy Alan. As the mystery is solved, a new dynamic (and probably more engrossing involvement) is created because the audience sees an evil character, who pretends to be something other than the audience knows him to be, go undetected. Mark Stevens is a good example as he marries beautiful and genuine Jennifer, as part of his plot to ruin Alan. At the same time, the viewer knows evildoers are ultimately caught. Suspense and anticipation involve not only the harm Mark can do until he is caught, but how and when he will be caught.

A key element of the storytelling is the concealment or revelation of information and its impact (Riley 1977; Rose 1979). One major piece of information creating and prolonging a story was Nola's use of Floyd to get pregnant so that she could trap Kelly into marrying her by making Kelly believe he was the father of the child. Eventually, Floyd was revealed as the father, but for several months Floyd remained unaware that Nola never loved him when he fathered the child. A series of partial revelations stimulate past experience and create opportunities to observe how characters respond to the revelation. Concealment (and revelation) "prolong the plot line, provide an intriguing kind of psychological suspense and maximize viewer involvement the way Hitchcock does" (Riley 1977:18).

The program continually stimulates and resolves the tensions and expectations of life in an ideal community.

> By community I mean something that goes far beyond mere local community. The word, as we find it in much nineteenth and twentieth century thought encompasses all forms of relationships which are characterized by a high degree of personal intimacy, emotional depth, moral committment, social cohesion, and continuity in time. . . . Fundamental to the strength or the bond of community is the real or imagined antithesis formed in the same social setting by the noncommunal relationship of competition or conflict, utility or contractual assent. These by their relative impersonality and anonymity, highlight the close personal ties of community. (Nisbet 1966:47-48)

> Guiding Light has traditionally created an ideal community that embodies these qualities. Enduring and familiar families and characters are involved in emotionally significant relationships. The few strangers or menacing characters ultimately disappear, are punished, or become familiar over time. A core of people affirm and embody the moral values of the community. While the Bauer family is involved in the conflicts and complications of life in Springfield and undergo their own problems, they are a relatively stable group whose actions create or reinforce the moral order underlying the chaos and conflict, the ambiguity and fluidity of life. The family undergoes trials and affirms the ideal values of the community.
>     One producer emphasized the importance of family to the nature of the program and the potential for experience it provides.

> What was GL about when it started? Family. Usually the formula called for two families that are opposing each other in particular ways. What has happened, and our show is an example of this, the family grew up, the matriarch got older, the brothers became professional people, doctor and lawyer, developed families of their own. Because of the nature of the problems of society with which we deal--infidelity, divorce, etc.--the families

experience the same kind of dissolution that
sociologists tell us is, was rampant in the
United States in the sixties and seventies.
What are we seeing now? We are seeing a conscious move by writers, producers, so on,
dealing with the question, a constant effort
to deal with the question, where is the emotional substance of the show? The answer
keeps coming back--the family. You think of
the show in terms of core family whom you care
about. You take Maureen and put her in the
disco with Katie, Hillary, etc. You don't
care about her, outside the family, but if
you see them, as a part of that family, that
chemistry is there. That sense of loyalty to
the family is so strong in our concept of
character and what our audience tells us they
want to see. We believe society is trying to
say to us, and we are therefore, mirroring it,
it is so strong. When we look at the show and
say where is its strength, we say the source
is family. Five years ago, while that ideal
was there is was dissolved . . . the problem
we face is how to get back into that family
feeling. The characters people care about are
characters who have some emotional attachment
tosome central core.

Given the existence of a domesticated world, of a family core, the program is an exploration of the relationships
of self to others, of individual to community. What are the
appropriate responsibilities of the individual to others and
to one's self? What are the limits of concern beyond which
that concern becomes personally destructive? One of the
ways this issue is embodied in soaps is in terms of the consequences of concealing or disclosing information about relationships.

Tension and suspense derive from the viewer's privileged knowledge of the behavior of the characters. There is
a feeling of power as the viewer watches and cares about the
consequences of disclosure or the concealment of information. The moral consequences become intensified as the tensions between self, others, and the ambiguity of social
reality and relationships are explored. However, despite all
the divorce, murder, duplicity, and conflict, the fundamental
rightness of the moral order is ultimately upheld and affirmed, even if only briefly.

Social cohesion is continually made problematic. The writer plays with the ideal of cohesion by creating relationships that bring people together only to drive them apart, frequently placing obstacles in the path of true love. The tension between the socially ideal condition of domestic and social harmony and the frustrations of reaching that ideal is at the core of the drama.

The dramatic hold of the symbolic world is also related to a sense of intimacy, which is created in a number of ways. Viewers come to feel they know the characters well--characters are continually there, and their most intimate feelings, desires, and behaviors are accessible. Continuing characters in continuing relationships with the audience creates the potential for an intense interest in, and identification with, characters. Intensity is also connected with the emotional depth derived from repeated experiencing of the performances. The personalistic, intimate focus on highly emotional themes can create an experience of considerable emotional depth and intensity. The viewers' involvement and investment of time and energy can embody a form of moral commitment as they vicariously participate in the symbolic world. There is moral commitment at issue in the symbolic world and the simultaneous moral commitment of the viewer to watching the program itself.

The character and quality of the relationships of the participants and the importance of social harmony are very evident when relationships are disrupted. On such occasions, virtually the entire community is affected as the news spreads and characters react. The well-being and appropriateness of the responses of major characters are crucial as characters express concern, proffer help, stimulate and re-stimulate the tension between the ideal expectations and the unpredictable outcome, and animate associations with past experience.

In one episode, aired March 29, 1982, Alan, the wealthy, powerful corporate executive who was in prison for past misdeeds, disappears. One major conjecture was that he escaped after overpowering a guard. While purportedly traveling to the capital, he was actually at the house of the prison warden. The ruse was part of a plan to determine who had been threatening his life. It was hoped that another attempt would be made on Alan's life during the trip and the victimizer would then be caught. A second conjecture was that Alan had actually been kidnapped. For Hope, Alan's wife, the occasion is a difficult one since she does not believe he would try to escape and she fears for his well-being. She is extremely indignant that people believe Alan escaped. The disappearance also has a major impact on Amanda, Alan's "illegitimate" daughter, who feels she has been betrayed. Alan signed over his stocks in Spaulding Enterprises to Amanda and made her the major power in the corporation. The disappearance occurs just before a crucial stockholder's meeting. Amanda feels that Alan has deceived her because she feels the value of the stocks will plummet with the news of his disappearance.

It is difficult to capture how the event stimulates and restimulates associations with past events and current tensions. For example, Amanda has been continually hurt by men and has a great deal of trouble trusting them. Alan's escape reactivates that issue or tension, particularly because she had become more trusting before Alan's escape. Hope has been very supportive of her husband and feels particularly protective of him. She is protective not only because his life is in jeopardy, but because she feels he has truly become a different person through their love for each other. He is no longer the manipulative, power-hungry individual he was.

Because virtually every character knows all other characters, and typically cares about them or is involved in an emotionally significant relationship, even if a hostile one, the disruptive event disrupts the entire social world.

In an early scene in the episode, Ed Bauer brings the news of Alan's disappearance to the stockholder's meeting. The affirmation of the personal ties and nature of the community is reflected in Ed's statement that his brother, Mike, "wanted me to tell you so you <u>wouldn't find out the news from a stranger</u>." [Emphasis mine]

Amanda reacts strongly and directly. "What a fool I've been to believe my father could turn into something I could trust or respect." Amanda's mother responds, trying to soften the blow, given Amanda's fragility and suspiciousness. "Now, Amanda, we don't know what is going on." But Amanda is convinced of her interpretation of the event.

Amanda:  He knew, he knew. When he called me yesterday acting concerned, he knew . . .
No wonder he signed over all those stocks to me. He planned it. He knew what was going to happen, all those stocks would plummet and he knew it. Well, I'm going to prove to him just how wrong he is if it is the last thing I do . . .

Ross, a lawyer, is present, and he, in the same setting with Amanda, expresses concern for Hope.

Ross:  Ed, how is Hope taking all this?

Ed:        Well, as you can imagine she refuses to accept
           it . . . Well, I think I'll get back to Hope.

Ross:      Listen, Ed, thanks for coming over here and giving
           us the news. And give my love to Hope. [Emphasis
           mine]

Ed:        I will.

     A personal and caring universe is repeatedly affirmed
with expressions of concern and offerings of love, as in
Ross's asking Ed to "give Hope my love." Later in the same
scene, Henry Chamberlain brings Ross news about Ross's
wife. Ross is concerned because she is late for the meeting. Her lateness calls into play associations of her lap-
ses of memory, finding herself in bizarre situations, and
the split in her personality.

Henry:     Ross, Carrie just telephoned to say she overslept,
           but that she'll be over shortly.

Ross:      Thank heavens. I was about to go over there myself
           before Ed came with the news.

Henry:     What news?

Ross:      Henry, several hours ago, Alan broke out of prison.

Henry is visibly shaken—he has a weak heart—and Ross helps
him in turn.

     The expressions of concern and interest in each other
occur throughout the episode. There are scenes with younger
characters, who are toasting Maureen's new job at the hospital and who are clearly upbeat, receiving the news that
Judy Collins, a popular singer, will be at the disco later.
This serves as a counterpoint to the heaviness or the intensity of the tensions triggered by Alan's disappearance. Two
of the younger characters, Kelly and Hillary, who are at
Hillary's apartment, receive the news about Alan and react,
making explicit connections with analogous events in their
lives.

Hillary: I'm sorry this news had to come tonight and put
           such a damper on the dinner party.

Kelly:   I feel so sorry for what it is doing to Hope. Bert [Hope's grandmother] could hardly speak when she got on the phone.

. . .

Hillary: Derek [Hillary's current partner, although she is more attracted to Kelly] said Amanda was really upset when she got the news. A lot of guests left the party. He said he wanted to stay and help out, so we should eat anytime we feel like it.

Kelly:   If it's all right with you, Hillary, I'd hold off on that business. Kinda reminded me of that morning you had to be over to the Reardon's and tell me Morgan had been kidnapped.

Hillary: I can certainly remember how I felt when I brought you that news. I'm sure it's the same way Ed felt having to tell Hope.

Kelly:   We've shared a lot of important times together, haven't we? Some good . . . some not so good.

Hillary: We sure have. I think that's what real friendships are all about—sharing the bad times and good times.

Again, the conflict between romantic interest and friendship is stimulated, and past events are explicitly associated with the present. The ideal of emotional and social solidarity is repeated and reinforced with the identification of past and present concerns.

The tension between self-concern and the concern for the well-being of others also is repeatedly created or restimulated. Carrie finally arrives at the meeting.

Carrie: On the way over in the cab all I could think about was my problems. Now all I can think about is Amanda and what she must be feeling, and Hope, too.

Ross:   Well, Henry is the one I'm worried about. He turned white as a sheet when I told him the news about Alan. Mark and I got him into this room, got him to take his medicine. I offered to call Justin [Henry's doctor] but he wouldn't hear of it . . .

Conflicting obligations are also stimulated in other exchanges. Mark, an executive to whom Vanessa is attracted, decides he will spend time with Amanda rather than with

Reacting to
the news of
Alan's dis-
appearance.

Close-up
of Hope.

Amanda and
her mother.

Amanda's
pain.

Vanessa. While he wants to share Vanessa's success with the disco, Wired for Sound, he feels he should stay with Amanda.

Mark:     . . . but I also realize Amanda needs people here to help her through this much more than you need me to share your successes.

Vanessa:     . . . I love you all the more for being so considerate of other people's feelings.

At times concern takes the form of overt advice and reflection on past experience. At one point Amanda says she hates Alan. Carrie replies that "I can't tell you what a destructive force hatred can be," reflecting on her destructive and self-destructive past after her lover committed suicide.

The episode illustrates the melodramatic character of the viewing experience, not only in the use of sensational incident to create intensified effects, but in weaving together a number of destinies in the context of a domesticated world.

[The] melodrama shows how the complex ambiguities and tragedies of the world ultimately reveal the operation of a benevolent, humanly oriented moral order. Because of this, melodramas are usually rather complicated in plot and character; instead of identifying with a single protagonist through his line of action. The melodrama typically makes us intersect imaginatively with many lives. Sub-plots multiply, and the point of view continually

shifts in order to involve us in a complex of
destinies. (Cawelti 1976:45)

A number of factors, many of which I discuss later,
combine to account for the nature of the experience the program makes available. Visually, the use of a limited range
of shots, particularly close-ups and extreme close-ups, the
reliance on gradually tightening shots as the scenes progress and emotional significance is emphasized, and the voy-
euristic framing of the action and point of view all contribute to the emotional intensity. The themes of romance and
quests for power and success combine with patterns of concealment and disclosure in the framework of situations of
mystery, jeopardy, intrigue, and suspense to create an emotional involvement in the lives of the participants in the
alternative world of the performances.

Also, the extreme concern shown, the overlapping and
continuing relationships in the context of the emotionally
charged situations, the heightened visual expressions and
explicit verbalizations of motivations and feelings, the
transparent and precise language, the overt moralizing and
the bounded character of the community as the characters
deal with the restricted range of discrepancies between the
ideal moral/social order and events within the frames all
create a potential form of social participation unlike any
other.

Guiding Light provides an alternative to everyday
experience that can be filled with mystery, adventure,
intrigue, spectacle, and glamor, largely as an adjunct to
romance. At the same time, the program is designed and
often experienced, as mirroring the reality of everyday
life. A realism of detail is created so that the programming resonates or articulates with dominant conceptions of
how we acomplish social life or should accomplish it.

The social world is largely white, Anglo-Saxon, Protestant, and upper-middle class. Social success and dominance,
wealth and power are valued and sought after, but only if
they do not destroy domestic or personal relationships.
Power and wealth are not to be used selfishly or vindictively. The motivations (and justifications) for behavior
are rooted in familial and interpersonal experiences, partic-
cularly romantic engagements. The world Guiding Light
invites us to participate in is a domesticated world, with
domestic romance at its core.

# 4

# The Economic Context

[Commercial] television is primarily a marketing medium and secondarily an entertaining
medium, but it is primarily a marketing medium. (Sonny Fox, quoted in Klein 1979:36)

The shaping context for the production of Guiding Light and
other soaps is the competition for daytime television audiences. This chapter explores how and why Procter and Gamble
provides resources for the production of Guiding Light in
the competition for that audience. I first discuss the
appeals of soaps to advertisers and networks; then I discuss
the conflicting interests and changing relationship between
Procter and Gamble, which owns Guiding Light, and CBS, the
network airing the program. Finally, I interrelate soaps
and commercials, giving priority to the commercial to emphasize the economic interests shaping the performances.
   Soap programming is compatible with, or complementary
to, the commercials at their core. The symbolic world of
Guiding Light emphasizes domestic romance, while commercials
emphasize romanticized domesticity. Taken together, they
simultaneously reach viewers, potential markets, and consumers in the context of an advanced capitalist society. From
an economic perspective, the never-ending tale that is Guiding Light is paralleled by never-ending viewing and consumption.

## THE APPEALS OF SOAPS TO ADVERTISERS AND NETWORKS

The economic interests supporting daytime serials are reflected in the conventional label "soap opera" or "soaps."
Sponsored by soap companies, but more accurately corporations
selling home and family care products, soap operas are created to attract a predominantly female audience, often referred to as "the lady of the house" or "the woman in the home"
by advertising executives. The close and traditional assoc-

iation between the programs and sponsors is easily overlooked with the familiarity of the label.

Soaps are created to reach women and to provide a context for advertising products used in the home. They are
specifically designed to reach women 25 to 54 years old and,
increasingly, to reach women 18 to 49. In both cases, it is
women at the lower end of the age scale who are the primary
object of the current programming and advertising strategy.
While women 25 and over are the largest spenders, garnering
younger viewers contributes to higher ratings and may lead
to network/program/product loyalty. They will become major
consumers as they establish their own households and rear a
family. Soaps are appealing to certain advertisers because
they largely reach women who buy their products. They are
appealing to networks because networks use programming to
sell access to markets to advertisers.

The economics of soap production and the fees they
bring in from advertising make them very profitable for the
networks and attractive to sponsors who wish to reach repeatedly the ideal female market for their products. Soaps are
relatively inexpensive to produce, and advertising costs are
relatively low compared to prime-time. The profits are enormous.

Daytime dramas have a yearly budget in the
range of $30 million and can earn their
respective networks upwards of $150 million
in profits. In 1981, daytime television
accounted for $1.4 of the total $5.6 billion
in network advertising revenues. (Brown
1982a:26)

Soaps are also attractive to the networks because they are
carried by almost all the affiliates upon whom the networks
rely for distribution of the programming. While no program
gets 100 percent clearance, soaps such as General Hospital
(ABC) and Guiding Light (CBS) are carried by 99 percent of
the affiliates.

For the networks and soap producers such as Procter and
Gamble, soaps are attractive because they are inexpensive to
make or lease. For example, it costs approximately $500,000
to make one episode of a prime-time situation comedy, the
same amount it costs to manufacture five episodes (five
hours) of a soap opera (Steinberg 1980:136). While the
advertising rates that networks charge are lower during the
day than for night prime-time, the total income from advertising is substantial given the low costs of manufacturing

and/or leasing a show. "For instance, although a 30-second commercial brings in only about $15,000 during the daytime hours as compared to $50,000 or more during prime-time . . . the proportion of commercials to production costs for a week of a daytime series more than makes up for the initial cost differences" (Cantor 1979:70).

During a one-hour program, and most soaps are now one hour long, approximately 12 minutes are allotted to advertising. Using a base figure of $15,000 for each 30-second spot, and allowing 12 minutes for advertising, generates advertising revenues of $360,000 for one episode, or $1.85 million for five episodes. The figures make it very clear that daytime television is an important moneymaker and, in fact, supports the costly and risky dynamics of prime-time production.

The producing costs for soaps are kept down in a number of ways. The shows are videotaped rapidly, with minimal rehearsal time. Most of the taping occurs in the studio, and a limited number of sets are used repeatedly. There also were economies of scale when the programs became an hour in length: some of the costs did not increase proportionately. Salaries for performers are lower than they are for prime-time. Stars are not essential to daytime soap opera and, as a result, actors gain less power on soaps than in other forms of production and command smaller salaries. Overall, salaries tend to be lower for many production roles compared to prime-time (Cantor 1979:69-70). Production costs have increased as performers have become aware of the profits from daytime because of the attention given to daytime, and production values have changed given the increased competition for the daytime audience. But the costs remain low relative to the profit they bring in.

Another factor that explains the attractiveness of soaps to sponsors (and therefore networks) is that costs are low for spots—between $7,000 and $30,000 for 30 seconds—and they can reach the same body of women frequently. Many women watch a show more than once during the week, and many watch more than one show. The stable, continuing audience is also a stable, continuing market or potential market. Advertising strategies are based upon a knowledge of viewing habits. Advertisers will place the same commercials on different networks and at different times on the same network as part of their strategy. Procter and Gamble purchases spots during the ABC soaps, particularly All My Children and One Life to Live, which are aired at the same time as Procter and Gamble owned soaps on CBS and NBC. They will also sponsor prime-time programs to reach women who are not home or who do not watch television during the day.

The number of female television viewers is considerable, and larger than the number of male viewers.

Women from 18 to 49 watch T.V. more hours than men the same age watch. In the fall of 1976, the viewing time of these younger adult women was almost seven hours per week more than that of younger adult men. Their total viewing increased by more than four hours in the last three years, and they remain above the overall average for individual viewing, with over 31 hours a week. (Steinberg 1980: 151)

The general pattern nationwide is one in which the number of women viewers increases during the day. By three p.m., "25 percent of all women 18 to 49 years old are watching T.V." (Steinberg 1980:152). The daytime audience is 70 to 80 percent women, with approximately 50 million women a week regularly watching soaps.

Another consideration is the relative stability of the profits and audience in daytime. Prime-time programming is very costly and extremely risky. Many shows are failures, the programming schedule is constantly being changed, and the initial high costs are covered only if a program lasts long enough to be marketed for syndication. Soaps are an area of relative calm compared to the unpredictability of prime-time.

The increased media attention to daytime television is related to the increasing popularity of prime-time soaps such as Dallas, Dynasty, and Falcon Crest. Among other qualities, soaps attract a continuing audience with greater loyalty to a program than to a game show, for instance. At the same time that prime-time has become increasingly unpredictable for programmers and viewers, the overall audience for network television has been shrinking as the networks compete with cable, videodiscs, cassettes, and other electronic innovations, and changes in the work force and popular tastes. Soaps are increasingly attractive to the networks as competition increases and the overall audience size shrinks since audiences are more loyal to soap programming in comparison to other types of network fare.

It is clear that both serials and series have advantages for programme planners: a timeslot as it is significantly called, can be filled for a run of weeks, and in their elements of continuity the series and the

serial encourage attachment to a given station or channel. (Williams 1975:60)

A soap is a continuing story that ideally creates a continuing audience. The audience member is a consumer of the
advertisements, program, and network if again, ideally, a
brand loyalty develops to the show, products and network.
From another perspective, the continuing audience is a product that is generated to consume shows, advertisements, and
products. As Williams notes, a brand loyalty can develop,
insuring a stable audience/market. In fact, the soaps on
ABC are identified by many viewers as the ABC soaps. ABC's
success in creating a brand loyalty to the soaps they owned
and the enormous profits from them changed the relationship
between Procter and Gamble and CBS.


ORGANIZATIONAL RELATIONSHIPS AND INTERESTS

Whereas the predominant pattern of program production for
network television is one whereby independent producers or
the network itself makes the programming, and the network in
turn sells spots or time to advertising sponsors, Procter
and Gamble continues the older pattern of sponsor ownership
and control. Procter and Gamble Productions owned six soaps
and now owns five. In addition to Guiding Light, an hour-
long show, it also owns As the World Turns, a one-hour show,
and Search For Tomorrow, a half-hour program. When I began
my study, all appeared on the CBS network, but on March 29,
1982, Search For Tomorrow was moved to NBC. Another World
and Texas (now cancelled), both hour-long programs, were
aired over NBC, and Edge of Night, a half-hour long, aired
over ABC. In addition to making these programs, Procter and
Gamble Productions also produces various specials for television such as the Miss Universe Contest and series such as
Shirley.
    The networks aired thirteen soaps throughout 1981. A
half-hour program called Capitol, owned by John Conboy Productions, replaced Search For Tomorrow when it moved from
CBS to NBC, making the total fourteen as of March 29, 1982.
The other soaps included four very successful ABC-owned
shows: All My Children, One Life to Live, and General Hospital, all an hour long, and Ryan's Hope, a half-hour long.
CBS also broadcast The Young and the Restless, co-owned by
Corday Productions, Columbia, and Bill Bell. NBC aired Days
of Our Lives and The Doctors (which is now also cancelled).[8]

Guiding Light is owned by Procter and Gamble Productions, Incorporated, which is part of General Advertising Services, a division of Procter and Gamble, Incorporated. Procter and Gamble Productions contracts with and through Compton Advertising to carry out the actual production, a practice dating from 1937. The producers, actors, directors, and other staff members of the program are paid by Compton. Compton also contracts with CBS for facilities, technicians, and other personnel necessary for making the program.

Procter and Gamble Productions leases the programs to the networks. It leased three, and eventually two, programs to CBS. CBS pays Procter and Gamble and, in turn, CBS sells time during a program to Procter and Gamble. Procter and Gamble retains not less than half the time allotted to advertising and retains some control over the time periods they do not use. Originally, this meant that other soap manufacturers could not advertise on the Procter and Gamble owned shows. As Procter and Gamble has extended the range of products it manufactures and markets—paper products such as toilet paper and paper towels, tampons, nationally distributed coffee, and others—it has negotiated with CBS on the conditions limiting the use of the non-Procter and Gamble time. For example, a limiting condition might stipulate that a competing manufacturer and advertiser such as a tampon manufacturer could not advertise on a particular show more than once or twice a week. Another consequence was that competitors such as Colgate-Palmolive Peet and Lever Brothers had corporate policies against buying time on the Procter and Gamble owned soaps. Procter and Gamble's continued involvement in soap production demonstrates the importance of soaps as an environment or domain, to use Barnouw's phrase (1979), for commercials to reach a particular audience/market.

Procter and Gamble's daytime serials have been and continue to be an important part of our overall marketing efforts. They provide an effective and highly economical way to deliver product messages to current or potential customers in the home environment, where Procter and Gamble's products are mostly used. (Procter and Gamble Customer Services)

Procter and Gamble's primary interest is in the cost of reaching the market, their cost per thousand viewers. The lower the costs, the better. CBS, on the other hand, is interested in selling spots to advertisers. The higher the costs for the spots, the greater its potential profit. The ratings and demographics of the audience directly affect the advertising rates or cost of the spots. Whereas CBS and Procter and Gamble once dominated daytime television, this is no longer the case. ABC is very successful in reaching a larger and younger female audience with soaps it owns directly. It not only controls the programming and establishes higher rates for the advertising, it also controls all the advertising time itself and makes larger profits.

The importance of ratings to networks, the differing interests of the networks and Procter and Gamble, as well as the uncertainty in media production, which I discuss later, are illustrated in the following comments of the headwriter of Guiding Light. He had previously written General Hospital and discussed what occurred at a meeting immediately after General Hospital rose to the number-one position in the ratings for the first time.

I remember meeting Agnes Nixon downstairs at the elevator because Agnes was a consultant for all the shows on ABC and it was the week that General Hospital hit number one solid—we wiped everything else out. The fact that this poor pathetic show was the solid number one show was like victory—this was the first story meeting I haven't dreaded. Agnes said, "Don't be too sure." I said, "What can they say, we're number one?" Jackie Smith came in and said, her opening remarks, she was a half-hour late, and said, "We're in terrible trouble." I couldn't believe it. Her maid that morning had said that the Laura, Bobbie, Scotty thing was boring, she didn't like it —all our eggs are in that basket. I said, "It was the basket that brought us here." She said, "Yes, now we have to find ways to stay there." "We can't go on telling the same story." I said, "The story isn't even over yet." I couldn't believe it. Agnes was totally right. She winked at me from across the room. There is an incredible instinct to panic. I have not found that at all with P & G. [Emphasis mine]

ABC had the three highest rated programs throughout the period I researched. The following are representative figures from January and February of 1982. General Hospital had a rating of 11.4; All My Children, 9.7, and One Life To

Live, 9.4. Guiding Light had a rating of 8.7 in direct competition with General Hospital. This translates into 13.07
million viewers tuned to General Hospital and 9.89 million
tuned to Guiding Light. The other major demographic factor
is the size of the female audience from 18 to 49.

ABC execs also pointed to the daytime ros-
ter's sex appeal among the all-important
women 18 to 49. The latest demographic data,
covering January and February, shows General
Hospital as the favorite with an average of
5,790,000 women per show in that age bracket
out of a total viewership of 13,070,000. ABC
also had the three other demographic biggies
--All My Children with 5,230,000 women 18 to
49 out of 10,750,000 viewers; One Life to Live
with 5,000,000 women 18 to 49; and Ryan's Hope
with 3,200,000.
  Their closest rivals for the women's affec-
tions were CBS's Guiding Light and Young and
the Restless, ties for fifth with slightly
more than 3,000,000 18 to 49 per episode.
Guiding Light had 3,120,000 fewer total viewers than General Hospital in the same 3:00
p.m. to 4:00 p.m. time period. (Forkan
1982:1)

  The differences between the costs for spots on General
Hospital and Guiding Light are considerable. For example,
in the second quarter of 1982, advertising time during General Hospital cost $27,800 for a 30-second spot. Guiding
Light could charge only $16,500 (Flax 1982:66). Not only
were the advertising rates on General Hospital nearly double
those of Guiding Light, but ABC controlled all the advertising time itself, controlled the program content, and made
the profits directly.
  One Guiding Light producer frankly commented on the
changing relationship between CBS and Procter and Gamble:

As the World Turns (a P & G show on CBS) was
the undisputed number one show for so many
years, and all the shows after it. They had
the top six shows and sort of "ruled the
roost" but that isn't the case anymore with
ABC's success. Actually, CBS, if they had
their druthers, would like to get P & G off
their network and force them into simply buying minutes. As you know, P & G gets a big

write-up by owning the shows. Half the commercial minutes CBS is able to sell, but the
other half P & G gets a tremendous discount.
This is why they can take Capitol, force out
Search For Tomorrow and put Capitol in,
knowing that Capitol will come in at a lesser
rating than Search, but they'll make more
money off it.

CBS was particularly frustrated because Procter and Gamble shows consistently attracted an older audience. Added
frustration followed from the loss of the younger audience
that the initial CBS daytime soap attracted. The Young and
the Restless, a CBS owned show, was followed by As the World
Turns, a Procter and Gamble soap.
     Figures from the Nielsen Second Report for November 1981
make the change in audience composition readily apparent.
The figures represent the season average for each age category for both shows as well as for All My Children, which
airs on ABC (see Table 4-1). As the World Turns lost many
younger viewers and picked up older viewers. In comparison,
ABC's All My Children had even larger numbers of younger
viewers, even fewer older viewers than either CBS show.[9]
     The same executive also emphasized the long-term impor-
tance of attracting a larger younger audience. While gaining a younger audience, particularly at the beginning of
summer, was helpful in the ratings competition, long-term
demographics were of even greater importance.


M.I.: Are you interested in the younger view-
ers--teenagers--in terms of what they'll do to
the ratings?

Producer: Sure. In the summer, yes. Going
for younger viewers--by that I mean kids,
teenagers, college kids--people think we are
out for some big number we are going to get
right away. What a lot of older viewers fail
to understand is they started watching the
CBS shows 25 years ago when they were that
age--either teens or young marrieds, college.
If we don't hook those viewers now we are going to lose them. Now ABC made a concerted
effort over the last 15 years to go for a
younger audience and that audience grew up on
ABC and that audience is the middle of the
baby boom. That baby boom grew up and went

TABLE 4.1
AGE DISTRIBUTION OF WOMEN VIEWERS
(Viewers per thousand viewing households)

| | Total | 18-34 | 18-49 | 25-54 | 35-64 | 55+ |
|---|---|---|---|---|---|---|
| The Young and the Restless | | | | | | |
| CBS | | | | | | |
| 12:30 - 1:30 | 895 | 290 | 468 | 395 | 374 | 362 |
| As the World Turns | | | | | | |
| CBS | | | | | | |
| 1:30 - 2:30 | 899 | -185* | -349 | -344 | +407* | +485 |
| All My Children | | | | | | |
| ABC | | | | | | |
| 1:00 - 2:00 | 910 | 465 | 653 | 476 | 309 | 224 |

*Minus (-) and plus (+) indicate change in audience size in various categories for The Young and the Restless and As the World Turns.

Source: Nielsen Second Report, November 1981.

71

home to have kids and they are sitting number one, a lot for that reason. At CBS we are very alone and some of our soaps have less younger viewers than NBC with a lower rating. What we have to do is get some of those younger viewers into the pipe line so that the person sitting at this desk ten years from now doesn't commit hari-kari. What's going to happen is if we don't get younger viewers now, our hunk of audience which is over 55 (which is the bulk of our viewers) they are going to be over 65. I don't mean it to sound terrible, but people pass away. I think we have to bring more people in at the bottom of the demographic scale or we are going to have problems.

CBS and Procter and Gamble had similar interests in long-term viewing habits and demographics. The comments of one Procter and Gamble producer reflected the point.

M.I.: Are you going after a younger audience because that audience is so important in terms of ratings? Or is it because they will be future consumers?

Producer: Both. They are going to be buying our product.

M.I.: You hope that if they are loyal to the show, they will be loyal to the product?

P: That's why these shows exist in the first place. It's a phenomenal thing that nobody understands in the first place. . . . And it is a fact that the audience that watches a soap opera is intensely loyal to that show and some of the audience loyalty certainly spills over to the products.

So while CBS and Procter and Gamble had conflicting interests in capturing the daytime audience/market, they both shared a concern for long-term audience loyalty; in the one case, loyalty to network; in the other, loyalty to products. Both interests are mediated by the soap performances and the commercials at their heart.

COMMERCIALS AS PERFORMANCES

The commercial works as a kind of "organic"
connector--linking together consumers, image-
makers, producers, networks, sponsors, corporations, economic systems--and contributes more
to the mediating of ideas than any other type
of programming. (Goethals 1981:137)

Whereas we tend to distinguish programming from commercials,
and consider commercials as inserts in programming, it is
revealing to consider both as part of one process and give
priority to the commercial. Soaps exist to provide a context for commercials just as news exists to fill the advertising spaces in newspapers.

[News] is news because it is necessary to
have something to fill the space between the
advertisements which are slotted en masse in
advance, into each day's projected paper.
(Schiller 1980:89)

    The economic or commercial basis to the communication
process generates soaps that are compatible or complementary
to the commercials. I distinguish two broad categories of
commercials that appear with soap programming. One category
advertises products that make household chores potentially
easier and less time consuming--laundry detergents, floor
polish, cleanser, paper towels, and others. Such commercials appeal to a sense of identity that values, or is
reflected in, happy children and husbands, approving friends
and neighbors. As many manufacturers have found out, commercials for products that claim to save women time or that
appeal to their desire to make domestic responsibilities
easier, are very successful.
    The second major category of commercials has to do with
personal attractiveness for women. Deodorants, hair spray,
panty hose, facial creams, for example, are presented as
contributing to social approval in general, but more importantly, to romantic success or appreciation. As many people
have observed, what commercials sell, in effect, is an
idealized self-image. Both home and family care products
tend to emphasize a romanticized domesticity. The first
category of commercials makes household chores important to
domestic relationships; the second category directly emphasizes social approval and romantic appreciation.
    The following representative sample of commercials for
the March 29, 1982, air show (script/episode 8865) illus-

trates the general themes. The commercials primarily romanticize domesticity and largely portray women as superior to men in the domestic arena. A young girl shows a male that Bounce is the right softener to use; Rosie shows the cost-conscious male that Bounty is more effective, thus cheaper; a woman tells her male companion that Crisco oil is light. Similarly there are the triumphs of using Coast soap and being refreshed and of using Ivory dishwashing liquid and having hands that stay young looking. Finally, many commercials begin with a problem and disapproval but, through the use of the advertised product, the problem disappers and social approval is regained. A woman finds "suds in her closet" but is redeemed through the use of Dash; another woman is redeemed by the use of Downy softener which "rinses in April freshness." Part I of the show is presented by Dash, "the detergent that rinses dirt and suds out of your wash," and Ivory, "Mild Ivory liquid, it helps your hands stay young looking."

1. <u>Ivory dishwashing liquid</u>: Commercial shows two women at ski lodge; they say they are 30, but one is really 44 and the mother of three. Ivory is described as helping her hands "stay young looking" and as getting her dishes "really clean."

2. <u>Bounce clothes softener</u>: A sister shows her brother that Bounce is the right softener to use.

3. <u>Dash</u>: A woman is advised she has "suds in her closet," and, disturbed by the charge, she rinses her washed clothes to find that they do contain suds. A child remarks, "Icky suds." The mother says, "I don't want this stuff in my family's laundry." Commercial ends after Dash is used, wash is free of suds, and child looks on approvingly.

4. <u>Bounty paper towels</u>: "Rosie" demonstrates to cost-conscious male that Bounty is a better buy than bargain brand paper towels since they absorb much more per sheet. Commercial ends with her joking about <u>her</u> fee to the cost-conscious male.

5. <u>Pringle's potato chips</u>: Chorus shown with a music teacher. The children break into song, "We've got the fever for the flavor of a Pringle." She joins children after tasting a Pringle in singing the praises of the potato chip.

6. <u>Coast deodorant soap</u>--"The Eye Opener": A tired mother is awakened by two children and reminded it is the day of the Chipmunk campout. She is shown in shower coming back to life with Coast, and at the end of the commercial she is shown hitting children with pillows, playfully and energetically.

7. <u>Doxidan laxative</u>:  A man is shown holding a capsule for a "unique laxative called Doxidan." The pill contains a laxative for constipation and a stool softener for discomfort. The commercial ends with the fact that the product has been "recommended by doctors and pharmacists for years."

8. <u>Secret deodorant</u>:  A husband and wife are shown preparing to go fishing in the morning. The woman doesn't want to use her husband's deodorant and insists she wants to use Secret which is "made for a woman, but strong enough for a man." The husband says the fish won't care if she uses his, but she says she does since it will keep her "fresh and dry."

9. <u>Crisco oil</u>:  A male is shown holding a salad, and a woman suggests he use Crisco oil since it is light and not oily. He tastes salad and says there is "no heavy oily taste." Commercial ends with woman remarking that she was glad there was room for the oil after salad ingredients fall out of man's over-filled bowl.

At mid-break there are promotional pieces, public service ads, program identification, and commercials for Kleenex Huggies disposable diapers and Thrift Drug – Theragran.

Part II of <u>Guiding Light</u> is presented by Downy clothes softener, which "makes your clothes smell April fresh," and Oxydol laundry detergent "for sparkling whites."

1. <u>Oxydol</u>:  Against the backdrop of a crowd at a ballgame, a woman stands in a white dress which reflects the improvement in Oxydol that makes for a "whiter white."

2. <u>Duncan Hines cake mix</u>:  A woman is shown in her kitchen with husband and family. She "tickles their noses" with blueberry muffin mix from Duncan Hines. Also, a farm setting and kitchen are shown.

3. <u>Downy softener</u>:  A younger woman, the mother of the baby in the scene, hears an older woman say that the baby's clothes don't smell fresh. It is suggested by another voice that the clothes are not fresh because Downy, which "rinses in April freshness," was not used.

4. <u>Charmin toilet paper</u>:  A man is shown displaying bargain brand products that his family did and didn't like. As he puts it, "what good is a bargain if they don't like it?" Charmin is approvingly displayed as a product they do like. Scene takes place in a kitchen.

5. <u>Dawn dishwashing liquid</u>:  Dawn is demonstrated to cut grease in washing dishes as glasses are compared. A glass done later with the same dish-water compares favorably with the one done earlier.

6. Folger's coffee: Mrs. Olsen is shown in a kitchen. She praises Folger's coffee and says, "Good coffee is like good cooking, you can taste the difference."
7. Ruffles Brand potato chips: A high school student decides that Ruffles Brand potato chips are best and that they win 2 to 1 and are the "champion chip."
8. Baby Fresh: Wipes are shown being effective with mother cleaning child. There are shots of a happy family and happy mother and child.
9. Aquafresh tooth paste: Aquafresh is shown to offer triple protection in the approving company of mother, child, and pharmacist.
10. 9-Lives cat food: Morris, the finicky cat, is shown.
11. Total cereal: Total is shown to have 100 percent of nine recommended vitamins and also to taste better than other cereals mentioned.
12. Nestlé Toll House chocolate chips: Taste test—chocolate chip cookies made with Nestle chocolate chips are shown to taste best.

In a fundamental way, the products and the commercials for the products help form both the audience for the soap and the market for the product. The advertised products create the possibility of giving the viewer more free time, or they cultivate the viewer's sense of efficiency concerning household chores. They may do both, but soaps and commercials from this perspective certainly create their own audience.

Reversing conventional priorities, soaps are carefully crafted to fit commercials. This process helps explain the criticism that soaps are unrealistic since there are no dirty dishes, unmade beds, and so on in the programming. Presenting such a symbolic setting, in conjunction with commercials that idealize domestic routines and their significance, would be extremely disturbing. A story with scenes reflecting domestic pressures—dirty dishes and misbehaving children—would contradict the aims of the commercials and threaten, from the sponsor's viewpoint, to distance the viewer. It might allow or force the viewer to step back from the program and critically relate commercial and program content. One of the characteristics of soaps is that they are constructed to be engrossing and engaging and, while they primarily deal with the drama of everyday life, they are inherently spectacular alternatives to everyday life. Commercials and programs are to be kept separate, not call each other into question, and yet work to create a context for each other.

Commercials seem to fit into soaps in a way that makes them seem less obtrusive than in other forms of programming

There is a ritualized character to the interruptions throughout commercial television, but the fit between program, commercials, and context of viewing for soaps is unlike any other in that they are all related to the domestic world. Soaps and commercials are largely viewed in the home, and the products advertised are largely used in the home or by family members.

Braudy's observations on the centrality of the family in television and the domestic-viewing context apply to soaps, although he fails to mention them:

The television image is only one of many visual items claiming our attention in the room, as opposed to the single focus on the movie screen. The continuity of television is not only within its own elements, but also with all the other objects surrounding it. The problem of attractig and keeping attention in television is, therefore, a much greater aesthetic-thematic problem than it is in the normal film. Since the television attention span is usually much shorter than that in any other art, an emphasis on family becomes very important--from situation comedies, to the variety shows with a continuous host and supporting actors, to the talk shows --because then the images on the screen can form a link with the people in the room. (1977:6)

Another way programs and commercials fit together is that both promote a life of high consumption and ease. The programming's alternative to ordinary reality is glamorous and spectacular, largely concentrating on the upper-middle class and upper-class people. The world of work is largely absent from soaps, and people have a great deal of time for each other. Commercials promote a life of ease through consumption, which at the same time promotes a sense of caring in the viewer--viewers could see themselves being seen as a concerned and caring persons.

Porter insightfully comments on the relationships of program and commercials:

The price the viewer pays for pleasure is the ad, but the ad is tolerated, even enjoyed on different levels for its own sake, because it functions like the formal device of retardation. More importantly, however, the ad is ac-

cepted because it interrupts without necessarily breaking the spell. But in order for this
to occur, it is essential that the unfolding
drama and its interpolated "messages" be kept
separate. 1979:94)

One way the messages are kept separate is through the
visual or storytelling conventions employed. In the soaps I
observed, different visual conventions were used at the
beginning and end of acts, versus scenes within the acts.
"Fades" are used to come out of commercials, and to lead
into commercials; "cuts" occur between acts. In most commercials, the participants look directly at the viewers
and/or speak directly to them. This contrasts with the conventions used in soaps. Commercials also provide a form of
dramatic counterpoint. Many commercials begin with a prob-
lem--a dirty collar or a dirty floor, for example--and end
with the problem solved and harmony restored in a matter of
seconds. This is in marked contrast to the never-ending
problems of the programs themselves. The simplicity and
speed with which the problem in each commercial is solved is
quite different from the slower and more complex resolving
of the problems providing the dramatic conflicts of the program.

There are a number of policies or practices designed to
keep programs and commercials separate. Actors who appear
on a Procter and Gamble soap are not permitted, by contract,
to appear in ads for their products or in ads for competitors' products. There are a number of reasons for this policy.

We don't want an actor on the show to represent our product when that product will appear in the context of the show. We go to
great pains to keep that from happening--the
reason being that if . . . Ed Bauer were to
represent Pepto Bismol, if Peter Simon were
to say . . . "This is Pepto Bismol. Drink
it. It tastes good, and you should use it to
cure your sour belly," the audience would see
that. They would know intellectually that he
is not Ed Bauer, that he is Peter Simon and
he is saying words that were written for him
by whoever owns that product to sell that
product. They would be identifying that back
to the show, which would imply an endorsement
of the product, because the show is in some
way related to the use of the product, which
we don't want.

> We don't want the characters, the actors, to be identifiable with the product. We don't want to identify a product with the show, or an actor with a product. That would be taking unfair advantage of the audience.

Having Peter Simon/Dr. Ed Bauer promoting a product would imply that since he is a doctor, he must know what he is talking about. One example of the practice alluded to occurred when Robert Young, who was well established as a television doctor, Marcus Welby, advertised a decaffeinated coffee, citing doctors' recommendations for the product. The advertisers made use of Young's persona as Dr. Welby by association in the commercial. There are other factors behind the separation of commercial and show.

> We are also concerned that if you see Peter Simon in a commercial selling a product, and the next second he is talking to Rita (his promiscuous wife), that also reflects on the product—possibly negatively. More important, it also interferes with your ability to say that an actor in the commercial is that actor on the show and it creates a violation of that "willing suspension of disbelief."

The aims of creating good will between Procter and Gamble and the audience would be undermined, as might the dramatic hold of the programming. Procter and Gamble associates itself with the programming by announcing at the beginning and mid-point of each episode that "Guiding Light is presented by Downy clothes softener, which makes your clothes smell April fresh, and by Oxydol laundry detergent for sparkling whites" or two other products (thereby also gaining free mention of their products). The ultimate intent is the same for show and commercials, which also helps explain the complementarity or fit between show and commercials, as well as the practices that keep the messages separate. As one producer noted, "The intent is the same—to make you feel good about character/show, character/product in an opposite context."

The processes of production and consumption of soaps, comercials, and products are all interrelated. There are parallel or simultaneous processes involved in the production and distribution of the programming, the commercials, and the products the commercials advertise as shown in Table 4-2.

TABLE 4-2
PRODUCTION/PERFORMANCE/CONSUMPTION

| Production & Distribution | Product/Performance | Consumer/Audience |
|---|---|---|
| Manufacture & distribution of program | Programming Context for domestic romance | Audience as consumer of show |
| Manufacture & distribution of products | Commercials Romanticizing domesticity and romance to promote | Audience as consumer of commercial and potential market of product advertised |
| Manufacture & distribution of products | Products Purchase of products used in home for family care | Consumer of products and self-image associated with use of product |

Source: Compiled by the author.

From a somewhat different perspective, the audience itself is a product generated to support the overall interrelated system of entertainment/advertising/production. Dallas Smythe forcefully argues that commercial mass media, particularly in North America, have important functions that include producing "people in audiences who work at learning the theory and practice of consumership for civilian goods and who support the military demand management system . . . [and] audiences whose theory and practice confirms the ideology of monopoly capitalism (1977:20).

My research on the practices generating soap programming, the fit between the programming and commercials, and the nature of the symbolic world supports Smythe's characterization of commercial mass media. His characterization gains even more force from a historical perspective on the creation of soaps and soap audiences. What we now take as a given did not exist 50 years ago. James Thurber proves to be an unlikely supporter of such a position in a series of articles he wrote on soaps for the New Yorker in the 1940s:

Hummert and Mrs. Ashencraft [two individuals in advertising who were to become major writers and producers of soaps] figured the largely fallow daytime air of twenty years ago could be transformed into a valuable advertising time.

Things moved slowly at first. Advertisers favored evening hours, because they were convinced that radio entertainment would not be popular during the day. Most men, and many women, they pointed out, worked from eight or nine in the morning until five in the afternoon. They admitted that the millions of American housewives acted as purchasing agents for the home, but they did not see how the peripatetic mass of busy women could be made into an attentive audience. The housewife was notoriously all over the place, upstairs and down, indoors and out . . . Hummert and his assistant decided to invent a daytime program first and then try to adjust it to the nature of the housewife. (1970:201)

The effort clearly succeeded. Soap operas as an art or entertainment form were virtually developed to help create an audience and, thus, support the larger pattern of economic, social, and ideological relationships. Changes over the past several years in the competitive context changed the relationship between Procter and Gamble and CBS and generated considerable pressure to alter the Procter and Gamble formula for soaps in order to attract and hold the ideal audience. Just as Hummert and his assistant developed and adjusted early programming to the nature of the housewife, so Procter and Gamble, with CBS's nudging, was seeking to change the storytelling to recapture the (younger) woman in the home.

# 5
## Soap Storytelling as Corporate Enterprise

Many television dramatists now write episodes for serials or series more often than they write single plays. They then usually find themselves writing within an established formation of situation and leading characters, in what can be described as a collective but is more often a corporate dramatic enterprise. Certain formulas on which the continuity depends are then the limiting conventions within which they must work. (Williams 1975:60)

[My] concern is to deepen our grasp of ideological structure by moving beyond fiction as something meaningful through purporting to be pictorial representation, to a grasp of narrative as stories which are tellable. In the latter sense ideology is not a distorted report but certain limiting presuppositions on how to report. (Chaney 1979:12)

In the following chapter I view soap storytelling as a corporate activity. I demonstrate how the story creation and selection process is (1) influenced by the perception and measurements of success in reaching the ideal audience with a distinctive appealing product in competition with other programs, (2) concerned with reducing uncertainty about the audience will be entertained--literally held by the story, and (3) designed to minimize the risk of offending viewers who might not only avoid the program, but also bring legal or political pressure to bear. These factors are intertwined with economic considerations important in all cases. The problem for the storytellers is one of creating sellable and tellable tales in the competition for audiences.

It is conventional to think of authorship entailing a creative individual working alone or a few authors working together in the case of mass media. This reflects the ideology surrounding artistic production and the tendency to focus on individuals and personalize what is a social process. Storytelling easily becomes a linear, chronological process beginning with the storyteller. Soap storytelling can be viewed as not only a collective activity or process (Becker 1974) but also as Williams suggests, a "corporate dramatic enterprise." While it may seem strange to think of a corporation telling a story, corporations provide the resources and approve the selection and realization of stories. Guiding Light has been on the air since 1937, and, whereas it was once the property of its creator, Irna Phillips, it is now owned by Procter and Gamble. Writers come and go, but the storytelling continues.

One series of events clearly revealed the corporate character of the creation process. The headwriter for Guiding Light during the period I carried out my research left the program in September of 1982. He was replaced by the same headwriter who had replaced him when he left General Hospital, which he had written previously. Writers not only come and go, but they can write stories that compete with each other and from where each leaves off, writing the same story.

The collective (and corporate) nature of the storytelling is also reflected in the importance of standardized conventions and formulas for the communication process.

While standardization is not highly valued in modern artistic ideologies, it is, in important ways, the essence of all literature. Standard conventions establish a common ground between writers and audiences. Without at least some forms of standardization, artistic communication would not be possible. But well-established conventional structures are particularly essential to the creation of formula literature and reflect the interests of audiences, creators and distributors. (Cawelti 1976:9)

Cawelti notes the importance of shared resources or agreements for any communication process, even though we tend to emphasize uniqueness and originality in discussions of literature and other forms of expressive communication. In soap production, there are many pressures to rely on conventions. On the one hand, they provide a common ground and establish patterns of expectation and response. On the other hand, they are necessary for a rapid production process involving many people who quickly and continuously generate a great quantity of material. The conventions, therefore, have a major impact on costs and profit. Conventions refer to social practices that generate a particular structure of images and sounds, as well as to the interpretive strategies or subjective reading of the visual and aural signs. Communicators produce potential forms of experience that the audience makes sense of through its engagement in the process.

Conventions make it possible for a large number of people to progressively realize what are lengthy episodes (scripts). Five days a week, a 75 page script is turned into more than 40 minutes of dramatic performance. I discuss the work process at greater length in the following chapter, but it is important to emphasize the degree to which shared understandings are at work. The headwriter for Guiding Light prepares a lengthy outline of each episode. The outline is turned into a script, largely through the creation of dialogue by subwriters. Each subwriter works on one script a week. The scripts, which provide minimal instruction, are turned into performances by a large number of performers--between 15 and 30 for an episode--with limited interaction between director, performers, and producer. There is not enough time. Formulas make it possible to turn out enough material rapidly, and they make the production process more economical and thereby potentially increase profits.

On the one hand, the storytelling entails hierarchically organized collective practices. On the other hand, the performances have to be engaging and meaningful to audiences. The corporate, public nature of the storytelling in pursuit of profit shapes the stories that are deemed tellable, as this chapter is designed to explore. The focus is not only on what stories are not tellable, but, in a more positive sense, on how and why the stories that are told take the shape they do.


MAKING A COMPETITIVE PRODUCT

The ultimate consideration in creating and selecting stories is that they garner and keep a sufficiently large and demographically appropriate audience. For Guiding Light the ideal audience was a younger, female audience. The competitive context found Guiding Light pitted against the most successful daytime show, General Hospital, which provided the model to be emulated in the quest for a younger, larger audience. One CBS executive provided a succinct characterization of the new direction that CBS desired and which to some extent was gradually being realized.

On Guiding Light we've asked for a number of things. Traditionally, it is like most P & G shows which are very talky and very slow moving and very character oriented. We've asked for faster paced shows with a lot more plot, focusing on less stories. It's carrying eight or nine stories now and it's very hard to follow the show. We've asked for less dialogue in the scenes. They are very overwritten. People tend to talk about what they are doing rather than doing anything. We've asked for more humor. By humor I mean funny things. I mean jokes.

One of the strategies adopted to capture a younger audience was to introduce a larger percentage of younger characters.[10] A number of older characters disappeared rather quickly from the show in the fall of 1981. The executive quoted above estimated that in 1978 more than 75 percent of the characters were over 40, whereas more than two-thirds of the characters were under 30 by 1982.

The ages of the characters had clearly changed, but the stories told and how they were told seemed not to have changed enough. The younger characters still acted as older characters traditionally did.

Now the problem is to tell stories that are right for those ages. Now you watch Guiding Light and Morgan acts like she's 40, Kelly is geriatric. That's a real problem. A party scene, Nola walks in and everybody hates Nola. Everybody sits there very quietly and calmly go, "I can't believe she is here." At a real party a 17 year old would have picked up a handful of pretzels and chucked them across the room. . . . That's how a 17 year old acts. They get drunk, have a good time and say what's on their minds. Ours talk in complete sentences, massive paragraphs and are very, very boring.

CBS research also helped shape the perception of what the program makers thought the (younger) audience would like and supported the drive to change the formula of Guiding

<u>Light</u>. The same executive noted how the research influenced his approach to the programming.

> They [younger viewers] also have a different
> attitude toward watching television. The
> older viewer will sit--do her housework, pick
> up the kids and watch T.V., just for an
> hour. The younger viewers will say, "Oh,
> yeah, I turn this on, and yeah, I'll turn
> that on." They are a much less commmitted
> viewer, I think, and you have to do more to
> grab her.

Given the importance of ratings, and the recent emphasis on upbeat stories, there is also a general tendency to
avoid stories which are downers or upsetting to the audience.[11]  Stories involving homosexuality, incest (where a
brother and sister unknowingly fall in love), wife-beating
and child-beating have been told, but they have been used
infrequently. All such themes appear to tear too deeply at
the fabric of domestic relations. Modleski makes a similar
observation. "An issue like homosexuality, which, perhaps,
threatens to explode the family structure rather than temporarily disrupt it is simply ignored" (1979:15). The
exploration of everyday like is constrained by the pursuit
of ratings, but also by the dominant ideological emphasis on
a romanticized domestic world.

Many factors associated with the look of the show
broadly summarized the new direction or changes in the program. <u>Guiding Light</u> had to be made more appealing and
engaging by emphasizing and fulfilling audience expectations. A competitive product, <u>Guiding Light</u> was to become a
unique product with a distinctive identity. Establishing a
look was important for promoting the programming as uniquely
filling a need.

<u>M.I.</u>: The concern for the look of the show,
is it for the audience to distinguish it from
other shows as something different, special,
or better?

<u>Producer</u>: So that we are different from
other shows, so we do something that says
<u>Guiding Light</u> is intrinsically unique. That
is like you buy a product . . . [interruption]
if a product is marketed to you as a consumer
you have to be convinced, and the product is
usually created because there is a need for

it, you have to be convinced . . . we have to
convince you whether you are an old viewer or
new viewer. We have to convince you that we
are somehow important to you. We fulfill a
need you have--romance, mystery, action--our
show has to have an identity, and that identity is--bang--the image that you saw!

Many factors are perceived as potentially important in
reaching viewers. The general configuration is a show that
is spectacular, glamorous, larger than life, vibrant, and
alive but involving characters that people care about.

M.I.: One term you hear is the look of the
show. What is it a shorthand of?

Producer: You think of an image, a picture.
What is the dominant take-away image you have?
It might be our costumes, which we have put a
great deal of interest in and emphasis on.
It might be our new logo; it might be something as specific as that. The look of the
show might be something more amorphous--the
contrast between the Reardons and the Bauers,
if that is a clear image to you. When you
are dealing with the look of the show you are
dealing with a specific take away. We want
the show to look different. It does look different because our people dress somewhat out
of the range of normal. Vanessa is abnormal
in her dress, Tony in his dress . . . the
costuming is carefully constructed so people
match, so that their material is coordinated,
so that their clothing when you look at it on
the air--that they are designed. The image
is that these people are not totally real.
They're a heightened reality, and the clothing reflects that. That's the look show that
you work for. A young look in fashion, the
new logo, the beat, the drive through, quick
cut. This is all part of the elements that
make us have a young look, attract attention,
trying to say to the audience, tune in, this
is vibrant and alive. Other elements have to
do with the way the characters are viewed;
you look at the Reardon family, and what you
get is a composite, you take away an image of

<u>caring people</u>. Part of what makes the show
<u>what it is is</u> this caring dimension. . . . The
look is also going out on remote. In that way
the show leaps out.

Increased investment in sets and costuming, casting of
performers, and changes in the storytelling conventions were
all justified by a concern for the look of the show. When a
veteran performer left the show, one of the reasons given
for the nonrenewal of his contract and a recast of his part
was that he did not fit the projected look of the show. In
the casting of a major part, a performer who was limited in
her acting ability was chosen because she had the right
look. The issue of the show's look reflected, I think, a
pressure toward a concern for form over content and a view
of the audience as consumer of a dramatic presentation. Put
differently, a basic consideration was product differentiation, a term usually applied to advertisements designed to
convince consumers a particular commodity is unique and
special.

The competition for audiences, and the measurement of
how successful a program is in reaching large and demographically appropriate audiences, affects soap storytelling
directly. Stories were written to appeal to younger viewers, but they were structured in such a way that the program
ideally garners the younger audience at the beginning of the
summer. This helps the ratings, which typically go down in
the summer, but they also, again, ideally capture the younger audience and carry the audience into the fall when they
return to school. Stories are written involving more of the
younger characters, and the stories are designed to peak at
the time students return to school, as a producer stated:

I think all year you try to have something
for everybody. Then in the spring, actually
maybe before that . . . anytime there is a
vacation, when the kids are home from school,
I think you push the people you are going to
tell summer story with, so they get a glimpse
of them. I think we have moved toward that.
You have to address the fact that the audience demographics shift in the summer. You
are talking of a three or four month change
in audience.

Another consideration is the measurement of program
success. Ratings, which reflect a national profile of the

audience, are compiled each week. Sweeps, which are important for establishing local ratings and, ultimately, local
advertising rates, also occur. Sweeps weeks occur in February, May, July, and November. One producer provided an
example of how the ratings measurement period affected the
programming.

> You just try to bring one of the peaks
> together of the story at that point. We are
> in one now. We are throwing in this big
> Busby Berkely thing, and we are hoping CBS is
> going to go overboard giving us promotion.
> We think it is a different look, something
> that hasn't been attempted on daytime be-
> fore. Little gimmicks like that.

The competition for a segment of the audience, the
means used to measure success, viewing patterns, and the aim
of product differentiation combine to strongly influence the
storytelling. These are only a few of the considerations
affecting the decision making.


REDUCING UNCERTAINTY

One characteristic of the production process is the development of strategies to reduce uncertainty.

> The task of those who produce commercial
> television is, of course, to generate pro-
> gramming which can hold an audience for
> advertisers hour after hour, day after day,
> week after week. This is no easy task, due
> first to the difficulty of predicting the
> behavior of both the viewing public and com-
> petitors and, second, to the relatively non-
> routine nature of the production process it-
> self. (Pekurny 1982:131)

As a number of people have noted, a basic characteristic of production for large mass markets is the uncertainty
of whether what is produced will be purchased (McQuail 1969;
Hirsch 1972; Elliott 1979; Pekurny 1982). In Elliott's
words, uncertainty "is particularly characteristic of cultural production because there is no way of knowing which
creative item will appeal to the audience and which, if
selected for production and distribution, will be the greatest economic success" (1979:160).

The commercial and competitive nature of television broadcasting and the high costs, as well as the potential or actual large rewards, make the risks in creating television fare considerable. This is the case because, despite past or present patterns of program acceptance, it is impossible to know in advance what viewers will accept (Gans 1980:71). As a result, communicators making soap operas, like others who produce fare for the public, tend to develop and rely on strategies to reduce uncertainty. Some of the strategies are embodied in work routines and occupational and professional ideologies (McQuail 1969; Tuchman 1969; Elliott 1979; Murdock and Halloran 1979), which come to play an important role in program making. But despite the strategies, the choices remain problematic and pressing. Changes in the competitive context, changes in technology, changes in degree of market control and success, and changes in the patterns of audience taste and choices combine to create a situation fraught with uncertainty.

A number of techniques or strategies are used to reduce uncertainty. One major strategy, common for virtually all types of entertainment, is to rely on people, whether producers, writers, or actors, who have a proven track record. The use of big-name stars is one way Hollywood film or prime-time television has employed this strategy. With soaps, however, a star system recently gradually developed, although it appeared unlikely that daytime status could automatically turn into prime-time or film success and status. The pattern of relying on popular soap performers, however, was illustrated by the luring of an actor from one soap to another competing one (from General Hospital to Texas), with hopes of luring the audience away also. The effect was minimal, apparently. Stars from other media recently were used for "cameo" appearances to attract viewers. Elizabeth Taylor, for example, appeared on General Hospital, and Guiding Light made use of contemporary singers and groups such as Judy Collins and the B-52's.

Many performers were hired who had appeared on other soaps. For example, out of 32 contract players on Guiding Light in March 1982, 15 had previous work experience on soaps and 15 were new to soaps. Most of the new performers were young and reflected the new emphasis on younger characters. Two other performers had appeared only on Guiding Light--one for 31 years, the other for ten years. The dependence on familiar performers was reflected in the choice to fill the role of Doctor Ed Bauer when the part was recast. An actor was chosen who had appeared on two other Procter and Gamble shows. One producer commented on the ten-

dency to hire familiar performers, and at the same time, illustrated the role of a look for the programming.

Producer: Ideally, you try to go for new
faces.

M.I.: But it seems to get weighted for the
known quantities because you see them all the
time.

P: Yes, but only because you know what you
are buying. With a Jennifer Cook you do know
what you are buying. She looks right. We
hope she'll improve over the audition, so we
go with that.

The writer for Guiding Light similarly had a good deal
of experience. He was once a performer on soaps and had
written for three other shows before coming to Guiding
Light. He had helped General Hospital in its rise to success, writing for younger characters. As with performers,
writers often moved from soap to soap.[12] This was true,
even if the program that particular writer was associated
with was not very successful. To some degree, this reflects
the limited number of well-known and experienced writers of
soaps. Elliott's observation that "media culture is the
product of a continual interchange of people and products
between the various cultural production and media systems"
(1979:161) is supported by the movement of people from one
soap to another, their promotion through magazines and talk
shows, and projected television series on soaps.[13]
Another major strategy to reduce uncertainty is for
communicators to rely upon what they perceive as successful
formulas. This may mean repeating what they feel has led to
success in the past and/or copying what they see as leading
to the success of a competing program. Repetition and imitation result.

[Formulas] help the industry cope with the
problem of generating new material much as
the use of track records do--what has worked
in the past may work again. (Pekurny 1982:
139)

At times a ritualism can result as a means of reducing
uncertainty. One writer I spoke with gave an example of the
tendency of network executives to resort to ritualism.

Gloria Monty on General Hospital had started
a system called the 49 steps, and it was simply 1, 2, the whole plot. Now we have to
have 49 steps through which the story moves.
. . . It's all security. . . . They have them
so they can see where the show is going to be
on June 18. . . . They pay you so much. You
can respect the sincerity with which they
attack their jobs.

A CBS executive noted a similar tendency when he explained the decline in the popularity of the Procter and Gamble soaps. He noted that many of the people responsible for
the successful ABC shows had formerly worked for Procter and
Gamble.

Somewhere along the line those key creative
people left. What people imitated was the
style and not the substance. Sometimes you
look at a show and try to figure out why it
is great and you say, "OK, there is a guy
with curly hair and they make a lot of
jokes." All of a sudden you see a lot of
guys with curly hair, or couples, and they
make a lot of jokes. And that is not what
the show is about.

A number of strategies were combined in the introduction of one program by Procter and Gamble. Texas was developed as a spin-off of Another World and scheduled immediately
after that program. The aim was to capitalize on audience
identification with characters on Another World, and, in effect, keep the audience by using an already familiar set of
characters and through scheduling the new program after the
familiar one. The program attempted to imitate the successful prime-time melodrama, Dallas, and also stole a performer
from General Hospital, which aired at the same time as
Texas, hoping to attract some of the fans of the performer.
Past experience, an internalized sense of what works,
is also important.

It isn't just focus (audience research)
groups, it's past experience. We know we are
on solid ground, we are not going to offend
anyone if we tell a truly romantic love
story. The letters constantly harp back on
Alan and Hope, when they went down on the
plane and had the island (to themselves). We

knew that was going to work. You can't go
wrong.

They are two people who can't stand each
other, (we) force them to be together on a
deserted island and watch their coming
together . . . they can't miss.

That kind of thing we are sure of. We try
to do that kind of thing again and again with
variations, throw in different kinds of complications . . . that's a known and we are on
solid ground when we do that.

With Kelly and Morgan, we did it another
way—their coming together and having Nola in
there to be the monkey wrench in the works.
But finally they come together. Now we have
to invent ways to bring them apart.

The same producer also indicated that a basic challenge
of soap storytelling was finding new ways to tell the same
story, with enough variation and novelty to keep the audience. Interestingly, many people working on soap opera production recognize the limited and repetitive nature of the
storytelling. One of their justifications for what they do
is that "there are only seven basic plots" although when
asked to identify them they could not do so.

Research is also used to reduce uncertainty. Focus
research entails observing a group of typical female audience members discussing their views, values, and other concerns in relation to the storylines and characters on various soaps. A discussion leader elicits opinions on a wide
range of subjects while the interaction is watched, with the
knowledge of those observed, through a one-way mirror.
Viewers of other shows, in addition to Guiding Light, are
observed and interviewed to determine their likes and dislikes. There are limits to the usefulness of focus research, as noted by a producer.

In the first place, you are dealing with wom-
en familiar with our shows. When you find
some of our opinions echoed in their voices
you tend to think all is right with the
world. We have to remind ourselves that
there may be eight or ten or twelve women
sitting around a table talking and the information is as valuable as the number of people
that day.

One writer of an ABC soap I interviewed particularly emphasized the importance of audience research to network executives.

We get incredible, unreadable ten page things.
. . . We have groups of women in about every
three months. One group will meet who watch
the show. Another group will meet who don't
like it. Another group is the other soaps
they like. We get full reports from that.
It's interesting, but that's it. They drag
them out of supermarkets on Long Island, drag
them in for a luncheon and to talk. People
love to respond. They are desperately honest,
but it is a small thing. It mostly seems to
give the network executives satisfaction or
dissatisfaction. They want every kind of
research they can have. The audience is so
enormous. The rules are constantly changing.
. . . The networks seem to feel the next step
will reveal the great mystical secret and no
one will ever have to do anything again. [Emphasis mine]

The problems of sampling and representativeness necessarily affect just how helpful the research is. While much research confirms what producers already believe, it can provide the justification for change. One of the ways focus groups were particularly important to Procter and Gamble was in finding out how women would respond to younger characters and storylines and controversial stories. But however extensive the research, it still cannot predict or guarantee success and is ultimately limited in its usefulness. Herbert Gans makes the point well:

[Much] media research seems geared to certi-
fying audience support for the familiar and
thus fails the need of content suppliers who
want an answer to an admittedly difficult
question: What will the audience accept next
time? (1980:71)

Ultimately, past experience and research cannot answer the question of what will work next time. One producer summarized the problematic nature and challenge of the decision making.

All of these things will tell you what has
worked, but I have seen the show's stories
that have been repeated on the premise they
worked once so "let's do it again." Bringing
back Roger Thorpe was a good example. He was
killed once. Suddenly, bingo, here he comes
back again. That particular one worked. . . .
I'm trying to think of another character that
was killed off and brought back again. On As
the World Turns it didn't work. Why not?
The same story, the same actor, same writer,
the same show with the same people and the
same audience watching it. Why didn't it
generate better [ratings]? . . . Because it
rained Tuesday. Who knows?

That's what makes the job so interesting,
dramatic. It's a non-quantifiable sort of
thing.

As I noted, what is perceived as contributing to programming success leads to the creation of a formula or set
of storytelling conventions. In the case of soaps, the formula has also entailed telling realistic stories, dealing
with everyday life, set in the present, concerned with topical contemporary issues. A fundamental tenet is that characters must be believable so that viewers can care about
them.

The aim of having the audience take the program as real
life involving real people was reflected in a number of
practices that were only changed recently. In the past,
Procter and Gamble avoided having performers appear out of
character and avoided using a crawl (the moving credits at
the end of a program) since both might lead viewers to distance themselves from the show and see the show as a show
and not as real life. One performer, who had been on Guiding Light for more than 12 years, commented on his experiences on doing publicity in the past.

There was a time when I first came on the
show, for example, that Procter and Gamble in
general, and the networks in general, were
afraid that if their actor playing a given
role were publicized in the print media,
specials on television, interviews, whatever,
it would take away from the audience's identification with the character. Absolutely, no
doubt about it.

I'll give you a perfect example. Only four or five years ago I did a star weekend thing in Atlanta for CBS with all the night-time stars for CBS shows and as it turned out, only two daytime stars went down to Atlanta to be available to the local affiliates from all over the country. [The actors] would say things by way of the promotions so each local affiliate would have a promo where the actor would give the call letters of the local station. The copy, none of which was checked with the actors, would read--only in the case of daytime--"Hi, this is Ed Bauer inviting you to watch Guiding Light. . . . "However, George Kennedy, who was doing a nighttime detective show would say, "Hi, this is George Kennedy. . . . "

I finally said, "I'm not going to do the promo that way. I'm going to say, 'Hi, I'm Mart Hulswit and I play Ed Bauer on Guiding Light. . . . '" They said, "But nobody knows who you are." I said, "I do." "Yes, but they don't care about who you are, they care about the character you play. . . . "

I finally told a lady from an affiliate, "Look, if Yul Brynner were doing a promo for his show, The King and I, would you say it made sense for him to say, 'I'm the King of Siam?'" Then she began to get an inkling of what I meant.

He credited his action with contributing to the adoption of a policy whereby daytime actors would identify themselves as actors. This performer felt that the producers gradually abandoned a position that "the character identification would be diminished by knowing that it was an actor playing a role. . . . "

The aim of having the audience take the performers as real people and the show as real life is also reflected in the remarks of one producer about the recently changed practice.

P & G used to feel very strongly about that. They downgraded the performers. They didn't want people to use the performer's name. They used to feel very strongly about that. They were saying to the audience, "These are real people in real life situations and we

want them to know them (the actors) as their
characters."
They used to resent the crawl, because
they had to do the crawl . . . that was tend-
ing to remind the audience that this is only
a show. . . . That is all changing now.

The fear of losing the audience by undercutting the
purported realism helps to account for another traditional
characteristic of soaps, their lack of humor. Writing humor
is difficult; problems of continuity may arise; the dialogue
for individual episodes may be written by different writers;
and actors vary in their ability to handle humor. But humor
also may threaten the hold of the drama. As one producer
noted, the past formula of soaps filled with "minute incidents of great calamity" was now changing. What conventionally was designed to create such an atmosphere might have
lost its salience if humor rendered the dilemmas and world,
in general, less threatening.
A related consideration is that the performances articulate with reality, particularly contemporary reality. Persuasiveness, the authority of a construction, is linked to
the sense that this is the way the world is now. Contempor-
aneity contributes to the dramatic power of performances.
Programming tends to adopt or use stories that articulate with what viewers have learned is current in society
(which partially derives from other dramatic programming).
Rape as an issue had been recently widely discussed in the
news and, in turn, was used for dramatic interest and topicality on not only Guiding Light but other soaps. News
often resonates with drama as they both partake of or contribute to contemporary "reality trends."[14]
At times, the relationship between fictional presentations and real world occurrences can be quite complex. One
of the risks is that in art copying life in pursuit of contemporary themes, coincidences might make a story untell-
able. At Edge of Night a story about a manipulative,
exploitative cult leader of a group of younger people was
being told when the Jonestown tragedy occurred. Over 900
people who were followers of the cult leader, Jim Jones,
committed suicide or were killed. According to the head
writer for Edge of Night:

It was sheer coincidence, but in a way it
wasn't a coincidence in that you always look
for contemporary stories about contemporary
social phenomena involving young people. . . .

When the story broke it would appear to some
people--so the network thought--that we were
trying to take advantage of the situation,
trying to make capital out of a tragedy. It
was nothing of the kind. The story had started months before, and I had never heard of Jim
Jones. Nevertheless, we had to truncate the
story. We cut if off very, very quickly.
[Emphasis mine]
The network was most concerned. Some
people in the audience thought we shouldn't
be doing this at this time. There was some
ill feeling toward the story. We do have
flexibility--we exercised that flexibility by
making the story shorter.

Understandably, one of the constraints on how quickly
the story could be killed was the amount of programming
already taped. Changes can be made more quickly and at less
cost if material is not taped too far ahead of its air
date. Not taping far in advance has another advantage:
interesting, fortuitous, real-life events can be written
into the show, thus exploiting the vent's newsworthiness.
Topics that might otherwise be considered too risky thus
acquire legitimacy, by virtue of the original event as precedent, and contribute to the sense of realism as the fic-
tionalized event and the actual event are linked.

An example of art copying life occurred in a story in
which a woman sued her husband for rape. National news had
recently reported a case in Oregon where a woman had sued
her husband for rape, and the story was seen as tellable
given the history of the program characters. Given past
character development, a husband's rape of his wife was
motivated as was her lawsuit. It is doubtful the story
would have taken that course if the national news had not
carried the Oregon rape trial story.

The tension between, on the one hand, being seen as
exploitative or, on the other, as topical and contemporary
is probably minimal. However, I think the dynamic is important. How and why occurrences are chosen and built into
performances would provide greater insight into how society
as source works its way into storytelling and performance.
I would assume that much of the awareness of the people
involved in story creation and selection would come from the
media, so their experience of the media culture would influence their work. Using Tuchman's perspective that news
involves the use of occurrences to construct news, so soaps
and other fictional fare make use of occurrences that are

part of the public arena constructed by news. News "imparts to occurrences their public character as it transforms mere happenings into publicly discussable events" (Tuchman 1979:3). A private event such as a woman bringing rape charges against her husband is transformed into a public event and becomes part of the resources of people in society exposed to such accounts.

Another factor that contributes to the believability and authority (realism) of the presentations is technical accuracy and the use of experts. Elliott suggests that one of the ways fictional programming, particularly a realistic series, would tend to "keep creative imagination within realistic bounds" would be through the use of advisors:

The term realistic series is intended to include programs based on known communities or occupations. Such series are often equipped with an expert advisor whose task is to keep creative imagination within realistic bounds. Moreover, the community or occupation concerned is likely to take an interest in how it is portrayed in the programs. Its success in influencing the production personnel and the television organizations will depend on a variety of factors such as the strength of any representative organizations and the social standing of the group concerned. (Elliott 1972:157)

The most striking example of the importance of the advisory process at Guiding Light is the reliance upon outside technical experts, chiefly doctors, lawyers, and psychiatrists. For instance, the writer dealt with the theme of alcoholism among teenagers and consulted a major organization concerned with the prevention and treatment of alcoholism. The production organization also has a number of experts it consults, again primarily in medicine and law. Advisors were consulted for the depiction of the medical treatment of two people injured in a car crash and for courtroom trial scenes. Accuracy in verifiable details plays a part in making the programming appear realistic and believable. At the same time, the presentations need to be dramatic, so compromise occurs in the form of dramatic license.

But some matters are too important to forego expert consultation. In technical matters regarding powerful occupations and legitimated routines, a greater concern for accuracy in the depiction of the technical work activities of doctors and lawyers, while characterizing their social relationships on the job and off in extremely romantic or idealized fashion. Again, the technical is handled carefully, while the social is shaped to the symbolic world.

The reliance on consultants contributes to story creation and legitimacy. Accuracy helps make stories believable and lends them an air of authority, and it minimizes the errors and the risks involved in dealing with serious issues and powerful professions. These are also built-in procedures for dealing with accountability, a topic discussed later in this chapter.

Making a character's actions believable also entails considering the audience's past experiences of the program. The communicators must consider how the audience perceives, or how they think the audience perceives, particular characters and what they know or remember of past story. A major constraint is this historicity. The dilemma for soap producers is the potential conflict between new and exciting story versus past character history as the embodiment of past story. Changes in character to fit story direction are ideally made very carefully.

The question of audience identification with character is discussed anytime that you bring in a new character or anytime that you are using a character in an unforetold way. For example, were we to take a Vanessa and turn her into a romantic lead, the immediate question, although put in very simplistic terms, is "Will the audience buy it?" Will the audience believe that the character can turn in such a way. And the answer is always, it depends on how you do it, and yes, they will probably believe it if it is done in a manner that is acceptable. The first premise is that it is gradual and that it is well motivated. . . .

If we tried [to turn Vanessa into a romantic lead], it would take a long period of time, it would have to be very well motivated, and there would have to be several serious incidents which would lead us toward having sympathy with the character, making the character human. I hate to use the word, making the character believable, but that's what it all comes down to. What can happen to the character to undergo the metamorphosis to a new person.

The continuing demand for a dramatically engaging novel story is often discussed in terms of the conflict between plot and character. The traditional emphasis on character in Procter and Gamble soaps is largely credited for past programming successes. The importance of a character as someone the audience can care about, find believable, and/or can identify with is cited as an explanation of the appeals of soaps but also as a characteristic that distinguishes daytime programming from nighttime (prime-time) offerings. Soaps are viewed as superior by people working in or viewing daytime television <u>because</u> they emphasize character over plot, although if a soap plot is compressed, plots are clearly incredible. But plot has traditionally been associated with prime-time television because of the emphasis on action, sex, and violence in such programming. "Formula" is often used pejoratively by people working in daytime. The term connotes an artificial structure created to manipulate an audience.

Again, the changing competitive context altered this emphasis. A question about the importance of characters people care about prompted a producer's response that reflected changing perceptions and approaches.

<u>M.I.</u>: Would you say that in daytime, characters that people care about is a basic ingredient?

<u>Producer</u>: Yes, it is the basic ingredient. I think that the <u>General Hospital</u> phenomena has changed that to some degree; plot is more important now than it used to be. If you don't have a strong plot your audience will rebel. The character relationships are the most important. The old style soap, I say that in the context of pre-<u>General Hospital</u> Luke and Laura--that concentrated development through "minute incidents of great calamity" --everything was important to them, I think, everything is overblown. My perception of <u>General Hospital</u> right now is that things are not that terrible, life goes on, they have a different fix on what is and is not important to the individual as he marches through Port Charles or wherever. The fix that says everything is important, dwells more on character development and the interpersonal relationship. Most of our shows tend to do that. <u>One Life To Live</u>, <u>All My Children</u>, <u>General Hospi-</u>

tal, tend to be playing around in a pleasant
manner with plot.

The considerations identified so far are related to the
dominant concerns of entertainment and competition. The
perceptions of the audience, the measurement of success,
targeted audience, perceptions of past and present successes, and the strategies to reduce uncertainty and produce
enough material quickly and cheaply enough are all involved.
However, there are other important factors if the audience
is viewed as a politicized being.


MINIMIZING RISK

Viewers can bring pressure to bear on program makers when
they are offended by the programming or consider it harmful. Organizations such as Action for Children's Television
and the Gray Panthers represent groups that initiate legal
actions and prompt congressional or legislative action.
Audience concerns can also be registered through actual or
threatened boycotts, thereby directly affecting profits.
But the economic strategy follows from the offense or perceived threat the programming creates. From this perspective the dilemma for the communicator is one of telling
tellable tales that minimize risk.
    Organizational vulnerabilities are important for under-
standing risk avoidance. Procter and Gamble has worked to
create and maintain a corporate image as a maker of whole-
some and helpful products for the home. Their continued
production of soap operas has meant control over the environment in which their commercials are placed. A corporate
ethos has influenced the process of production and affected
what stories have been considered tellable. Procter and
Gamble is clearly identified or associated with soap programming and is very careful not to offend viewers with the
programming it sponsors (and produces).
    The tendency for Procter and Gamble soaps to shy away
from socially conscious topics was reflected in a statement
by a writer who had been interviewed by Procter and Gamble.

I had a meeting with P & G about five years
ago. One of the things they wanted to know
was if I would insist on doing what they called "Agnes Nixon stories." I said what are
they? They said, "They are stories about
these troubled times and using socially conscious themes. We don't like messages in our
shows."

Interestingly, it was Agnes Nixon's writing and supervision that contributed greatly to the rise to prominence of the ABC soaps. She was associated with the success of both All My Children and One Life To Live on ABC.

Another vulnerability concerns the nature of the products Procter and Gamble manufactures and markets.

Food and drug companies dependent on constant and rapid flow of products via supermarket shelves, have generally been most afraid of antagonizing anyone; the thought of protests or boycotts has easily terrified them--as in the blacklist period. Their fears translate themselves into policy timidity, along with stress on ratings and demographics. Thus, Procter and Gamble, in a memorandum on broadcast policies, decreed: "There will be no material that may give offense, either directly or by inference, to any commercial organization of any sort." (Barnouw 1979:112)

One indication of this vulnerability was the early reaction of Procter and Gamble to the warnings of the Moral Majority that they were considering a product boycott. The chairman of the board of the company delivered a statement that Procter and Gamble was withdrawing or avoiding sponsorship from 50 prime-time programs because of excessive violence. There was, however, no mention of daytime programming.

CBS's organizational concerns are also significant. They want to avoid concentrated criticism of their programming and do not want to lose any affiliates. Pressure on local level distributors (stations) can be transmitted back to the network. Also, CBS has attempted to maintain a corporate image as a broadcaster of tasteful entertainment and quality programming.

One editor at CBS's Program Practices, which monitors program content, related her role to these corporate concerns. She stated that editors "must have a feel for company policy," have an idea of the image the company wants to project, have an overall picture of what the picture of CBS should be, and know where the line is drawn of what is acceptable and in good taste.

One institutionalized process for minimizing risks entails the use of censors or editors. Censorship has to do with the network's conscious monitoring and control over program content. At the CBS Television Network, Program Practices is responsible for the "standards of material broadcast"; at ABC it is the Department of Broadcast Standards and Practices. The practices of Program Practices itself, ironically, clearly reveal the factors influencing programming.

At CBS there were two editors, and now one, assigned to Guiding Light from Program Practices. One editor is assigned to Edge of Night at ABC. Story projections, and the breakdowns that are used as the basis of specific episodes, are read by the editor at ABC who conveys her concerns to the Programming Department. At CBS it appears that the long-term story is not monitored in the same way, although the producer of the show may offer advice about issues, scenes, and language that might be controversial. At times, the editors perceive that there may be something sensitive in the future "from where the story is going." In both cases, the editors receive a copy of the script the week before taping, about one week before the program will be aired. The scripts alert the editors to issues they may discuss with the producer, and on occasion they will request that changes be made. Also, the scripts are used to pin-point scenes, issues, and language whose acceptability will depend on how they are performed and shot. At CBS, Program Practices could monitor the rehearsals and taping from their offices since they had a direct feed from the taping studio. The ABC editor submitted a written statement approving the script or indicated changes that had to be made. She would also view the dress rehearsal or final taping of the show. In both cases, if there was a need, tapes of the programs were available for viewing.

The relationship between the departments and programs was such that at both Guiding Light and Edge of Night, people in the control room or studio wondered aloud what specific editors would do about a particular scene or bit of language. "I wonder what -- would think" at Edge of Night, or "I wonder if -- is watching" at Guiding Light. In fact, one producer of Guiding Light would often ask the technical director to have the monitors that fed into the control room "go black" to avoid disruptive calls. They were concerned that what was seen during rehearsal or in preparation for the rehearsal of scenes would be taken as the ultimate performance. They could avoid annoying phone calls by turning off the monitors.

People at both production companies felt different standards were applied to daytime and prime-time programming. They felt decisions were arbitrary and difficult to predict. Most of these complaints came from people directly involved in the production process, often in the control room. One producer complained that "nothing was written on paper" and that "you are at the mercy of the person." Program Practices, however, does not see the decisions as arbitrary. At the network level they are concerned with purported different audiences watching programs at different times of the day. What seems arbitrary at the production level, where the show is made, does not seem arbitrary at the network level.

At times the joking about the rules took the form of wondering aloud about what the current rules were. For example, in one lunchtime discussion at Guiding Light it was decided a current rule was the program was allowed to show a couple in bed after sex without straps on the woman only if they were married. Another rule was that you could not lead up to a couple having intercourse, but you could come out of a scene that implied intercourse. One scene that was allowed, for example, involved Floyd and Nola. Nola was seducing Floyd so that she would become pregnant and then contend Kelly made her pregnant and force him to marry her. The scene was allowed since (1) when she started to undress she had a blouse on under her coat, (2) when she was in bed after intercourse she had a shirt on, and (3) it was "shot tight" (only the tops of her shoulders and head were shown) as she dressed and, although no straps were evident, she was away from the bed.

At times there was amusement and amazement as well as frustration expressed. One example of Program Practices' intervention at Guiding Light was cited by production personnel as representative of the editor "seeing something that wasn't there." In one scene in which Amanda is in bed thinking about Ben's attractiveness to her, Program Practices insisted both of Amanda's hands be on top of the bed covers.

Both departments are concerned with the efficacy of "standards of material broadcast" in identifying and resolving potential problems. The list of rewards and negative sanctions regarding content and presentation is considerable, although understandable given the number of constituents or audiences involved. These sanctions and rewards must take into account legal, regulatory, or self-regulatory codes; potential or actual Congressional, pressure group, and audience actions; and concerns and demands of sponsors, producers, and affiliates. Ultimately, all have an impact on corporate image and financial well-being.

Since soap programming is fictional, the production organization is freed from some of the considerations that apply to news programming. But at the same time, the programming has to be realistic to create a sense that the presentation is a picture of society as it really is or as it really works. People are not supposed to use the programming as they potentially might a news report, yet the programming must be persuasive. Accuracy or correspondence to previous experience, particularly mediated experience, contributes to persuasiveness as a reflection of how things really are.

However, ambiguity or tension is inherent in the communication process since a fictional presentation can potentially be used as a basis for acting or justifying behavior in the real world. Something viewed on a program might be copied and carried out in real life. One example, cited by an editor at CBS, involved a fictional incident of a girl raped with a broom on a program broadcast by NBC. A similar act was carried out in real life, and part of the defense was that the defendants had seen the incident on television and it had influenced their behavior.

Even though the program is a fiction, the social basis of experience and communication requires the use of recognizable or correlative groups and activities. Viewers and organizations take fictional programming seriously, even if the program is a cartoon. Politicized viewers, for example, might consider the characterizations of the relationships between males and females in a cartoon as stereotyped, negative, and harmful. As a result, even a fictional presentation can be held accountable for social behavior and conditions; thus, there are practices that are motivated by a concern to avoid problems that might arise. The recognition (1) that by presenting a certain view of society, people may be made aware of behavior they had never considered before and (2) that some members of society might consider certain images of behavior and language objectionable constrains communicators to tell less risky stories because the audience might view the programming as concrete evidence of the communicator's point of view. What is a neutral presentation to the communicator can be viewed as advocacy by the viewer. Put differently, all realities must be persuasive and read for their intentions and purposes and assessed for potential consequences.

We are much more censored than we were then. For example, we cannot have someone go to a fortune teller. And we can't even have in a scene someone look at the other person's palm and say, "That's your lifeline." Our censors will take that out. <u>They don't want the audience to think that we are advocating anything</u>. [Emphasis mine]

The problematic nature of avoiding risk is compounded because the programming is received by a large, heterogeneous, changing audience. The public character of the communication process, the complexity and ambiguity inherent in the interpretive process as meaning is inferred, the shifting politicization and varying attention of the audience, and the potential conflict of fictional stories versus nonfictional real world events all affect storytelling.

One of the risks is inaccuracy. This is also one of the reasons experts are consulted.

I remember once on <u>As the World Turns</u> we did a complete about-face because of the letters. We call it the "Elaine Super Story" because her name was Elaine Super. Irna Phillips went to her doctor and said she wanted to find an illness that a character could have that people would care about. She was going to kill the character off. This doctor she talked to came up with lupus. And so we played it on the air. When Bob Hughes was told his girlfriend has lupus, he said, "Oh, my God, no!" We played it that she was practically dead. Well, the phones lit up. The National Lupus Society mail came in. It seems there are many, many forms of lupus. You can live with lupus all your life.

I remember one letter specifically that we got from a woman who said she hadn't heard from her daughter in England for some time. The day before she had just gotten a letter from her daughter in England saying, "Mother, I was in the hospital, but don't worry. I'm fine now. I had lupus and it's all going to be fine!" The letter from the mother said, "Do I jump on the next plane to London now that I know my daughter's going to die?" We just turned around fast and had her live. We allowed the writer to do the research instead of checking on it ourselves.

A good example of risk as an organizational concern involved a scene in an episode of <u>Guiding Light</u>. The CBS Program Practices unit objected to the making of a match bomb in an episode. They were worried that a viewer might make a bomb following the detailed description and visualization of the process in the episode. In this context, too much accuracy might be potentially dangerous.

Risk is also minimized by avoiding mention of specific diseases or miraculous cures. Typically such a concern would be voiced at a story conference.

You have to be aware of your responsibility to the audience in terms of people who are handicapped, who have diseases which could be terminal, you are better off portraying things in general or generic terms rather than specifics. For your story reasons you decide one of your characters is going to die because of a particular disease, generalize the disease. It is a rare blood disease as opposed to leukemia, a disease of the central nervous system as opposed to cerebral palsy. . . . The idea is not to take hope away from someone who may have the disease. By the same token, if you want to save a particular individual or character from the throes of death because of some miraculous turnabout, you don't want to offer false hope among the audience who have that particular ailment. The writers may want to name specific diseases.

Accuracy also pertained to legal issues.

If you are going to get into various areas of law you better have documentation to back it up. Specifically, what is the latest ruling on a current kidnapping, or a parent kidnapping? "Snatching" is the technical term for his own child. Up until recently there were only six states that had reciprocal custody laws. I understand that it has broadened, but that is the kind of thing you have to get into if you are going to do a story along those lines. People watch these things, and there you do have a responsibility because there they are learning. If you are dealing with information you are dispersing to them as being true, they are going to believe you. You have a responsibility to make sure the information is true, is accurate.

Characterizations of disease and legal procedures—areas that are technical and reflect valued occupations and institutions —are usually carefully checked. Producers rely on accuracy and generalization to avoid legal problems. Such concerns would be checked at story conferences so that changes would not have to be made later in the production process. By catching potential problems early, production costs are lowered. The differences of opinion over the match bomb episode is an example of how misunderstandings occurred even when there had been communication between Program Practices and the production team. Corrections had to be made through editing the scene.[15]

Another risk in storytelling is potential audience reaction if they feel that immoral behavior has been condoned. Retribution for immoral acts, with evildoers punished, is one way in which the potential negative reaction can be minimized. Some of the elements that go into story creation and storytelling are apparent in this statement by the headwriter. He is referring to the sexual involvement of Kelly and Morgan, who fall in love and have sex even though Morgan is seventeen and they are not married.

About censorship. Sometimes I'll argue violently against. We had a big problem last year with the first Morgan-Kelly sex scene. They certainly got very uptight and weren't going to let it happen. Codes and Practices got very strict and said they were not going to let them go to bed together. There is a year and a half story down the drain.

Their feeling was that, since my projection had them marry a year and so many months later, wasn't I really saying to teenage girls--17- or 18-year-old girls--that if you have sex with this boy it means a happy ending? They marry a year from now. I said, No, that's not what I am saying at all. There is a lot of interim story where she suffers a great deal. What I'm telling is that you can be physically ready for sex at a lot of ages but are you ready for it emotionally, for the responsibilities that go along with a sexual relationship? I said the moral of the story was she was not. She is going to go through a lot--she is not going to marry Kelly a year from now because she had sex with him this year. That's not the story. To me, I said, there is a moral point of view and a very good lesson for a lot of teenagers.

They need to know that along with physical satisfaction goes an emotional responsibility and you have to be ready for it.

M.I.: They think you are really teaching the world out there.

Headwriter: I said, if I'm teaching any-thing, yes, she can be in love with him, physically ready, but is she emotionally ready, is she mature enough? They said, if she gets pregnant we'll let you tell the story. I said I don't want to tell that story; it's an old boring story. That's not the story I want to tell. This is 1980 for Christ's sake.

M.I.: It's true. Everytime somebody has sex they get pregnant.

Hw: Right. And not only that, it's such a chauvinist attitude. Why can the boy walk away from it and the girl pay. Why must the girl be paying for it. And the boy can walk away free. I stuck to my guns, and the head of programming for CBS was totally behind me, and we fought and won.

M.I.: Is there a conscious concern that there be retribution?

Oh, yes and much of it is dated, I think. And they are not people who watch the show every day. They are people who suddenly tune in because they got flagged on a certain incident, who can't possibly know what led up to it. They pick a story point, they pick the one point a year and a half later when they are going to get married and ignore everything in between that happens to these two people.

A complementary statement by a producer notes the role of Program Practices in story creation. Kelly and Morgan's affair has painful consequences, although pregnancy is not part of the punishment. The nature and degree of suffering does not fall equally upon both participants in the sexual relationship, nor is sex in or out of wedlock treated equally.

We were aware of the law that in some states there is a statutory rape. Also we were aware of our social obligation as pointed up by Program Practices in terms of we mustn't portray teenage promiscuity as totally rewarding, not without fault, not without problems and complications. The one major problem we were agreed upon was that many times, although physically capable of enjoying a sexual act, a 17-year-old girl may be emotionally immature and not understand what the responsibilities are. We have tried to portray Morgan as a child-woman.

There was some talk about Morgan becoming pregnant. I must say that the writer fought that. It was not the story we wanted to tell. He did not want to go back to the old Victorian ethic that if you do something morally wrong in the Moral Majority's eyes, "God's gonna get you for it." Because the kids of today know that that isn't necessarily true. It could happen, but it doesn't always happen. Because of that we wanted to deal within a more broadened scope of the responsibilities two people have toward each other.

We have to look at it from the standpoint, what has this girl been through since she slept with Kelly. Number one, she ran away to Chicago, was picked up by a pimp, almost sold into bondage and rescued by her one love, Kelly. She returned home to find out he had a liaison with another woman, as told to her by one whom she thought was her best friend. She ran away to Chicago again, went back again, with painful memories and was spotted by these desperadoes, one of whom was in prison, and she was almost killed once again. Only then to come back to Springfield to the safety of home to be kidnapped, raped, beaten, and almost burnt by this desperado. So if you want to talk about outside influences if you will, she has had it both ways. She suffered both the emotional stigma and gone through and tried to learn from it. Kelly in a roundabout way has never suffered from any physical stigmata. We have gone back to the Victorian ethic—the scarlet letter.

The issue of balance in fictional storytelling is sought by using the same strategy employed in news reporting. Both sides of the story are told. One member of Program Practices made the link between network organiza-tional concern and programming explicit.

We haven't gotten into problems with Guiding Light. A woman could make an argument that was pro-abortion saying it was her baby. Our concern would be not to make CBS sound as if they are for abortion. We have to balance the portrayal.

A producer expressed the same concern in his statement that the program had a responsibility to be accurate in telling a story.

There again, you don't want to draw an editorial point of view. We don't want to say that the laws are right or wrong. We just want to state what the law is. That is your social responsibility. To go beyond that and make a statement regarding the law is editorialization.

What is particularly significant is that while there is no Fairness Doctrine that requires that broadcasters "must afford reasonable opportunity for the presentation of contrasting viewpoints on controversial issues of public importance" for fictional production, the result is much the same. Legal interpretation of the Fairness Doctrine has meant that "only news or public or personal attacks on an individual are considered issues of public performance" (Cantor 1980:51). But the concern for balanced presentations leads to a similar result. Usually two viewpoints are presented or stressed, and controversial issues are avoided.

One producer made a distinction between a controversial topic and an argumentative one that also helps illuminate the thinking behind the decision making.

If, four or five years ago, you would have come to me and told me I have this great story for you, you should do on your show, Guiding Light, involving an abortion, I would have said to you, it's the wrong time. I won't touch it. That's not controversial, that has become argumentative in the community and you have polarized factions. They

are not going to give on either end. Neither
is willing to see the benefit of the other's
argument. They have their own point of view.
What you end up with, portraying such a
story with a subject such as that--the people
who are pro your side of the story, you are
going to alienate 50 percent of them because
they are going to say you didn't tell the
story strongly enough. That's number one.
You immediately alienated another 50 percent
of the people because they didn't like your
point of view. So you have alienated 75 percent of your audience.

There is always the concern to avoid being seen as
glamorizing, romanticizing, condoning what many would see as
immoral or harmful behavior. The example of the problems
Kelly and Morgan experienced fits this general concern.
Such monitoring is reflected in the comments of one individual at CBS Program Practices who reviewed the promotional
presentations. She permitted one "promo" (as they are
called) even though it touched on a problematic issue:
teenage alcoholism. The particular promo showed Tim, a
teenage alcoholic, drinking, but the promo did not glamorize
the drinking by showing him having a good time at a party,
for example. His drinking on the program, in general, was
characterized as having a very negative effect on his
life. Tim was lectured about the evils of drinking by a
major character, who was a former alcoholic, and, thus,
balance was provided.
While a purportedly realistic characterization of
everyday life and, as such, a reflection of society, it is
illuminating to note what is omitted. The programs are
carefully crafted to avoid certain images and issues. At
Edge of Night, one incident made it very evident how much
the networks avoid identifying commercial products and services in a program. In some footage that was considered for
use, an airplane taxis up to a passenger ramp. The director
wanted to show something more than the usual interior of a
plane represented by two seats and a window, or a door
through which passengers would be pictured entering the air-
port. The network's Division of Standards and Practices
forbade the use of the footage because it included the logo
of American Airlines. That such conflicts are infrequent is
proof of how internalized such practices become. In fact,
the Program Practices representative in charge of monitoring
Guiding Light praised the staff of the show for remembering
to turn the whiskey bottles in a scene so that the labels
were not visible.

The justification for such a practice is that competitors of a manufacturer or service would consider the appearance of the logo, the presence of an identifiable name, as free advertising. If they have to pay a certain amount to advertise their product or service, why should a competitor receive free time to have its name before the audience? This practice assures that virtually no mention or visualization of the product or service of a corporation large enough to sponsor advertising on television will ever appear. The corporate structure that undergirds the system as it is becomes invisible in the world it sponsors—other than through commercials or credits.

There are occasional conflicts between the commercials and the content of a program. At Edge of Night, commercials were inserted into the actual tape of the program at the studio during the editing process. On one occasion a scene in a restaurant or coffee shop ended with a character saying, "If I have another cup of coffee, I'll be up for three weeks." The line conflicted with the commercial for Folger's coffee, which immediately followed it. As a result, an executive decision was made in the editing room, and the line was dropped. Such conflicts are rare, and, as can be seen in this example, a very brief edit of the problematic line removed the problem. The commercial message has priority over the program.

The examples demonstrate how the programming renders invisible the corporation that makes the programming possible. It is an enduring paradox that the extraordinary number of advertisements and commercials that confront us in real life are nowhere to be seen in the programming itself, and that those corporations with the greatest power and wealth are the ones most able to effect such a result.

Networks and production companies are also alert to avoid potential legal suits based on libel. For example, when Morgan goes to Chicago, the name of the club in which she appeared had to be changed because there was one with the same name in Chicago. Portraying the club in a negative way, as a setting for disreputable, immoral, or illegal acts, might have left the network open to a lawsuit.

Another risk entails the potential action of special-interest pressure groups. Risks of commission include, for example, portraying a particular group negatively, while risks of omission include failing to include a group in the programming. During the spring of 1981 , the representative of Program Practices at CBS stated she was meeting with the Gray Panthers, a group representing the elderly. She cited the character of Dr. Steve Jackson as a positive characterization of the elderly on Guiding Light. That he took Bert

Bauer, the matriarch of the Bauer family, dancing was cited as an indication of how "old people were not shown on the shelf." Shortly after that, major casting and character changes were made to attract a younger and larger audience. One of those changes was that the actor playing Dr. Jackson was not retained on a contract and, in fact, did not appear on the show in the future. The problems and afflictions of the elderly, as well as their triumphs and satisfactions, largely conflict with the traditional concerns of soaps. The potential response of the elderly would appear not to have been a major concern, other than the general desire on the part of the Procter and Gamble to keep its traditional audience.

One group, or general social movement, that did seem to have an impact was the women's movement. I am not arguing, that by taking into account specific requests for changes from ABC Standards and Practices, that the characterization of women on Edge of Night would satisfy most politicized women and men. What did occur was a reflection of the sensitivity of Program Standards to particular women's rights concerns.

One example cited entailed a change in a story line. A woman--Emily--who was originally scripted to be killed, wound up being catatonic and at the mercy of a sadistic intern, who was in a position to victimize her sexually. There were numerous script changes that reflected a general concern not to show Emily as totally passive and a victim. Broadcast Standards and Practices suggested that Emily be portrayed as actively seducing Sharkey and not as his passive victim. Their primary concern was to avoid presenting women as passive, helpless creatures.

Other changes were requested in scenes in the psychiatric ward where Sharkey worked. These changes reflected a desire to not portray patients in mental hospitals negatively. Substitutions were made for such phrases as "funny farm," "loonies," "nutty ones," "crazy," and "nut case." Often the terms "mental patient" or "mental institution" were used instead and found acceptable by Broadcast Standards.

Approaching the story creation and selection process as a collective and corporate effort leads to the identification of a large number of factors influencing which stories are tellable. More than a matter of taboos, the same factors had implications for which stories were told and how they were told. Many of the considerations are attributable to the commercial competitive nature of the storytelling as an adjunct to marketing and to its public nature whereby performances are experienced as participation in a way of

life and contribute to our vocabulary of collective con-
ciousness. Such participation can potentially lead to boycotts of programming and products and to objections to the
kind of society we participate in or are invited to participate in by the programming.

The aim of reaching the ideal market/audience with
stories that have characters people care about, that are understandable, believable, contemporary, and deal with real
life, the need to minimize risk, reduce uncertainty, and
generate an appealing (addictive), distinctive stream of
experience largely shaped the community Guiding Light invites us into. The dominant justifications for the programming derive from an emphasis on entertainment and
competition.

# THE WORK PROCESS

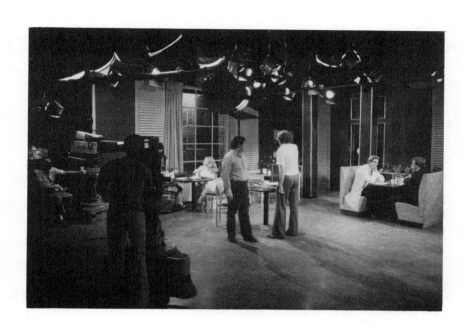

# 6

## Soap as Industrialized Cultural Production: Authority and Work

[Much] of the behavior of creative and performing artists in mass media setting can be
viewed as work.  They write, perform and produce in highly organized teams that demand
coordination; they face routine work pressures, try to handle mistakes at work, control the activities of colleagues, and cope
with the risks of personal failure.  (Faulkner 1971:5)

As a form of industrialized cultural production in an advanced capitalist society, the serial format of Guiding Light
entails a continuous work process.  Work takes place in a
hierarchically controlled organizational setting involving
an elaborate division of labor and the use of complex tech-
nologies to generate scenes, acts, and episodes as part of
the on-going storytelling.  While each scene, act, and episode is unique and discrete, each is also standardized and
part of a continuous product, a continuous potential for
experience.  Using Woodward's typology of industrial productions, soaps entail a continuous process of unit and small
batch production (1970).  Phrased differently, soaps are
industrially manufactured live performances for continuous
consumption.
    Many production practices can be described as aspects of
roles.  Important questions concerning how and why performances take the form they do entail looking at the work process and determining how individuals (and roles) adapt to
the conditions of soap production.  Issues regarding authority, autonomy, creativity, risk, work pressures, failure,
and satisfactions all have consequences for performances.
Viewing work as participation, what is the nature of that
participation as various roles/individuals attempt to deal
with the pressures, risks and rewards of making Guiding
Light?
    The complexity of the production process is reflected in
the  number and variety of roles, their organization and or-

121

ganizational relationships (see Table 6-1). More than 100 people are directly involved in the daily production process. The process is particularly complex given the ongoing work on performances at various stages of realization. While an episode is taped each day, preparations are made for future episodes, some many weeks in the future. Every role is important to the successful realization of an episode, but I have concentrated on six roles shaping the performances.[16] Initially in this chapter I describe the roles and relative power of the supervising and executive producer and the headwriter whose decisions affect long-term story, casting, ultimate realization of the programming, and budget. In the final section I discuss the activities of performers, directors, and line producers realizing or creating performances.


MAJOR DECISIONS AND MAJOR DECISION MAKERS

Three major roles concerned with all areas are the supervising producer, executive producer, and headwriter. Traditionally, the executive in charge of production at Procter and Gamble Productions oversees the making of all six soaps, while a supervising producer works directly with one or more soaps, riding herd on the shows' budget and costs, ratings, story creation and realization, and casting. The executive producer is also involved in all of these areas, but works more closely with the actual production process in the studio. The degree of involvement of the supervising producer for Guiding Light changed during the research period. Formerly, one supervising producer had responsibility for three shows. With that individual's promotion, one supervising producer was assigned to Guiding Light.

The executive producer participates in budget and story meetings and casting sessions, but also works on a daily basis with other phases of the work process. He works directly with the headwriter, discussing and making script changes and cuts, and with the line producers and production staff handling creative, logistical, and personnel problems. He is the immediate supervisor of the line producers at Guiding Light, who are even more involved in daily production activities.

The executive producer's degree of involvement in the rehearsal and taping process can vary considerably, although at the shows I observed the executive producers tended to leave decisions regarding how each episode was played and shot to others, particularly to directors and line producers.

TABLE 6-1

THE ORGANIZATION OF PRODUCTION

---

Procter and Gamble Productions, Incorporated

Executive in charge of production
Supervising producer

Advertising Agency Personnel

Production Staff for Guiding Light

Executive producer - 1
Producers - 2 (line producers)
Associate producer - 1
Assistants to the producer - 2
Production assistants - 2
Casting director - 1
Assistant casting director - 1
Production office coordinators (secretaries) - 3

Creative Staff/Talent

Headwriter - 1
Dialogue writers - 4-5
Actors - Contract actors (approximately 30-35)
         Day players
         Under-fives        hired on a daily basis
         Extras             (number varies)
Directors - 4

| # Technical Staff | # Stage Crew | # Support Staff |
|---|---|---|
| 2 technical director | 2+ electrician | 2 Music supervisor |
| 2 video director | 2+ carpenter | 2 set designer |
| 2 audio engineer | 2+ prop | 2 set decorator |
| 6 cameraperson | 2 studio supervisor | 2 stage manager |
| 4 boom person | 2 prod. supervisor | 2 hairdresser |
| 4 utility person | maintenance | 2 make-up |
| 2 music cartridge | | 1 costume designer |
| operator | Advisors | 1 assistant designer |
| 2 videotape editor | 1 legal | 3 wardrobe |
| 2 lighting director | 1 medical | |

---

+ Head plus assistants.
Source: Compiled by the author.

Traditionally, Procter and Gamble has given considerable authority to headwriters, often more than to the executive producer. One individual with considerable experience in soap productions explained the conventional framework in the following way:

P & G historically has given all the power to the writers because they have had trouble finding writers. They have always hired pro- ducers they could control and manipulate. They have constantly gotten themselves in trouble with writers. They went into the business when the writer would own the show. Irna Philips owned the show. That was their training, their background. When the con- tract was up, Irna could damn well pull that show away from them. And the same people who now run P & G were trained in that milieu.

Their orientation to soap production has been one where the programming is primarily a vehicle for marketing. Creative decisions could be left to others as long as the programs were successful in reaching audiences as markets and poten- tial markets.

The increased attention paid to daytime by various media, CBS's strong interest in increasing their profits from daytime, and the succcesses of the ABC shows had led Procter and Gamble to attempt to consolidate its control over its programming. One producer described the changes:

P & G has come up with quite a new concept. They have put more power in the hands of the executive producers than they used to. For many years they placed the writers on a pedes- tal, and let the writers run the show. That's changing now.

He used an example of a decision he had fought. The show had recast the role of Dr. Ed Bauer, after the same performer, Mart Hulswit, had played the role for twelve years.

For instance, with this Mart Hulswit thing, if this new system had been in effect at that time, they are saying I could have had the right to say, "No, this is my show and he doesn't go." And they would be willing to go

out on a limb to tell CBS and everybody else
who wanted to replace him that the producer
has said no.

The authority of the headwriter, for both Guiding Light
and Edge of Night, was considerable. The work involved in
story creation, realization, and other aspects of soap production is unique and considerable and helps account for the
traditional pattern. Headwriters for both Edge of Night and
Guiding Light spoke of the satisfactions of writing for daytime television because what they write is largely realized,
as opposed to prime-time television where scripts undergo
considerable change, particularly at the hands of producers.

There is a division of labor in soap writing, even for
half-hour shows. The headwriter, who is largely responsible
for story, hires subwriters, dialogue writers, or associates,
who are under contract to him. There were five dialogue
writers for Guiding Light. They provided the appropriate
dialogue for a particular episode, based upon an outline or
breakdown of the episode prepared by the headwriter. The
scripts, in turn, are edited by the headwriter.

Because soaps are a never-ending story, writers come and
go. Guiding Light has been on the air since 1937. A headwriter, given an on-going program, has to consider past
story, character development, and cast in creating stories.
Past story, character history, performer's capabilities, and
other elements are both resources and constraints, having
implications for the stories that can be told.

The demands of soap writing are considerable and unique.
There is overall responsibility for producing storylines,
breakdowns or outlines, and editing or writing the scripts
for five programs a week for 52 weeks of the year. A headwriter has to create about 250 scripts a year, which in the
case of an hour long program adds up to about 17,500 pages
of material. This work must be done while monitoring the
program that is aired, participating in decision making, and
remaining aware of and juggling a large number of variables.

Headwriters will monitor the realization of the scripts,
analyzing and evaluating the performances. Changes in a
number of areas may be suggested through this feedback, as
well as from feedback from other sources. Continuing interaction with the programming influences the storytelling,
particularly through the interaction of headwriter and performer as the headwriter shapes character and story to fit
his reading of the performer's characterization of the part
and his or her personal mannerisms, strengths, and weaknesses.

Many factors have to be considered in story development and writing specific episodes. Budget considerations affect the number of contract performers hired or retained; the number and character of the noncontract players (day players, under-fives and extras) hired; the number, size, and quality of the sets and props used each day; the quality and quantity of costumes; the support personnel including hairdressers and costume designers, technical facilities and crews, administrative and/or production staff and directors available; and whether location shooting can occur. The complexity of the production process the requirement of producing five programs a week, within budget and time limitations, and the continuing dependence upon a number of individuals or roles all affect the storytelling.

Additional factors include what are considered appropriate stories for daytime, given past successes or failures, perceptions of the audience, sponsor or network taboos, concern for corporate image, demographics of the audience as market or desired potential market, current programming successes or failures on competing shows, as well as the resources dependent on budget, along with the historicity of the show.

Briefly elaborating on the constraints, for example, much of the action occurs indoors. The writer has to write basically for an indoor world embodied in a limited number of sets. Budgetary and space limitations control the number, variety, types, and size of settings that can be used in general, or on any specific day. In terms of contractual agreements, all actors have contracts which guarantee how many times they are to appear on the show in a 13-week period. If they are not used that guaranteed number of times, which does happen, they are still paid as if they had been used. And again, because there is a continuing dependency on a large complex production organization and because there is a short period between the time shows are taped and aired, illnesses, accidents, or other contingencies such as the pregnancy of a performer might require changes in scripts and storylines.

There was a continual process of interaction between the headwriter and the executive producer, as well as the supervising producer and network representative. One executive distinguished three types of story conferences. There is a more formal meeting where long-term story is discussed.

Those major conferences tend to solidify direction of the story--what the company wants (P & G), what the network will accept and the writer gets a feel for what he can and cannot do, given the story he has created.

Other meetings are semiformal, often with fewer people present where "we talk about questions we have about where the
story is going, what do you think of going in this direction
and sometimes talking about more specific steps of a given
story." Finally, there are more informal meetings at the
writer's house, for example, where ideas are presented that
will "work their way back into the other meetings or into
the long-term story."

There is also a continual monitoring of the story by
Procter and Gamble and CBS in terms of its fidelity to the
original conception and the more specific realization in the
scripts and performances. A producer gave an example of a
script change that was made as a result of the monitoring:

We just made a change in the script. It came
in in a breakdown. We want Tony to be a
strong, virile guy, to be his own man. And
continually we were getting things where he
was strong until Vanessa opens her jacket and
then he can't help himself. We have done it
two or three times in the past. We said, no,
no more, so we had him change that. The
writer could not see that this makes the guy
weak; it doesn't work if you want to make him
a hero.

There is daily contact between the headwriter and the
production personnel, particularly if cuts have to be made
in episodes that are too long or if there are questions about
continuity or realization that will affect later episodes.
The executive producer, and less frequently, the line producer will call the headwriter about cuts. Suggested cuts
are ideally identified early to help in the process.

We'll take the script, if one comes in 75
pages, we know we are going to be five
minutes long. I'll look through it, call
Doug and say, "We are looking like we are
going to be five minutes long. There are
three minutes' worth of cuts I'd like to talk
about before we go into production." . . .
Sometimes he'll say, "No, I'd like to leave
that in because such-and-such is going to
happen and link back to next week." And then
after the fact we have cuts. We do it
through him since he's really the only one
who knows where we are going and what's
important.

The on-going storytelling process also has implications for the contracts that are offered performers. For example, the guarantees offered performers are linked to how important they will be in future story. "Guarantees" refers to the number of times performers are guaranteed work during a 13- or 26-week period. If they appear less than that total, they still are paid according to the guarantee. They are also paid for additional performances.

> For instance, I'm talking with Nola's right-
> hand-girl--Gracie--she has not been a con-
> tract player. She came on for one or two
> shots. It worked so well she stayed on. And
> now we'd like to make sure she sticks around,
> so we are going into a contract. He says,
> "Let's do it, but don't guarantee her more
> than one a week. She'll probably work more,
> but hold the guarantee down." That affects
> the money we pay her.

A number of unexpected incidents affected the story and its realization. One example was the pregnancy of the performer playing Amanda, a character who had recently suffered greatly. The headwriter noted the strategy adopted to handle the problem.

> We were forced into finding a way to get her
> out for a period without losing the character
> completely. We have her a recluse. She was
> in a perfect mental state to do that, and we
> used Chet's death (her uncle) as the final
> blow that she couldn't deal with. We pre-
> taped a lot of scenes, which will feed in
> through the summer while she is having her
> own baby. We were forced to come up with it.

The use of videotape and the ease of editing made it possible to insert scenes of Amanda, secluded in her room dressed like a child, playing the piano throughout the actress's pregnancy. On another occasion, the actor playing an important romantic lead part, Kelly, broke his arm. This was handled by simply injecting lines into the script that conveyed the news that Kelly had been hurt at home.

The creation of story entails making use of characters who have a history (as well as performers who have various strengths and weaknesses as actors), something that was spoken of by an advertising executive as a character franchise. Characters are resources; therefore story direction and char-

acter changes are approached very carefully.  For instance,
a major character with great appeal to the audience, Alan
Spaulding, was transformed from an evil, power-hungry business magnate into a loving person through his love for his
wife Hope and her love for him.  His redemption through love
meant that he had continuing use for the storytelling because
he was no longer so evil that he had to be "killed off."  But
even though he was transformed, he still had to be punished
for his crimes.  His punishment, a brief prison term, was
made to coincide with the vacation and break the actor wanted
to take from the role.  Scenes were pretaped of his kidnap-
ing while he was in prison so that he not only appeared in
the show during his vacation but was a central figure who was
in jeopardy.

At times characters will be given an extended life, particularly if they are played by extremely popular actors.
This was the case with Michael Zaslow, who played the part
of evil Roger Thorpe.

M.I.:  Did you want to get more mileage out
of the performer/character so you had him
come back again?

Producer:  It was working and the ratings indicated it.  We all had a good feeling about
it, we sensed this was something good we had
going.  Could we indeed find a way of carrying him on.

M.I.:  What was the way you did it?

P:  Well, Holly was going to shoot him and
he was going to die.  Really at the last
moment we made this decision -- a week or so
to go. . . . We had him (Roger) in the
hospital.  He called Alan Spaulding and said,
"I won't tell on you if you get me out of
this hospital. Get
me off to recuperate." . . . Alan had this
clinic down in Puerto Rico so they shipped
him down to Puerto Rico.

Then we, of course, had the scene where
his father went in, talked with him and he
seemed to be O.K.  His father went off for a
cup of coffee and came back, and they were
making up his bed.  He said, "What's the matter?"  They said, "We're sorry."  He just
sneaked away.

The performer himself needed the time off
. . . so we had him disappear and the audience
knew darn well he probably wasn't dead.

The casting of characters and the way performers realize
a particular character is considered extremely important in
soap production since audiences have to identify with or
care about the characters if a story is to work. There is
an interactive process involving the relationships between a
performer/character, the writer, and the audience that in
turn affects story creation and realization.

There are various categories of roles that are cast in
differing ways. "Extras," the smallest part and the least
paying, have no lines to speak and typically play background
roles such as a disco crowd or traffic around the nurses'
station in Cedars Hospital. "Under-fives" have fewer than
five speaking lines. A bartender, for example, might be an
under-five if he simply asks one or two people what they
would like to drink. These categories of parts are handled
primarily by the assistant casting director.

The highly competitive nature of acting as work and the
large number of actors without work was evident from the
many postcards the assistant casting director received each
week. She estimated she received between 250 and 350 cards
each week from actors seeking work as extras or under-fives.
The cards were piled on her desk or in the box for mail in
the production office. They served as a reminder of the
scarcity of work for actors. The cards typically consisted
of a photograph of the performer on one side of the card,
with name, phone number, and union memberships. They generally read as follows:

Please keep me in mind when you are casting.

Please keep me in mind for work on Guiding
Light. I have worked steadily for [name of
G.L. director] and I am always looking for
more.

Hi! Just a quick note to remind you of my
availability. Have a good summer!

Need anyone for an under-five? I'm ready. I
hope we meet again soon.

"Day players" are hired by the day, have no regular contract, but are important to the story. A detective investi-
gating a case, for example, might be involved in several episodes. Contract players are given contracts that guarantee

a certain number of performances for a 26-week period, but their contracts can be cancelled in 13 weeks in the case of the less important or less powerful performers. There are about 35 contract players on a one-hour show at any one time. The casting director auditions the day and contract part performers and calls them back if they pass the first screening. The performers are then taped to determine how they come across on camera and so that the headwriter and supervising producer, who may not be in the studio, can judge the performer's suitability.

The casting process entails filling a part with a performer who comes across in a way that is appropriate to the characterization. The interactive process is such that the headwriter and producers may see something in the performer's playing of the character and interaction with other performers/characters that is utilized in the future. Gracie, in the example given above, worked well so she was given more of a role. The audi- tions are taped, and it is then that a determination is often made about the appropriateness of the fit between performer/ character. Again, the major decision makers make the ultimate decisions, although the writer's desires often are paramount since he or she has to write for the performer. If there is a conflict or a dislike of the performer's acting, the headwriter can use them poorly or not use them dramatically very often, and ultimately write them out.

Performers who are taped are often considered for parts other than the one they auditioned for. They also may affect story, especially if they have what is called the right "chemistry" with a particular performer. Chemistry refers to the experiencing of performers in relationships, particularly romantic relationships. Production personnel discuss performers in these terms, using their reactions to the ways the performers come across to them. The term implies a strong emotional involvement between performers.

If we see a chemistry there, then that is a good person to go with, if the chemistry is there already in the audition material. It has happened we liked a performer, but somehow we don't see the chemistry between the two and we know they are two people we ultimately bring together, so we don't go in that direction. We might go with another performer.

Occasionally, chemistry will be noticed between two performers who were not originally considered as working together in the same story.

When we brought on Leslie Dalton, she played
a scene with Mike Bauer and we immediately
saw chemistry there, so we began to slant the
story in that direction.

At times, a series of performers may be brought on for a
day or two to see how they work with a character. Most time,
however, the writer does not have that option. The show was
looking for a performer to play a friend of Morgan, the
young female romantic lead. The headwriter commented on the
strategy he employed:

Headwriter: I brought in three or four girls
at the high school until I found the one I
felt was going to do the job for me.

M.I.: One at a time?

H: Yes, there's no point of going into a
contract with somebody if it is not going to
work. It wasn't that I needed her immediately for major story. I needed her for a
confidant of Morgan, and eventually a love
interest for Tim. As I said, I'll just keep
writing in certain friends from school, cast
them, and when we see one we like we'll get a
contract. It's a much safer way of casting
when you have that kind of flexibility. You
don't always have it.

In various episodes a new performer/character will be
introduced to the other characters. This strategy serves
two purposes--seeing how particular combinations work and
getting the character accepted by the audience.

You bring on a Josh--we know where we want
him to end up ultimately, but in order to get
his face known, yes, we throw him with everybody we can on the show so the audience gets
to know he knows all these people. That's
the quickest way to get him accepted, as part
of the group.

Initial casting decisions are quite important, as I
indicated. When auditions are taped general reactions are
gotten from anyone who cares to comment on the performance--
although the producers and the headwriter are the primary
decision makers. The fit between the actor and the way their

character is to be perceived and experienced is most important. The headwriter commented on one casting error he made
when he let himself be swayed by the reactions of the people
in the studio. Usually he based his decisions on what he saw
on a television screen.

Once we were casting a part who shall be
nameless for a sensual male character. I
only judge what I see on my television screen
when I look at the tapes of the audition.
Once I was told, "Oh, the secretaries are
crazy about him. They think he is the sexi-
est. . . . " I let that influence me once,
and I said maybe I'm missing something. Went
with the actor. Total washout.

One producer commented that, while initial casting decisions are important, they are still uncertain since the audience's response to a performer/character is what ultimately
counts.

If you are looking for somebody to play a
sympathetic character, somebody the audience
is going to identify with, then that's the
kind of quality you have to look for in the
performer who comes in to audition. You can
take an exceptionally fine actress who is
supposed to be sympathetic, you just take one
look--her eyes--it's a physical thing she has
going for her that would be wrong for that
character. You have to use your reactions to
anticipate what the audience may say, or how
they are going to react if that particular
actress gets the part. . . .
You have to have an awareness of what the
writer hopes the character will portray and
how your audience may respond to that particular performer playing that character. You
have to prejudge it, no two ways about it,
you are guessing.

Casting is also affected by the look of the show. One
performer who was considered overweight and neither young
nor dashing enough was replaced with another performer who
appeared if not younger, at least thinner. The performer
seemed to have become a symbol of the look that the producers were trying to change. Some personnel spoke of a "Procter and Gamble look" because of the predominance of beauti-

ful/handsome, largely "WASPish" performers. The issue of look surfaced when the producers avoided casting "too many blonds," for example, which they felt might create a sameness to the look of the show. Recasting does occur, sometimes to temporarily replace a performer who is having a child, for example. Recasting is done quite carefully. One part was recast only after the character disappeared for a while and was not featured on the program. After a period of months, a new performer was hired.

A major recast was, as I mentioned, for the part of Dr. Ed Bauer, which had been played by one performer for 12 years. Although the recast was fought by the executive producer, the change was made. There was a very negative reaction from the audience, protesting the change, and it took several months for the mail to stop coming in complaining of the major recast. Recasting of major characters is approached extremely carefully.

There are various strategies, which I discuss in the following section, that performers adopt to handle their vulnerability to being fired or replaced. But it is important to note that while performers can attempt to assert more authority if they have been on a show for a long period, they still can be replaced. Popular performers, performers who are closely identified with a character, are replaced only if absolutely necessary. For example, one performer who played Morgan, a teenage heroine in an important major storyline, was replaced because she continually disrupted and slowed down the work process by being late, disappearing from the set when she was needed, and not knowing her lines. Actors and directors were very vocal in their complaints so that she had to be fired, or as one producer said, "We would have had a revolt on our hands."

Soap stars generally cannot come to have the power that a prime-time or film star can. Actors know this. As part of their knowledge of the business, the firing of two major popular performers on Another World (LeMay 1981) established a precedent. During prime-time the close association of a particular performer and a program, such as the Mary Tyler Moore Show, means that, in a sense, without the performer there is no program. This is not true of daytime, even though the production company might be very reluctant to make a change. As I mentioned, the part of Ed Bauer was recast, despite the popularity of the previous actor.

The roles of supervising producer, executive producer, and headwriter clearly make the major decisions within the production organization. The process is even more of an interactive one than my description of the work process indicates. These three roles also monitor the episodes that are taped and aired. This can have a direct impact on the daily production process, particularly as their observations are communicated to the line producer who oversees each day's taping.

The relative authority of the writer and executive producer is particularly important in shaping performances. Since, as a writer put it, "they always need you tomorrow," and the show is dependent on a writer's knowledge of future story (which may not be revealed to the other executives), writers have tended to garner a great deal of power. The hour-length format, the need to coordinate and control the complex process of production, and the assertion or reassertion of Procter and Gamble's control over programming have led to increased authority for the executive producer. Ultimate authority rests with Procter and Gamble Productions, and while headwriters are scarce and valuable, they can be replaced. It is largely producers who remain and writers who come and go.

The role of CBS and its programming division in the production process had increased. Their role was limited, however, because they did not own the show and it would be difficult to dislodge Procter and Gamble from their production power given Procter and Gamble's major role in television advertising. It is also very costly and takes a good deal of time to create a new and successful show. The three major roles also indicate the fusion of creative and business interests and the way Procter and Gamble has traditionally looked at the content of the shows as a vehicle for marketing.


STORY REALIZATION: PERFORMERS, DIRECTORS, AND PRODUCERS

The daily work process involves producers, directors, and actors, as well as the other skilled and technical personnel. It occurs within the confines of the resources provided, including the story and its embodiment in scripts for each episode. The supervision of the results of the collaboration or work of directors and actors is in the hands of the line producer who represents management.

Taping an episode depends on a number of previous events. To mention only a few, scripts have to be typed and delivered to the performers, directors and producers, the technicians must know what equipment will be needed, the sets must be constructed or erected, costumes purchased, and all personnel informed of the production schedule for the day.

The production day for Guiding Light is divided into two segments. There is a morning taping in one studio, Studio

51, and there is usually an afternoon taping session in Studio 54, on another floor of the building. The scheduling of the various activities is handled by the assistants to the producer. The considerations that go into scheduling are apparent in this statement by an assistant to the producer. I have related much of her statement, since she is explicit about the decision making.

When we do determine the schedules, we do tape in a film style (taped out of sequence compared to the way the scenes are ordered in the final program). We tape about 60-40; 60 percent in the morning, 40 percent in the afternoon, and we try to make the combination of pieces, sets, and pages come out to that amount. That's one of the things we take into consideration. The first priority is to leave sets standing where they were standing before, so any existing set we want to leave in the same studio if at all possible.

We then try to minimize the numbers of actors who have to double--in other words, working in both studios on the same day.

Obviously, the continuity, or the dramatic content of a program is something to consider. Generally, we try to put the heavier dramatic stuff in the morning when people are fresher. Fifty-one happens to be a little more technically sound--it has a higher grid, voice seems to be better. There are a number of technical reasons why we do it that way.

We have then to consider a few oddities, like a few sets, only a few sets at this point only fit well in 51. Cars can only go in 51. When we have actors with problems, a pregnant woman who is much fresher in the morning, loses her stuff before four in the afternoon.

Those are the main variables. The most costly thing--most of the priorities are based on money, although at times we throw those considerations out of the window if the dramatic quality is particularly outstanding. Like the time we flip-flopped two days because of the shoot out--rather than have the same director do that two days in a row--both days there were 16 pieces, we flip-flopped so we

had him do one of the shows, then had a different director come in and do a different
show, which was not supposed to be in that
sequence. Then we had him come in for the
Friday. In other words, we flip-flopped the
Thursday/Friday shows so there was a day's
rest for the director and the actors. Occasionally a day like that comes out where we
go out of the way to accommodate the dramatic
material.

The most costly thing by far is studio
time. So moving sets we try to minimize that.
Actor's overtime is not so much of a consideration at this time; financially at this
time, it's more a consideration in terms of
the fatigue of your cast. The third cost
variable is the director's payments. If you
move things around, do pre- and posttaping--
directors have to be paid extra. That's a
cost variable. Running over in studios--if
the day is very heavy and the following day
is not, it is better to take some pieces from
one day so that they are both medium, so that
both get out on schedule and they don't have
to go into overtime.

The primary considerations are economic. Minimizing the
amount of time working with sets, keeping the production
process within scheduled time limits, and controlling the
amount of pretaping and posttaping to avoid extra payments
to the directors are major considerations. The fatigue of
performers and directors are lesser considerations. Scheduling may also be affected if a performer has a conflict
because of another commitment or requires special consideration. An actress who was pregnant, for example, was accom-
modated by having all the scenes she appeared in scheduled
for the morning.

One relatively recent practice affecting production has
been the use of location shooting--the taping or filming of
scenes out of the studio. Location shooting has a major
impact on the continuing production process in the studio.

One of the problems we face in getting out of
the studio is that we are pretty lightly
staffed anyway in the studio. When you start
to take people out--staff and actors--you are
suddenly dealing with a skeleton group somewhere. Time is of essence; you usually don't
take more than a week.

The overall costs for studio production as opposed to location shooting apparently are not much different, but a major concern is the scheduling problems location shooting generates.

There is a pretty good indication that when you do something in the studio and give it an exterior look it runs into a lot of time and a lot of money in terms of sets. Probably the biggest effect location shooting has on cost is the overall scheduling. You have to really rework the schedule for a couple of weeks—plus the toll it takes on people.

The daily rehearsal and taping process can vary considerably given the number of factors that have to be considered. The most frequent schedule, however, is a morning and early afternoon rehearsal and taping, and an afternoon, early evening rehearsal and taping.

The first rehearsal is dry rehearsal and takes place in the rehearsal hall, a large room with chairs and tables. It usually begins at seven in the morning. The performers needed for the morning taping, the director, associate director, and production assistant are present. Performers and director come prepared with ideas about how the scenes can be played. A major responsibility of the director is a plan for shooting the episode.

Taping usually begins at 10:00 a.m. and continues until 2:00 p.m. If the morning schedule is not completed, there may be more taping after the lunch break at 3:00 p.m. A similar sequence is repeated for the afternoon taping on a regularly scheduled day, that taping often lasting until eight or nine in the evening.

The rehearsal sequence and taping of the scenes can vary. The director will block the scene on the set while technicians, particularly boom and camerapersons, observe the movements of the performers and get directions on how the scene is to be shot. Dress rehearsal will be taped and used if a scene is simple and has gone well or if there is a great deal of pressure to meet a deadline. Another way time and money are saved is by taping consecutively scenes that are continuous, with only a brief "dip to black" between the end of one scene and the beginning of the next scene.

Directors (there are four for Guiding Light) are responsible for blocking the movements of the actors, for the dramatic interpretation of the episodes, as well as for the way the episodes are registered on tape. Directors attempt to create a fit between the actions and presentations of the performers and the way in which the performances are framed by the studio cameras. Some directors will come prepared with quite specific plans for the framing of each shot; others will develop and alter their plans throughout the day. It is the associate director's job to note the shots required and to relay them to the camerapersons before the shots are taken.

The styles of the directors are ultimately similar in that the taped episodes must be compatible. This entails more than questions of continuity or tracking, which virtually everyone pays attention to, particularly the producer and the production assistant who times the programming and takes notes from the producer for the director. The pressures of meeting production deadlines and the need to rely upon conventional understanding of how soaps are made produces a similar, or compatible, style. Also, footage directed by two different directors may have to be utilized in the same episode, again creating pressures toward uniformity.

Directors largely determine how each episode is to be shot, but the line producers may suggest or demand changes if they do not approve of the director's choices. At times the producer's comments are based on knowledge of how past episodes have been handled and how the current episode fits into the long-range storyline. Overt conflict was very rare.

The producer will often give the director notes or comments about the quality of a scene after each stage of the rehearsal on the studio floor. Whether and how the director gives the notes to the performers is an area in which the director has some leeway. Directors pride themselves on getting good results quickly, which at times means letting the producer feel he or she influenced the performance or that it was the actor's choices that made the scene. At times the director will not pass a note on, or he or she will interpret the note depending on the capabilities and attitudes of each performer. One director gave an example of the shorthand necessary to get results quickly.

A producer might give me seven notes about individual things, usually the cause, what is behind the notes, is that the attack of the scene is not as it should be. Many times it is as simple as passing actress X and saying, "You are shining a bit." That means, as I understand how she responds to that statement, she pulls back, she divorces herself emotionally. I know what she is going to do with it. It is a shorthand that has evolved over the years.

Another capability that directors emphasized was not
only getting results quickly, but leading the performers to
feel their idea or choice was involved.

Example number two. An actor who is no longer on the show would always overact and feel
sorry for himself. You'd do the same trick
over and over again and say you had no notes.
Once you got into notes with him you were
there for over an hour. He used to call me
the director of little note. And I would say
to him, then I would step back, turn away,
and say, "By the way, I want to compliment
you on what you are doing. This script is so
self-indulgent, self-pitying, any other actor
would have fallen into that trap. Not you, I
appreciate that." That's exactly what he was
doing, blamed it on the script, congratulated
him on it, doing this, telling him I had no
notes whatsoever, to get him to kneel to propose. You would never get him to kneel to
propose to this girl. I know he always wants
to feel big and to help people, so I got the
girl seated, said it was the wrong angle, too
high. They were by the fireplace, I blocked
her, he said, "Why don't I just stoop down
there?"

One director indicated that some of the work involved in
directing went on over the phone or over lunch. Interpretations and cuts were typically discussed, again because of
the limited rehearsal time in the studio.

Two differences in directors' styles had to do with
whether they relied upon one camera for capturing a performance instead of using two or three and intercutting, typically from head to head, action to reaction. Another difference concerned how closely scenes were shot. As I note
later on, there is a dominant pattern of using close-ups or
extreme close-ups and cutting from one head to another. One
younger director attempted to use one camera much more and
also to frame scenes visually in such a way that performers
were shot from farther away and more foreground and/or background appeared in the frame. The younger director felt the
overreliance on close-ups was a matter of laziness, but a
more experienced director felt the younger director used one
camera more since that director didn't have the timing down
on shots and couldn't call them quickly enough.

Director: The basic requirement, as much as
I don't like to say it, for a soap is speed.
You have to meet the schedule because that's
the dollars and cents. If you don't meet the
schedule, you are out, period. They might
coddle somebody for a year or so, but ultimately you are out of the business.
There are certain things I would do on the
outside that I can't afford to do here. For
instance, when you're shooting something--the
reason the style of soaps have evolved as
they are, they started back in the early days
when everything was shot in close-ups. Everybody talks about the glorious days-- which
makes me sick. It is all bullshit. They had
a week to do everything. The screens at that
time were so small that they shot waist up.
The ultimate shot, the most interesting shots
are those where you get depth, and depth of
field and foreground.
    Everytime I attempt to do that, maybe I
will, maybe one show, one favorite scene, it
takes me at least half an hour to chase the
boom shadows. I don't have the luxury of a
ten-day rehearsal as in the old days. A lot
of the close-up, even though it is not as
necessary now as it was then, purely cuts out
the background and the shadows. It is as
simple as that.
    The establishment of close-ups in the
field is totally due to a lack of time.

M.I.: There could be more visual variety?

D: Absolutely. There is nothing more boring
than going, "Take One, Take Three."

Relief from boredom was evident in scenes that departed from
the routine. Overt fantasy scenes, such as Nola's film-based
fantasies, were literally treated as fun to do.
    A major limitation on directors is that they must adhere
to the intent of the scenes, which is, in a sense, the property of the writer and ultimately Procter and Gamble. One
director referred to a director who had been fired.

D: If you start going outside the intent,
they object. It affects storylines. That's
one of the reasons that--isn't working for the
show anymore.

M.I.:  What happened?

D: He wanted to experiment.  He did some
beautiful things.  I think he was one of the
best directors the show ever had.  He expanded on things and sometimes the outer
boundaries of that expansion infringed on
what the writer wanted to do later on.  He had
to pull back . . . he was terribly creative
and when you can't accept what the writer has
and want to expand on it, especially on soaps.
. . . It's different on an hour-and-a-half
special because there you can take that kind
of license without having to worry about anything down the line.

The same director noted that as a result of a writers'
strike he missed knowing the story even only two weeks in
advance since it limited him even more than usual.

One director justified the work he did by saying that he
had to remind himself that viewers saw the show only once.
In general, getting the show done on time, within the limits
of the formula and the expectations of Procter and Gamble
and the on-site people, oriented and justified what had to
be done.

The pressures on directors are considerable since they
are responsible for getting the episode on tape, which
entails the contributions of many individuals, and they have
to do it within a time schedule.  One performer spoke of a
good director as having endurance, being able to work with
performers and being able to use the cameras well.

A good director for a soap has to have a lot
of endurance.  They have to have not too much
ego because in some of the shows they are
relegated to being camera pushers.  A couple
of our directors are wonderful in that they
can not only swallow the inequities, being
pushed around, they are also good directors
of actors.  They know what a scene needs and
what to do with it.  And not get the cameras
pushed around but get them pushed around ar-
tistically so the camera speaks as well,
which is a big part of any visual medium.
What you see is the director's job—a picture
makes a comment, a shot makes a comment.  I
don't think the director in soaps has the
authority he really should have.  I think we

would have much higher quality work if they
were given their proper place.

Another performer viewed the director's role in the following way:

It is a complicated mixture of things that
are required . . . awful lot of patience,
sensitivity, knowledge of saying something or
not saying something, how to deal with a specific actor. . . . In many ways the most ef-
ficient thing to do is to make sure you've
got the shots and see what the performers
want to do within that framework, if you can
accommodate them.

Directors often rely a great deal on performers, and as
this performer noted, a director's primary concern can become
visually capturing the performer's choices. Some performers
often resent the lack of direction. They would like more elaborate planning and involved discussion of scenes. On the other
hand, some actors appreciate that they can more actively participate in the work process by bringing their own interpretation
to a scene or episode. As a technical director noted, the number of elements that have to be satisfied are considerable.

There are so many elements. You have to satisfy the P & G people in Cincinnati; you have
to satisfy the on-site people; you have to satisfy the formulas. . . . Time is a big factor
because time is money.

From the producer's viewpoint a good director is one who
is creative and inventive and yet conforms to story or production requirements.

Well, someone who is creative and inventive
without taking that script off onto a tangent.
We let one director go because that was a
problem because in his efforts to be creative, too often he would take license with
the script and move off into other directions
. . . once a director does that then the next
director comes in the next day . . . how do
you get back to where you have to go today?

Directors are generally not involved in the editing and
tend to rely on their associate director, who called the

shots for the taping and has noted how scenes are to be presented. Directors will edit their own shows when it is shot
film style or when location footage has to be integrated into the episode.

Much of the editing process involves inserting corrections or "pick up edits" after an error has been made. Editors, with the associate director, assemble the program.
During the taping of the show, many of the important editing
decisions are made, particularly through the camera takes or
cuts that the director calls and that comprise each scene.
The way the episodes are shot must meet the approval of the
line producer and very much depends on the degree to which
the producer is involved in the daily production process.
As I indicated, the authority of the line producer is itself
delegated by the executive producer. The actual overseeing
of the day-to-day production process in the studio is the
responsibility of the line producer—whether holding the
rank of producer or associate producer. In the case of the
hour programs, with a continuous, long-run story, there is a
need for an organizing overview or viewpoint. Directors,
for example, may tape only three shows every two weeks, and
even on those days they will not be familiar with edited
versions of what they directed since they are very rarely
involved in the editing process. It is the line producer's
responsibility to deal with continuity of interpretation and
dramatic development on a day-by-day, firsthand basis.

One performer described the producer's role as that of a
"traffic cop."

Joe is worried about what the bold print says
here, are you going against what the intent
of the writer is? He is very worried about
that, and he is very worried about, is that
too graphic, am I going to get into trouble
from Program Practices? How many "gods" have
we said today, how many "gods," how many
"damns." . . . A lot of time Joe is really
structured by those two worries. He really
gets excited when they have done something
that will advance what the bold print says
and make it better. That's when he gets to
do his job; I'd say he gets to do that two or
three times a day . . . the rest of the time
he is traffic cop.

Monitoring what the director and performers do with a particular script, as well as monitoring inconsistencies and
heading off potentially time (and money) consuming problems

with Program Practices limits the creative involvement of a producer.

For both directors and performers, who traditionally work closely together, one of the frustrations is the authority of producers who often are better versed in the business as opposed to the creative side of the performances. The trend in recruitment at Guiding Light appeared to be one in which individuals moved from the position of producer's assistant, who handles scheduling and coordinating production, to associate producer or producer. The route to the role of director entailed experience as production assistant, then associate director and finally director. This career pattern seemed to reinforce a separation of business as opposed to creative or craft experience.

There can be considerable pressure on performers since they may have to learn their lines for several scenes the night preceding the taping of an episode. Occasionally a script was only available the day before it was to be shot. Actors must also perform with consistency so that production is not delayed, come to terms with the commercial and melodramatic nature of the writing if they wish to keep their job, and be able to make last-minute changes in their parts under the close scrutiny of the television camera. Even though shows are now taped, which takes some of the pressure off performers, there still is an expectation that performances should be gotten right the first time. When it is impossible to edit a brief segment, as in disco scenes with live music and considerable movement, there is even greater pressure to accomplish the scene without error.

For many reasons, working on soaps is attractive to performers, despite the limitations and pressures of the work.[17] Work on soaps pays well and can be very steady compared to the generally short-run work in theatre, film, or other forms of dramatic television. Because Guiding Light is taped in New York, performers can pursue other career interests, including work in commercials. Female performers, however, are considerably limited by contractual agreements since Procter and Gamble does not allow soap performers to appear in competitive commercials for products they make, nor are they allowed to appear in Procter and Gamble commercials. Work on soaps was looked on and justified by some younger or newer performers as a way of learning to work on television. Several referred to work on soaps as the "summer stock of television." Finally, prestige is associated with soaps. They are increasingly seen as legitimate work, and, accordingly, provide a potential basis through the visibility and prestige for work in other media, particularly theatre and film. Many performers return to work in soap opera after a period in Hollywood.

Most performers will only read the scenes they appear in in an episode. They all speak of making choices about how their parts were to be played, and discussions between directors and performers were usually very brief. There is little time for disagreement. What is extraordinary is the degree to which collective or routinized understandings are at work in realizing a scene when performers and directors do not know the ultimate meanings of an episode or performance in relation to long-term story.

One of the ways performers' ambivalence toward the work and the pressure they are under surfaces is during rehearsal hall. Rehearsal hall occasions a good deal of joking on everyone's part, but particularly for performers and directors. Performers will make fun of the parts, language, and conventions of soaps. For example, one performer would mockingly throw back her head and put her forearm to her head and exclaim, "I think I'm going to have a 'flashback.'" Asked about the joking, performers responded:

That's to release the tensions, get the garbage out of the scenes.

* * *

The morning is a good time to lighten things up before you hit the floor, so they don't get too tight. You do have to go through with this. It gets it out of your system, plus it helps you edit--I have to hear it first.

* * *

Personally, you need to. Sometimes there is a serious scene and you really need to work on it. But so much of it you really can't take seriously. I had a coach who worked like that. He directed, and he was a private coach. All of a sudden he would say, "Do everything wrong." What does that mean? "just do everything wrong." So you'd wind up . . . it pushed you so far in certain directions that there was a freedom that came about, any self-consciousness about the lines would kind of evaporate because you had been so ridiculous with them that when you pulled them in it was like a whole new insight.

It's a defense mechanism in the morning, to cover embarrassment and because you are so sleepy-eyed, how can you be passionate and upset. It is such a loose rehearsal in the morning. I think you need the freedom in the morning to get rid of all the silliness in the morning without bitching about it. It's a way to face that stuff without complaining, bitching, and moaning. . . . Then most of the time when we get upstairs it's nice most of the time to get down to business. There are situations up there where you do fool around. It's a way to not get bogged by the incredible pace and all the nerves--it's a release. It's almost our own comedy relief, we have our own built-in gesture.

* * *

When you don't feel comfortable with the writing or you think the scene is silly. . . . or you think you have done it for the fourth week in a row.

* * *

The joking is not derogatory toward the stuff; it's only to get you to where you have to go.

Frustration with the material led Guiding Light staff members to make a take-off of the show called "Guiding Plight," which satirized soap conventions and content, as well as commercials associated with soaps. One scene in "Guiding Plight" involved the use of voice-overs whereby viewers are made aware of the internal thought process of a character. The scene was humorous because every character in the frame could hear the thought process, not just the individual having the thoughts or the viewers. Another humorous theme satirized the use of euphemisms in soaps. When a female character says she has "been with" a male, the woman she is speaking to, a revered matriarchal figure is puzzled. "Been with?" she asks. The reply: "Yes, you know, humped."

Performers often attempt to exert some control over their work, both as a matter of integrity and as a way of attempting to keep their job. A producer described the process.

What happens after a performer has been on six months or so is that they begin to feel that they are the guardian of their character, and they really aren't. It still is in the hands of the writer, but actors do get to

that point. You hear, "I would never say
this," or "The character would never say
this." We have that problem continually.

During a writer's strike, when the scripts were being
ghost written, performers were particularly vocal about lines
they thought were repetitive, didn't "track," or were out of
character. A producer noted the occasional legitimacy of
their complaints.

Yes, sometimes it can get lost, because the
scripts can be passed around to writers that
haven't been on that long. It is true they
are funneled through the headwriter, and he
should catch these, but sometimes he misses.
You do get inconsistencies.

The relationship between performer and character, in
terms of what the performer feels is consistent with his
character's past, can also partake of how the performer feels
the audience views his character. One performer who was
particularly protective of his character, and was very vocal
about what he felt were compromises for the sake of plot,
was ultimately replaced by another performer.
One reason performers attempt to protect their character
is that they rely on their personal characteristics to play
their parts. Several spoke of "playing yourself."

M.I.: Do you feel responsible for the part
you are playing?

Performer: Of course I do; she is me. She is
what I make her. Yes. I've got words to work
with, but nobody but ------- is playing Trish
Lewis.

Another actress commented:

I think most of us have a line delineating
between who the characters are and who we
are, except these characters are basically
built on our personalities and what we do.
Even if you are playing a "bad guy" like I
did at one time, you use, within the framework of that, your bad feelings or your ani-
mosities. There is a part of us in any of
those characters so that consequently, when
anything gets changed, it is like something

in your life is being threatened. There is a
very fine line.

The variety of approaches to the work and underlying
dynamics were spelled out by one actress:

M.I.: Do the longer-term actors take a stronger interest in how the character develops?

Actress: Not necessarily. I think it is
probably the newcomers and some oldtimers.
Everybody is pretty gung-ho in the beginning,
as people stay on they sort of give up or
stop fighting so hard--"phone a lot of stuff
in" [don't invest in their acting] or they
just ride with the tide or in some cases they
are very protective as in ---'s case--although
I think now he has cooled it in fighting for
character, although I don't do as many scenes
with him so I don't really know. I don't
think it is necessarily that way--there are a
lot of people that have been on the show a
long time now, and I never really hear them
speak about it. I got less protective as I
knew that I was not going to be with the
character that much longer. I've been getting ready to leave for some time and also
because you see the frustration . . . that
those who, like --- who would be beside himself trying to have a new writer or different
writer changing things slightly. He would
come to work and be frothing by the end of
the day. It can be frustrating trying to
keep it in a mode that is your idea. It is
very frustrating and then spend hours rewrit-
ing. It got to be a thing with me where I
said, it's not really my function to do this,
to rewrite or to change in terms of my interpretation of the character, even if I know
best. You do get new writers or subwriters
who don't know the character development as
well.
If I was doing a Broadway show I wouldn't
have any say with Tennessee Williams about
how to do his play, and everybody is a potential Williams in their eyes I'm sure. I think
there is a point where you have to resign

yourself to the fact that you are going to be
frustrated most of the time, unless you decide to write the show yourself or resign
yourself to the fact that you are an actor
and you are here to read the script and do
your best with it.

Headwriters were critical of this tendency of actors
protecting their character and of actors not liking what
their character was scripted to do. I mentioned one romantic male lead who found himself becoming a grandfather on
the show.

I'm sure he hates it. . . . That's his problem. He's paid to act.
I don't think that actors are necessarily
the best judges of what story is good for
them anyway. Certain actors who have been on
the show a long time--you never find it with
new actors--after they are on a long time,
they decide their image is such and such.
They become image conscious in herms of what
their character is to the audience--an image,
a self-image which is very destructive.

Actors are very aware of where they think their character is "going." Protecting their character is protecting
their job. One major fear is that they will be simply written out of the show. The casting director phrased the dynamic in the following way.

I don't want my character going this way. I
don't want my character going that way. It
scares people if they think their character
is going to go off, "go upstairs" to get a cup
of coffee and never come down again.

Some performers try to keep from being written out, particularly if they think they are becoming an irredeemable
evil character, by playing against the way the part is
scripted.

Performer: I've been on the show eight
months and not really giving them and constantly changing the way the character thinks
to remain evasive so they don't trap you--if
you are too good at being good they can't
make you bad, if you're too bad they can't

save you--therefore, you paint yourself into
a corner and they fire you. Or kill you off.
So the actor's job is one of playing a master
psychologist in trying to figure out how to
maneuver as if the writer's job is to paint a
tapestry in which the character can maneuver.

M.I.: Do most performers approach it with
your awareness?

P: The ability is important in order to sur-
vive.

Another performer made a similar observation:

I saved myself, I think, from getting fired.
It is always good if you are playing a villain to find all the moments you can--I mean
these lines are so simple, they realize you
are a villain--but find the vulnerability,
find a moment somewhere to bring in humor or
sympathy for your character.
I always play opposites. If you are real
good, find something nasty to snap at somebody. If you are being real bad, like I say,
find those moments of humor and softness and
balance it out. Oftentimes you can manipulate
the writer's mind.

The degree to which performers actually influence story
is problematic. There is an interaction between writer-
character-performer as I just noted, but at times performers
may exaggerate their influence. One writer commented on
this tendency:

We are amused, sometimes infuriated, to read
the stories of how they personally took over
the character and turned it into a brilliant
thing when the writers didn't know quite what
to do.

Writers, however, will pick up on the mannerisms, personality, and special skills of a performer and write them
into a part. A performer with skills in karate and another
with skills in fencing had scenes written for them in which
they could employ those skills. Personal mannerisms or
interpretations of a scene may be written into future scenes.
This contributes to a sense of participation in the work

process as does the opportunity to change language, largely in a paraphrase.

One of the latent consequences of a successful scene or paraphrase is that performers may have to repeat themselves.

Steve and I were talking this morning, "Here we are; we are going to do this scene again." That's one flaw or drawback of doing a scene well, because if you do it well and the writer likes it, you'll see it again.

You get a lot of paraphrased scenes [from the writer] and that's not a knock at the writer. And something that you do well, they'll also latch onto that. It's odd. Different kinds of frustration set in when you are doing a long run.

There are limits, however, regarding paraphrasing with some performers allowed greater leeway. One general rule that could not be broken was that tags, the final lines in a scene, had to be played as written. Tags are important for the director in calling the camera takes as well as for dramatic content.

Lately the tag line has been sacrosanct . . . it is a bridge to the next scene and usually the whole intent of a future storyline will depend on someone's reaction to what's been said. The golden rule is you can get away with screwin' around with a lot of stuff, but not those tags.

You always have to say what is written for a tag. . . . The actors hate it because you have to sustain something when it might be really close to nothing [sustain last shot of scene], for a lot of moments while they cut across and get back to you. That's why they call it "egg." They are hard to pull off, and the best thing to do is absolutely nothing.

One of the risks or vulnerabilities for soap performers is ending up with "egg on their face." The convention of long, close-up final shots, particularly for emotionally intense, melodramatic reactions augmented with music, was one of the occupational hazards. As a performer noted, they are at the mercy of the director/camera as the shots are called. Another noted the dependence of performers on the technicians and overall technical process because they could either "make you look bad or look good."

The vulnerability for performers derives from the fact that it is their presence, their face on the screen that a viewer sees. There is a complex division of labor, work process, and authority structure behind the performances that performers must come to terms with, but it is their performance that viewers see. They are the only part of the work process that is visible to the audience.

You are dealing with a creative situation. Actors are creative people, writers are crea- tive people, they all have their opinion. In the whole entertainment business and theatre, everybody is important, but the bottom line is . . . your ass. We are the one on the screen. We are the ones, more than anyone else in the industry, who have less continu- ity in employment. The dime a dozen theory. It is not that we are subjected to it mali- ciously. There are a lot of people who are willing to, who want to be performers. Cast- ing and directing people have a huge choice. You may have a problem with the script or with the way you want your image to come across; certainly if your work is to sustain a career in daytime and develop a strong au- dience, it is absolutely valid you should have some input about it.

Another frustration is the repetition, particularly "re- cap"—a recapitulation of what has occurred earlier so that viewers who might have missed some episodes can be brought up to date on story:

You find yourself doing the same scene over and over and over again. That's another thing that's hard . . . it's out of sequence so you feel, you have to get over the feeling it is pointless. If you do the same scene in a Broadway show it has a build within the whole context; you don't have that disjointed empty feeling. But if you come and do that same tiny fragment again and again, it is very hard to find any kind of justification in reality for it.

One of the consequences of the fragmentation of the performances as scenes are shot out of order, and the never-
ending story, is a lack of a sense of closure, completeness.

In an actor's training in the theatre you are
always dealing with scenes that have a beginning, middle, and an end. You are always
dealing with what is the general thrust of a
scene. We have nothing like that--it started
in 1952. You are doing bits and pieces.

One frustration of it, what I miss from having done so much theatre--I miss a beginning,
a middle, and an end. Soap opera is all middle. A storyline will end, but the soap opera
never ends. It's peculiar to the acting world
in that regard--it just keeps going on.

Finally, another frustration followed from the close camera
work and restricted movements of soap performers.

The movement is very confining, very simple.
You walk in the door, you sit down, you walk
around the couch, you pour a drink.

The problem with this kind of acting is you
get very small, and it gets to the point of
restraint where you feel you can't move. Your
voice gets tiny.

Performers have to orient their movements and speaking
to the cameras and booms. It is incorrect to consider the
visual realization of a soap as solely a matter of camera
conventions. Actors, particularly those with only stage or
film training or experience, have to learn how to work with
the camera. Actors must learn to restrict the range and
pace of their movements, to restrain the projection associated with stage performance. They also have to work with two
or three cameras at one time in an uninterrupted performance.
This contrasts with film production in which one camera is
used, lighting is adjusted for each shot, and where there
are continual stops and starts and repositioning of actors,
cameras, lights, and other equipment. Teleprompters are
available for the performers if they need to rely upon them.
They provide dialogue and ideally are exactly synchronized
with the actors' deliveries. However, they tend to be used
very rarely. It is risky for performers to rely on the
teleprompter because any shift in their gaze from the focus

of concentration or attention in a scene is readily picked up by the cameras. Given the close-range and intimacy of the shots, particularly the emphasis on the eyes of performers, there is a danger of breaking the dramatic focus of a scene. One rule for camerapersons is to always keep the eyes in focus, even in an extreme close-up. As one cameraman put it, "the nose can be out of focus, but the focus on the eyes has to be maintained." One type of scene where it is less risky to use a teleprompter is one in which a person is using the phone and not looking at anyone. A person talking on a phone might look in any direction while he or she listened to the speaker on the other end of the line. This is particularly true in scenes shot with a "limbo." Such sets are minimal and starkly representative of a setting. Phone booths, office desks with a small backdrop, the interior of a car are typical limbos.

One of the rules that characterize soap acting, and television acting in general, is that actors make slow moves. One cameraperson spoke of the "T.V. sit," referring to the appropriate way for performers to sit; that is, gradually and smoothly. Rapid or jerky movements created problems for the camerapersons framing the action and following performers' movements. One actress was particularly prone to very rapid, small movements; such movements seemed spastic in the context of the conventional manner of moving.

Adaptations to the pressures and risks of the work, efforts to garner some control over their work, and the opportunity to express their values or creative convictions varied. But there was a generally shared conception of what it meant to be professional. Professionalism meant meeting work and organizational requirements. Performers spoke of:

"doing your homework" and "being prepared to perform when it comes time to deliver the goods."

"being on time for rehearsal or taping."

"being there for your partner [another actor] if they need you--some people like to 'run lines' a lot."

"you think about things to make things run more smoothly. So when they start a dress rehearsal you are already where you are going to be cued from. You are in position. The stage director doesn't have to usher you there. You try to anticipate."

The pressures of time, which are related to organizational pressures to keep costs down and produce material on a fixed schedule, are evident in what performers identify as being professional. Anticipation, the precise coordination of activity so that the work process flows smoothly was also noted, for example, in what is considered professionalism for camerapersons and in the skills of other occupations, such as the coordination of music.

One of the ways performers are limited in their assertion of autonomy or control over their work was that knowledge of future story was largely withheld from performers. Several reasons are given for this practice of producers and the writer. The headwriter gave the following justifications for not revealing future story for more than three or four weeks into the future.

I think there is a tendency sometimes to play the result much earlier than you should arrive there.

The story could change. It could change drastically. They have it in their head they are going to play one thing, and for some reason or another it can change.

From the writer's viewpoint, the actor's conception of character might work against the direction the story will move in. Another justification for not revealing future story was that just as in real life we do not know what is going to happen tomorrow, so soap characters also wouldn't know! There also is concern that, if future story is revealed, suspense and the audience's desire or need to "tune in tomorrow" would be undermined. This is particularly the case with mystery stories. Guiding Light taped four different endings to one mystery story so that the production staff would not know "who murdered Diane." Future story is also the life or death of a character, and because it is often unknown, actors feel vulnerable. The limited creative control performers have was reflected in comments by one performer who had been with the show for 32 years. Only once in all those years had she been asked for her opinion about future story.

While actors may voice concerns about the parts they are asked to play, and minor changes can be made, it is the intent of the story, the direction the story is designed to move in, that dictates what a character will or will not do, and the intent of the story remains the property of Procter and Gamble. If there are questions, the performer and executive producer will discuss them so that differences do not hinder production.

The work process reflects its hierarchical and collective nature and the importance of costs and profits. Major roles, whose decisions may affect every detail of the process, are those of the supervising producer, the executive producer, and headwriter. Budget, casting, story, and its realization are their direct or indirect concern. The executive producer works directly with the headwriter; the line producer directly oversees the daily production process. The changing relationship between CBS and Procter and Gamble led to greater authority for the executive producer and the assignment of one supervising producer to Guiding Light.

Directors and actors are limited by the authority structure, pace, and nature of the work. Their exclusion from story conferences, their limited knowledge of future story, and the breakneck production schedule generate a great deal of frustration and pressure. Having to work very quickly with often less than satisfying material that had to meet the approval of the production hierarchy (and audience) limits the variability and innovativeness of performances. Professionalism largely means meeting organizational requirements. It also, importantly, means that "form" again takes precedence over "content."

# 7

## Conventions for Expression and Experience: Visual, Audio, and Musical

Art, after all, _is_ artifice. It is not "real," although art may depict, or represent, or interpret reality. And in doing so, any art form can choose the course of verisimilitude, that is, the imitation of reality; or it can choose the course of stylization. If verisimilitude is the course taken, artifice must be disguised. . . . Television serial drama, like Hollywood Cinema, tends toward verisimilitude rather than stylization. Popular audiences, after all, prefer the familiar, and in modern society, mundane reality is familiar. But verisimilitude requires that the art always keep its guard up, so that its techniques of artifice never obtrude into the viewer's consciousness. (Schroeder 1979:415)

This chapter focuses on the activities of the audio, video, and music personnel and the conventions, or ways to structure the cultural products they employ. I also discuss recently introduced script writing conventions which are part of the new look of Guiding Light. Conventions not only contribute to the nature of the potential experience, but they also help make the production process routine by facilitating the coordination of activities. My emphasis here is not on the human relationships between the people behind the cameras or those who work the booms, but on the uses and nature of the conventions themselves.

The effectiveness and meaningfulness of conventions depend upon the participation of the audience. Ideally, the activities of the program makers as they are mediated through the taped performance are appropriately interpreted by the audience, a process whereby what is implied by the program maker corresponds to what a viewer infers. Changing conventions alter the fit, so the changes I discuss were introduced very carefully. From the viewpoint of the program makers, the audience's experience with prime-time television and film, particularly the extensive experience of younger viewers with television, meant that the audience was more sophisticated. This was an important justification for many of the changes.

Technical developments affected the conventions. The development of good quality videotape made the adoption of the hour format feasible, but the decision to adopt that format was largely made for economic reasons. It is cheaper to lengthen a 30-minute program into a 60-minute program than it is to introduce a new 30-minute program. The starting ups costs are considerable; it takes several months at a minimum to build an audience; and it is difficult to compete with an already established soap. The hour-length format is also an expanded environment into which commercials can be placed, although Procter and Gamble initially fought hour-long programming. At one time an effort was even made to extend another 60-minute soap program into a 90-minute program, but the experiment was unsuccessful. The increased budgets for programming, the improved technological capabilities, and their impact on the forms of expression and potential experience made available are derived from economic considerations--the adoption of the hour format and the increased competition for a different and larger audience and potential market.

The nature and structuring of the scripts/episodes is intimately related to the employment of the visual, audio, and musical conventions. As part of the new look to the show, the pace of the show was increased so that the show would move faster or _seem_ to move faster. Scripts were lengthened by the writer so that performers were forced to speed up their deliveries to get the entire performance on tape within the prescribed limits of 41 minutes. The episodes are divided into several acts with a few scenes in each act. There are typically 22 to 24 scenes in seven acts, so the many changes of scene can contribute to a sense of movement and increased pace. Shifting scenes ideally decreased the likelihood of viewer boredom.

Another change involved varying ways of informing the audience about past story. One conventional criticism of soaps is their tendency to repeat material in the form of recap, or recapitulation. The headwriter made use of a number of techniques as a way of summarizing story--through flashbacks, character's fantasies, layered conversations, telephone conversations, and overheard secrets. One convention that still remained, however, was the use of characters' names each time they entered a situation or began a conversation. Characters who obviously know each other well continually use first names as if they were strangers.

One of the innovations introduced by the headwriter was to have individual episodes entail action occurring over more than one day. Activities purportedly occurring in one day typically stretch over a number of episodes, but it is not conventional to tell a story involving more than one day on a single episode.

M.I.: You try to have the script conform to real time, all the things happening in one script happening in one day.

Producer: Doug is the first writer I have worked with--he'll often have somebody late at night at two-thirty in the morning after Wired for Sound or whatever, at the end of an act and in the following act pick up at eight-thirty in the morning. I've never done that in daytime before. Used to be a day at a time. You could have two, three, or four or five scripts dealing with one night, but to go from one day into the next day in the body of one script, I've never done that before. You have to throw in some late night scenes so when you go to a commercial and come back in it's hours later. We're getting away with that on this show.

Again, the aim was to create an impression of faster movement in the story. Also, scenes were begun in such a way that the action was already in progress. Two people are in the middle of a conversation, for example, and the viewer/ listener enters an on-going situation, some of which hypothetically is missed, but which the viewer ideally eagerly participates in to catch what is happening. All of these changes are designed to create more movement and action.

The question of pace in soap opera also may be related to the pace of commercials. I suspect that, given the extraordinary cost and care put into commercial manufacture and the intentions behind their realization, they might also have a major impact on technical quality, production values, and conventions of programming itself. Given the competitive process, programs have to compete with commercials. Anecdotal evidence for this is the familiar comment that at times the commercials are better than a particular program.

VISUAL CONVENTIONS

The development of videotape is a major technological development that affected the program, particularly in conjunction with computerized editing. At Guiding Light each scene is taped as if it were a live performance, unless there are highly complex moves involved, in which case it is shot movie-style. An example from Guiding Light was a scene in which Kelly swings down from the rafters of a barn to confront Duke, who has raped his love, Morgan. The scene made use of an elaborate studio set to represent a barn and a double for Kelly. There was much more movement than is characteristic of soap scenes. Such scenes are pieced together in the editing process. For most scenes, however, the selection and sequence of shots are determined by the director in the taping process itself.

The half-hour program, Edge of Night, generally tapes episode scenes in sequence, leaving time and space for the insertion of commercials. At times, scenes will be shot before (pretaped) or after the day (posttaped) on which the bulk of the scenes for an episode are shot. Half-hour programs, before the development of adequate quality tape, were performed in such a manner. The move to one-hour programming, the logistical and financial costs involved, the demands on performers, and the development of more sophisticated editing equipment have contributed to the use of film-style shooting in which scenes are taped out of sequence. But scenes are performed continuously, as if live.

The current technology of soap production has affected the work process in a number of ways. One technical director commented:

Prior to having tapes, you wouldn't consider doing these shows any other way than live. There was the tape itself as a good reproduction that got the shows thinking of going to tape and not going on the air live. That would be the first major breakthrough. Since that has happened, I would say the entire television picture has changed.

Computerized editing on one-inch tape has also contributed to the way in which one-hour programs tend to be shot. Before computerized editing, the editing process was much more difficult and time consuming.

An earlier system was still used at Edge of Night, except for scenes involving complex activity, when a computerized system was rented. The program relied more on the technical director to create effects through a control panel (switcher). Editing also was more time consuming because sections of the performance had to be literally marked on the tape with audio "beeps" and physically marked with a line in the editing process. Locating a specific portion of the performance and coordinating and integrating it with other portions of the performance was a time-consuming and difficult job. With the earlier system, "edit points" were important and reflected the greater dependence on the actual taping process. The video editor at Edge of Night described its operation.

M.I.: An edit point is where they change cameras?

Editor: Definitely on a camera cut and hopefully there will be no audio. There is what we call a "small hole." There is silence before a word and they edit right there. You can't really edit on the same camera shot. It is very difficult. If you have a whole scene on one camera you couldn't edit where an actor "went up" [forgot lines]. Music is a problem too. They go from scene A to scene B, and the actor in scene B "goes up;" they have to at least go back before the line where there is no music in scene A.

At Guiding Light the computerized system allowed for greater ease in locating and editing in material at specific points. The performances are coded, there are 45 frames identified per second, and the computer locates a specific frame at the editor's command. Similarly, audio and music tracks are separate and can be manipulated during the editing process. One technical director noted the impact of computerized editing.

The editing technology having changed through the computer operated editing and the one-inch tape has made everybody basically thing of shooting out of sequence. When it was the old type of editing, I would say the shows stayed live for a longer amount of time until they moved into computer editing. They would spend too much money and too much time on editing until the equipment became more so-phisticated. The end result was not tech-nically good--you would have problems. There was an overlap from the time videotape came into being and the shows at the half-hour level--there were no hour shows--until they decided to go fully onto tape with an editing process. One of the reasons the half-hour shows taped from start to finish was to avoid editing because of the technology of editing at that time. They would do a minimal amount of editing--it was not easy to edit with any degree of sophistication.

You can do virtually anything you want to do. You can remove the audio, change it, put it forward, put it backwards, put in new audio, all with relative safety--you can have one track with audio, one with music, it can be multitracked.

One social consequence of the computerized system is that directors or others in the control room will say, "They can fix it in the edit" when a scene has not gone ideally but they do not want to retape the scene. While editors then have more work, they also have a greater influence on the finished product, given the increased technical capability and greater reliance on the editing process.

The use of videotape and the improved editing technology have also contributed to the increased location shooting. Footage can be shot relatively cheaply and integrated into episodes primarily shot in the studio. For example, an important location shot made use of a Jamaican setting (although there was little to distinguish the setting from other tropical, romantic settings), primarily for beach and patio scenes. These scenes were interspersed with other scenes shot in the studio, occasionally in conjunction with scenes that, while shot in the studio, were identified as occurring in Jamaica. One limitation of videotape is its poor quality for night scenes. This contributes to the interior, well-lighted look of soaps.

These technological developments have, however, ultimately been fit into the commercial context, and while introducing new possibilities, have also been limited. For example, location shoots have been used to depict romantic settings and/or action-adventure settings on Guiding Light. The shootings fit the style of the show and have been used consciously that way.

Even with the use of tape, the picture quality still retains the quality of live television. Several performers remarked that some audience members think the show is "made-up" or improvised, it seems so real. Hoggart captures this quality of many television performances:

Television has a peculiar "immediacy" and
"fluidity"; it strongly suggests that "it's
all happening," gives a sense of "thereness,"
"thisness" and "nowness," and it tends to
break down existing categories. It resists
stage acting and even cinema acting, breaks
through the picture frame or mental prosce-
nium arch, and merges the spectator with the
picture, on its sidelines if not at the centre. On television everything tends to become an instant report from the front-lines.
Or television can make a funeral in a back
garden seem heavy with the meaning of life.
It heightens even the most "ordinary" ordi-
nariness of life and seems to give it dramatic significance. Because of its sense of
actuality, of its Brechtian breaking of distance, we are all sidewalk spectators of the
drama of life when we watch television.
(1970:170-71)

The fact that, even with the use of tape and more complex editing, the programs retained the quality of being live
is important for the nature of the performances. Similarly,
the visual conventions employed also contribute to the realism and presentness of the performances.

Though we readily see the importance of cinematic codes in film (camera angles, lighting,
setting, camera movement, editing . . . ) we
neglect to notice the effects of formulaic
camera moves in soap opera and in doing so we
succumb to the "realist illusion": the idea
that the camera simply records reality. We
assume that the soap opera is a utilitarian
tool, not an expressive one, and so we see
this kind of cinematography as dull, routine,
obvious--of no import. And that is what the
makers of soap operas count on. [The] very
obviousness of the cinematic codes of soap
opera keeps people from thinking about them
and thus makes them effective in doing their
job: to shape and direct the audience's
point of view. (Timburg in press)

For the camerapersons, shooting soaps becomes an extremely routine matter. The limited and repetitive nature of the
way soaps are conventionally shot meant that many cameraper-

sons paid little attention to the director's blocking of a
scene and needed little direction. At both Edge of Night
and Guiding Light the associate director would prepare camerapersons for the next shot, which would then be taken by the
director. The practice at ABC's All My Children was different. A "shot-sheet" was given to each cameraperson which
listed the shots and framing. The shots/takes in a scene are
numbered sequentially, and the cameraperson would know where
his shots and their composition fit into the sequence. In
addition, they communicate with the technical director, not
the associate director.

Professionalism for camerapersons consisted of carrying
out routine activities well. Rules for good camerawork included:

1. Composing a shot appropriately, such that there are "no
lamps sticking out of the tops of people's heads," and
objects in the background do not interfere with the emotional focus of the shot.
2. Keeping the boom or its shadow, if there was one, from
showing in a shot.
3. Keeping a focus on where there is a key light.
4. Maintaining a focus on the eyes, even if the nose is out
of focus.
5. Knowing which side a performer looks better on.
6. Being able to anticipate the next shot, for example, a
fast rise. A camera rise is slow, but performers may
rise too rapidly and potentially move out of the frame.
The good cameraperson can anticipate such moves.
7. Showing the furniture and set to its best advantage.
8. Using furniture to create depth in a set. This is done
by using a piece of furniture in the foreground.

The types of shots employed are limited. On soaps there
is a virtual absense of some shots, for example extreme long
shots, and a greater reliance on others. This is partly a
function of the size of the sets--their depth, width, and
height--camera capabilities, and time. However, the shots
can also be related to the social significance of distance.
Gaye Tuchman (1973), discussing camera conventions in television news, relates news/film (tape) conventions to the
social or cultural significance of distance. She labels
four major categories, using a framework developed by Edward
Hall.

Significance varies on a continuum, so one can distinguish between close personal distance and far personal distance and, similarly, between close and far social distance. The following drawings (Figure 7-1) are labelled

Figure 7-1          VISUAL CONVENTIONS

Intimate Distance
Extreme Close-up

Close Personal Distance
Close-up

Far Personal Distance
Medium Close-up

Close Social Distance
Medium Shot

Far Social Distance
Long Shoot

Public Distance
Extreme Long Shot

with terms that Tuchman uses (reflecting their social significance) and also with conventional television production
terms. In television news film there is a reliance on far
personal, close social, and far social distance. On the one
hand, news avoids extreme close-ups and close-ups that are
associated with intimacy. News film is supposed to be
objective (read "distanced") and close-ups imply subjective
involvement with what is in the frame. On the other hand,
television news tends to avoid shots that fit the public
distance category because such shots are seen as too
impersonal and television like to personalize the news.

| | |
|---|---|
| Public space | Beyond 13 feet |
| Social distance | 4 to 12 feet away |
| Personal distance | 1-1/2 to 4 feet away |
| Intimate distance | 0 to 18 inches away |

Soaps emphasize a limited range of shots. They
avoid public distance or long shots, as does the news, but
make much greater use of initmate and personal distance or,
put differently, shots of the shoulders, head, and extreme
close-ups. One characteristic readily associated with soaps
is the use of close-ups. They contribute to the identification of a program as a soap.

The emotional intensity of soaps and their personal
or individual focus are relatable to camera conventions and
the social significance of distance. Some of the reliance
is attributable to the size of the sets and budget (time),
but even in location footage there is a reliance on the same
types of shots. Budget factors conspire to keep out elements that do not fit the symbolic world of soaps. Even
outdoors, for example, we rarely see crowds or get a sense
of impersonal forces that dwarf the individual.

The headwriter of Edge of Night spoke directly to
the issue of the absence of "strangers." They used strangers in episodes in which Mike Carr, a detective/lawyer, was
outdoors, walking blindly with a cane.

We didn't pay the strangers anything. We made sure nobody was identifiable. With crowds you run into money problems. You can't use anybody in your drama without letting them know they're on the air. Strangers are really extras and are extraneous.

One soap that I observed did employ crowds of strangers. Search For Tomorrow filmed chase scenes on the streets of Hong Kong. Apparently the same restrictions do not apply in an alien society since they will not see the program.[18] A combination of factors works to keep the focus personal and limited.

The patterning of shots tends to reflect the change in social distance for dramatic effect. Opening shots in a scene are often from a greater distance that those closing a scene. An establishing shot will provide a context of significance for the scene and then the camera typically moves closer. The use of the zoom lens to "tighten in" or "squeeze in" is quite common. Generally, once a camera is positioned it seems rarely to be repositioned. A partial explanation for this practice is that it is risky to move the camera and chance creating noise or confusion. Another is that it can be confusing to the viewer to have the perspective changed, particularly since the camera will partially reflect the point of view of one of the participants in the scene. The general pattern for many scenes is a gradual tightening or concentration of focus, a decreasing distance, and an intensification of emotional involvement and identification. Many scenes end on a close-up or extreme close-up. When directors wish to emphasize the isolation or loneliness of a character, they will visually pull back from a scene.

The use of studio cameras and their relatively permanent positioning has also to do with the need to avoid rapid movements, both on the part of the actors and cameras because there is such a reliance on close-ups. The tighter the shot, the greater the magnification of any movement. Use of a hand-held camera would be disturbing given the conventional style of shooting, although portable cameras are used for scenes that require unique camera positions or more than the usual two or three cameras. Occasionally, hand-held cameras are used to present the point of view of someone who is being chased and/or in some form of danger.

Cameras tend to remain fixed and to follow the movement of performers from that position. The cameraperson is much like a gunner, tracking a target until it is properly framed. In the case of head-on shots, the figure's nose is framed in the exact center of the picture. When someone is moving across a set, the camera frames that person to one side of the screen, leaving the other side empty. As one cameraperson put it, "You let them move into or look into a space and follow them into that space."

The hand-held camera and "steady cam" are used a great deal, however, for location shooting.

The hand-held camera is used a lot outside. They are shooting with hand-held almost exclusively when they go on location. There is a steady cam device which allows a man to man a camera on his person and move around and keep the camera movement down to an absolute minimum. There are also a lot of mounts —if you want a 14-foot high shot, you need a 14-foot ladder, put the camera on the ladder with a clamp, put the camera on it, shoot your sequence, and take the camera off—it doesn't take any major dismantling. And that, of course, is time. You can put it on a very lightweight tripod. So the flexibility gives you anything from studio mode of operation to actual hand-held usage—you can go into airplanes with it, put it in cars.

Camera placement in soaps also reflects a pattern. They are placed in the rooms or sets where action occurs and also partially reflect the point of view of participants in a scene. For example, when a person enters a room, he is captured by a camera placed to the rear of a person already in the room. If that person is at a desk in an office, the camera is positioned low on its pedestal relative to the height of the person entering. If both the participants in a scene are seated, both cameras would be low on their pedestals.

The camera tends to be in a position that corresponds to the height of a person. There are no shots from a boom or from a place high over a set. Similarly there are few shots from extremely low positions. On one occasion (at _Edge of Night_) a camera was taken off its pedestal and placed on a sled (a wood platform with small wheels) so that the platform was only a few inches above floor level. The camera on the sled framed two seated people in such a way that an expanse of floor did not appear in front of them and a large window appeared behind the performers—the scene takes place in a dance studio.

The height of the sets does place limits, but, again, shots from extremely low or high positions would break the

frame of soaps. Because of the realism and psychological
focus in soaps, they shy away from an emphasis on physical
stature. For example, The Hulk, a show about a doctor un-
able to stop his transformation into a green muscle man when
he becomes angry, is often shot from extremely low angles.
In this way his physical stature is emphasized or exaggerated. Conversely, shots looking down tend to diminish the
stature of individuals. There is a general avoidance of
these camera conventions in soaps I have observed. Again,
this has implications for the surface realism of soaps. The
physical exaggeration of human dimensions would change or
threaten to change the "key" used to interpret the action,
perhaps into something more readily identified as fantasy or
fiction.

There is also a reliance on a fixed plane and an avoidance of "vision in motion," which would occur if the camera
were to keep changing its position. The use of hand-held
cameras would produce just that, as would the use of dolly-
ing or trucking. For example, conventionally, when someone
moves, the camera follows that person and "pans" with him.
A technical director who had extensive experience in television, including experience doing early live television
drama, commented on the limited uses of the cameras.

The soap writers, up until this point, have
not written for camera movement, and the
directors tend not to use camera movement as
it would be used on location or in the making
of film. Even against the days when we had
live dramatic shows, we had very fluid camera
movement--because the cameras had four lenses
on them and the cameramen being able to pick
any of the lenses. We had tremendous amounts
of fluid camera movement in the, for instance, Studio One dramatic series, Ford Theatre. The concept was different in that
nighttime format. They have yet to get involved with that in the studio.

It is time consuming to rehearse movement. In our framework they try to get so
much done in a relatively short time that
they do tend to oversimplify camerawise.
Also, the fact that the studio camera is only
equipped with a zoom lens makes it very difficult to move the entire camera unit and
zoom at the same time. The lens is designed
to be used from a steady position and use the
optics of the lens to actually pull the scene

in and out, from close-up to wide shot. It
is an awkward camera to use when you start
dollying--it is not designed for that. You
may arc a little right or left, but none of
the sweeping movements we used to do with the
straight lens. There is a definite restric-
tion on the camera movement using this opti-
cal equipment.

Through the rehearsal process and final taping, there
are a number of monitors in the studio and in production
offices. In the control room there is a monitor for each
camera's picture, as well as a monitor for the image taped
(on line). Throughout the process there is continual feedback, which aids the process of generating the appropriate
images.

In film, image sequences would normally be related to
editing events. In television soap opera production, editing can occur at a number of different points. Zettl's
Television Production Handbook distinguishes four senses of
the term editing:

1. Emphasizing the important and de-emphasiz-
   ing the unimportant.
2. In film and videotape: cutting out un-
   wanted portions and gluing the desired
   pieces together into a continuous show.
3. In live television: selecting from the
   preview monitors the picture that is to go
   on the air.
4. [electronic editing] Inserting or assembling of program portions on videotape
   through electronic means whereby the tape
   does not have to be physically cut.
   (1968:508)

The degree to which "pick up edits" (repeating a performance after a stop has been called) or "inserts" (the taping
of limited segments that are inserted into the larger more
acceptable sequence) are used depends greatly on the technical capability of the editing equipment. At Guiding Light,
inserts were used more frequently. But the overall editing
process basically entails assembling the show, shortening
the final take in a scene, or doing an insert.

Shortening final takes is particularly important since
the pace of soaps has changed greatly over the last four or
five years. This is reflected by the use of fewer lingering
close-ups or extreme close-ups at the end of scenes. Often
the dramatic significance of scenes was emphasized by

lengthy shots of reactions to dramatic news. Actors often spoke of being left with "egg on their face" in such scenes. In general, final takes were one area where the tape was manipulated to fit the program to its proper length and to avoid the exaggerated lengthy final shot.

A recently made stylistic change at Guiding Light was the use of cuts at the end of scenes as opposed to the traditional use of dissolves. The gradual fading or dissolving of the final image has been replaced by a (rapid) cut in order to increase the pace of the show and make it move faster dramatically. One problem with rapid cuts is that they can be disorienting.

At times, the cut comes so rapidly you don't know effectively that a change of scene has taken place.
Let's say they are in Hillary's apartment and the last shot is close-up. And the next shot going into the next apartment scene is a close-up of somebody else. When I go from here to here I don't see any background scenery. The audience doesn't know that you have changed the location. A dissolve is a change of location and a lapse of time, generally. It can be confusing at times.
We always used to dissolve from scene to scene within an act. A dissolve always denotes a change in location and many times a change in time. In soap opera, it could be the same time. It could be eight o'clock in the morning one place, to eight o'clock in the morning another place, but you'd still be dissolving to show the audience you have changed your location.

The writer for Guiding Light made extensive use of close-ups, which contributed to the possible confusion in the mind of a viewer. The overuse of close-ups was criticized by one technical director.

The overuse of close-ups is an arbitrary thing brought on by the producer and/or the writer. We went through a phase of Guiding Light where we had a certain group of producers in Cincinnati and they just wanted close-ups. We went through a number of months where we shot 60 percent of the show in close-ups to a point where people would make an entrance in

the room and they'd be discovered in a close-
up. That went the way of all arbitrary
things--it disappeared.

One innovation on Guiding Light was the use of fantasy
sequences based on Nola's experiences of old movies. A number of fantasy sequences were filmed that copied the original films--Casablanca and Shipmates Forever, for example.
The visual conventions employed imitated the film conventions. For example, a camera was suspended over the dance
floor to capture the choreography as Busby Berkley had done.
Visual conventions, as well as audio and musical conventions, "key" different frames of reference. Dreams, fantasies, and flashbacks are often shot so the images are soft
or hazy, but they may be associated with audio and musical
conventions also.


AUDIO CONVENTIONS

One audio convention creates a sense of distance, when
combined with the visual images. Booms are placed in
different locations, with the boom that is located at a
greater distance, or behind a door, set at a lower volume
level. This was referred to as "perspective sound." The
audio director makes reference to a scene in which one
character listens through a door to a conversation on the
other side of the door.

In the last scene Nola leaves and stands in
the hallway, listening to them inside. I had
a boom out in the hall, a microphone out in
the hall, and I had a microphone inside.
What I do is increase the volume; you have
the boom in the hall at the normal level, and
I knocked down the boom in the room. So it
picks more from the hall microphone than from
the direct microphone. That gives you an
effect of hearing through the door. That
gives you a perspective sound.

Another basic technique is the use of filters for phone
calls. The person heard through the phone sounds different
from the person on camera when he or she speaks into the
phone. The viewer is hearing the person on camera directly,
and the person off-camera indirectly through the filter.
Filters are also used for thought processes, although these
are distinguished in part from their use in phone calls by
less of a filtered effect.

Audio conventions are also employed in flashback and dream sequences. Echo effects are added to the visual component to make the context distinguishable from present time. Echoes are typically combined with a blurring or softening of the visual image. Tape has made it much easier to employ flashbacks, which are particularly useful in soap storytelling because they provide a way of recapping material. Flashbacks acquaint viewers with what they may have missed, reinforce the knowledge viewers already have, and stimulate associations. Flashbacks are also useful as they express or reinforce the psychological focus of the programming, allowing psychologically significant past events to occupy the present consciousness of a character.

Before the use of tape, both dream sequences and flashbacks could be created, but they were done much more infrequently. Done live, flashbacks or dream sequences were captured by cutting from one set, in the present, to another where the flashback or dream sequence would be enacted and then back to the scene in the present. The computerized editing process has made it even easier to use these conventions than mechanical tape editing. All programming is coded so that specific sequences can be retrieved quickly through the computerized process.

Another audio convention is the voice-over, which allows access to a character's inner thoughts and takes the form of an interior monologue. Typically the visual component involves a close-up of a character, usually motionless with an appropriate facial expression, while the viewer/listener hears the voice-over. Again, the technique contributes to the drama by providing access to intimate thoughts and feelings. One audio convention that is used less frequently is the use of multiple echoes to create a bizarre effect. One word is repeated over and over to create a sense of disturbance.

MUSICAL CONVENTIONS

The use of music to create or emphasize emotional effects continues to be a characteristic of soap operas. As melodramatic performances, structured around romantic and sensational incidents, relying on music as an integral element to create or enhance moods or meanings, and sponsored by soap manufacturers, the label soap opera has stuck despite the many changes in soaps over the years. The label also calls attention to the use of music itself. Traditionally, a solo organ provided the music for most soaps, creating an air of almost religious solemnity to the performances.[19]One music supervisor commented, "I tell people what I do, I'm the music person for <u>Guiding Light</u>. 'Oh, organ.' In fact, there is no more organ music. It is all very well orchestrated."

Music remains important, but the greater ambitiousness in their production and the overall effort to change the look of the show has led to a wider and more varied choice of music. Organ and piano, once replaced by strings, are now being superseded by a reliance on a greater variety of instruments and sound sources in different combinations, such as synthesizers, solo drums, or vibraphones.

Music production houses are contracted by the soaps for music. The production company provides a catalogue of musical pieces appropriate to the style of the show, which is continually revised to fit changes in story. At <u>Edge of Night</u> the theme of the program, played with the opening skyline of a city (Cincinnati, corporate headquarters of Procter and Gamble) at dusk, evoked the mysteriousness appropriate to the program. <u>Guiding Light</u> changed its theme during the period I carried out my research. Originally the program opened with harps and strings along with a visual of soft sunlit flowers. This image and theme were replaced by a series of takes from the program emphasizing drama, romance, and action with light now associated with the flash of photographers' cameras and the reflection of light from the mirrored surfaces in a disco. The music, also, emphasized this different image. The religious, inspirational "guiding light" of the earliest programming had changed to a more secular light promising a more exciting way of life.

In April 1982, <u>Guiding Light</u>'s musical catalogue had 1,114 separately numbered musical pieces, from four seconds to three minutes, recorded on cartridges. There were also other unnumbered pieces--cocktail music, disco music, wedding music, or synthesizer sounds. The music supervisor for the program selects the pieces thought appropriate to an episode and directs the music technician, who physically plays the tapes.

The pieces are catalogued by number (slate number). There is a very brief description of the mood of the piece (vague fear), a description of the sound sources used (vibes, strings), and a notation on the length of the piece. The music supervisors will often add their own notations to help them remember or differentiate the pieces.

For example, this "cart" is described as a "scheming feeling." When I go through and listen to it myself, I put my own [label] on it to help me identify it. What somebody else feels is a tense piece of music, could also to me have a feeling of being "ominous" or "heavy" because there are so many little moods. One time there will be a sad scene, and the next time there will be a little anger behind it. You have to find the right piece of music to fit the mood.

The supervisors receive scripts of the episodes they are responsible for in advance. If scripts are not available in advance, supervisors are given breakdowns describing the scenes in the episodes. The scripts generally do not indicate where and what music is to be used. The coordinators rely upon the scripts, as well as familiarity with past performances in making choices.

You get the feeling after watching day after day how the character is going to play it. You read the script, and you will think, "Ah ha, this should take a lot of time, there is a very warm mood." Then when they come on, it isn't always that way. But you also become attuned to the way a performer plays the role. You get used to that. After being here a while you know exactly how that character is going to play it.
For example, yesterday, there was a scene between Nola and her mother where her mother says, "Since you came back from London, are you happy?" She said, "Yes, why shouldn't I be? I have everything. I have a new baby, I live in this beautiful home. I have a chinchilla coat." Then the mother says, "You don't seem happy." "But I am happy, on top of the world." In the script it said, tears are coming down her cheek. But in reality, that wasn't the way they played it. She didn't do that at all. It was must faster and she was sort of depressed.
I just put in a little sad cello underneath when she was saying her last line, "Oh, yes, I'm very happy." At the end of the scene as it faded to black, the mother and she put their arms around each other. And there was just a sad chord.

Timing is particularly important. The music, to point up something ideally, or be most effective, must enter at the appropriate time. Anticipating what happens in scenes and having a good sense of timing is an important part of being professional.

There has to be a sense of timing with what
the actor is going to do. . . . A lot of it
is a sense of performing, a feeling.

There is a sense of the musical and dramatic
moment‘ and being able to combine them.

All three of the music coordinators I spoke with had been or were also professional singers, particularly of opera.

There are various categories of music, some defined by their function, such as opening or curtain music, others by their mood, and others by their connection with an individual or theme in the form of a leitmotif. Curtain pieces, for example, are used at the end of a scene, although they can also be used as an opening if they "don't sound too finalized." A curtain, "neutral serious," would be used for the close of a scene while another, "curtain-pretty-vibes," could also be used as an opener. Since it was pretty and played by vibes, this meant "it was up" and was usable as an opener. Other curtain categories, for example, included "curtain-mystery," "curtain-eerie mystery," and "curtain-mystery strange."

Musical leitmotifs are also employed, particularly as themes for individuals. An identifiable theme is created for an individual, and variations on that theme are created to reflect different moods. For example, the theme for Hillary had various forms, one a "sad curtain," another "bright and happy." The supervisors themselves will develop thematic statements for individuals, even if the pieces originally were not composed with that use in mind. One of the factors influencing the choices of music is whether the musical piece will "give something away."

If we know something and know something that
is coming up two or three weeks down the road,
we have to be careful not to give that away in
the music. For example, Carrie. It is evolv-
ing that she has a split personality. A while
back, say a month ago, when she was on her
honeymoon, another coordinator wanted to use
strange music, "Carrie Two music" we call it,
electronic music. This was before it came out
she had a split personality. He wanted to use
the music when she burned a picture up, but
the director said not to "because it would

give the audience a clue and we don't want to drop that clue already."

Music is used at the beginning of a scene to "set the scene," but then removed. It is also used at the end of a scene.

In the beginning of a scene, unless it is important, if they are just talking back and forth, the music wouldn't help. In other words, you bring the music up to set the scene, and get out with the music. It's ridiculous and silly to keep the music there just for the sake of keeping it there. That's number one.

The use of music to put a "button on a dramatic moment" is particularly important at the end of a scene.

What really dictates it is if there is a very strong ending--if a new and important piece of information comes at the end of a scene that requires a much stronger tag . . . there usually is not time for subtext at the ends of scenes because it is usually a fairly fast ending. It depends on what kind of feeling you want to leave--if it is a suspension thing, a question, a declaration.

Musical pieces that emphasized a point are termed "stings" and have a close connection with what are called "take notes" in the musical catalogue. In both cases, music is used to "draw the viewer's eye quickly, even more than just with a camera shot." Take notes are played by all the instruments and last about three or four seconds. This category was being used less frequently than in the past and was referred to as part of the "old-fashioned soap opera style." Music adds to the emotional complexity of a soap by underlining the subtext of a scene.

Subtext. That's where music plays a big part. A couple may be playing what seems to be a love scene and yet maybe one or the other is cheating, maybe the audience knows he is cheating . . . that could be a sub-text. In a happy scene and we know a char-acter is going to die, the music could bring that out. I would play a sad piece if I chose to bring out that aspect. My choice depends on the storyline--how strong that storyline is playing elsewhere. It is the music's job to underline what is happening and to bring out a subtext.

"Bridges" are used to move from one scene to another, to create or identify the emotional underpinnings of the scene. For example, when there is a shift from a troubled moment to a lighter moment, bridges are used across the scene break. Since the scenes are shot separately and usually out of sequence, the music has to be "fed over" the end of the scene into the next scene, and special note has to be taken to shut off other sound sources while the music continues to be taped. Later, in the editing process, the video and audio signals are combined or added to the music, which has already been recorded. One supervisor stated that music is not placed with a dramatic moment in the middle of a scene unless it involves a flashback or dream.

In the old days the organ would be doing lit- tle bits and fills all the time. In the mid- dle of a scene, it would sound very artifi- cial to add something at that point. That would be a no-no. However, if there is a flashback or a dream sequence, you might use music to accent the fact that there is some- thing out of the ordinary going on.

Music is also not used when a scene begins with the action already underway. For example, someone might be in- volved in a phone conversation. Music is viewed as distract- ing in such a context. One exception to the rule that music accompanies the end of a scene is when a following scene is extremely dramatic.

Even if the end of one scene does have a reaction from an actor, but you know from your script that the next scene coming up is the more dramatic scene, you want to be underplaying with some music, you'll lay off for that previous scene.

Another major rule was to use music to fill a "dead spot."

If the scene calls for it, you put in as much as possible. Also, if there is a "dead spot," if at the end of a scene they do a "take," somebody says something and they do a

take of one person, and then the (other) person before they switch to another scene, you
"fill the gap," help hold it together.

One of the ways music was being introduced into the program directly was through the use of popular entertainers
who appeared in the disco, Wired for Sound. Also, two major
performers, John Schipp who played Kelly and Tom Nielsen who
played Floyd, were performers themselves. The use of contemporary music, in the context of a disco, performed by
characters on the program or guests such as Judy Collins,
was justified on the basis that it would appeal to and
attract younger viewers and add entertainment value to the
program. The use of music in the storyline itself created a
number of problems. The sound levels for the music in the
disco scenes made it difficult to hear the dialogue; at
other times the selections contained vocals, which also conflicted with the dialogue. In addition, since the music was
recorded live from the studio floor, any stops in the taping
of a scene meant that the entire scene had to be retaped.
Music continues to be an important and integral element
in Guiding Light. It functions in a variety of ways--
generating suspense, emphasizing a subtext, and filling a
dead spot. New music has been composed and utilized to
create a new look to the show. Musical, audio, and visual
conventions are combined to "key" the meanings of the performances. They are carefully fitted together to create an
ideally distinctive pattern of experience. In whole, or in
part, conventions are important for the expression and
experience of Guiding Light.
Technical developments have affected the work practices
or conventions. Better quality videotape and computerized
editing are the two major developments; the zoom lens, a
lesser one. They have largely been incorporated to make the
programs longer and more profitable and fit within a style
derived from the traditional forces generating the perfor-
mances--attracting the afternoon female television audience. The specific pattern of current conventions, the
recently introduced changes, are a part of the competitive
process. Scripts and their content have been structured
differently; musical, audio, and visual conventions have
been altered to create a more appealing experience for the
audience in the competition for that audience.

# 8
## The Audience as Viewer, Statistic, and Social Being: Letters and Ratings

> Popular art is that work produced to appeal
> to a perceived audience in terms of their
> probably unarticulated expectations rather
> than correspond to formal features derived
> from traditional or academic conventions.
> An implication of this assertion is that the
> core difference between capitalist and social-
> ist societies in relation to popular art must
> be in how "perceptions" of audiences are ar-
> rived at rather than in some aesthetic essence
> of the meaning of popular. (Chaney 1979:8)

One of the more highly charged issues in discussions of mass communication and popular culture in advanced capitalist societies is to what degree do communicators impose their choices on the audience and/or to what degree do audiences impose their preferences on the communicators and thus determine what gets produced? As Chaney points out, perceptions of the audience play an important role in shaping and justifying what is produced given the distance between producers and audience members.

A range of positions is taken on the issue of the relative power of audience on communicators. At one extreme some observers see the audience as relatively powerless in affecting what is made available; others attribute much greater influence to the audience (Cantor 1980). But despite the evident importance of studying the actual interaction between communicators and the audience, there is little systematic information on the topic. Cantor, citing a number of researchers, summarizes their position as "agreeing the impact of information about audience preferences and viewing on the communicator has rarely been scrutinized systematically. Although they wrote over a decade ago, the above statement is still true" (Cantor 1980:111). Production studies are clearly a way to empirically explore the issues involved, and to

go beyond media "folklore," or occu- pational, organizational and political ideologies.

The interaction of communicators and the audience is complex, unique, and more important in soap production than in
other forms of media fare. That soaps are on five days a
week, 52 a year, has a number of consequences, as does the
fact that the programs are not produced far in advance of
their air date nor syndicated for domestic broadcast.[20]

Ideally, scripts for particular episodes are ready about
four to six weeks before they are taped. This allows time
for the distribution of the scripts and careful planning of
the production process. Quite frequently there are only two
or three weeks for preparation. The episodes in turn are
taped about five to seven days before they are broadcast.
This schedule contrasts with other dramatic programming for
television where production may occur several months before
the program is aired. In such cases, there is a considerable
time lag between production and broadcast, so that the main
sources of audience feedback—letters and ratings—stand in
a different relationship to the production process. For
soaps, the potential significance of letters and ratings is
quite different because producers have access to pertinent
information they can use in decision making.

The dynamics are also different because soaps as serials
are continuing stories which need to generate a continuing
audience. It is generally agreed that it takes from several
months to a year or more for a soap to build an audience and
good will toward the show. This realization followed the
failure of many early soaps that were given too short a
period to develop an audience. What is important, according
to the communicators, is that the audience comes to know the
characters and care about them. As a result, decisions are
made in a time frame that does not exist or apply to programs
that have only a few weeks or months in which to prove
themselves.

Very often suppliers will attempt to build on the core
of viewers that a program does have and to make changes to
add to that core, even if the core and share of the audience
is relatively small and ratings are low for the program. In
fact, many of the innovations made in General Hospital occurred during a period in which the program had very low
ratings, was at the bottom of the barrel and had nowhere to
go but up. Even though cancellation was scheduled, executives chose to work with an established show rather than
start a new one. Texas, an extremely unsuccessful soap,
pitted against both General Hospital and Guiding Light, remained on the air for more than two years with very low rat-

ings. Attempts were repeatedly made to improve the program by changing personnel and, ultimately, by changing air time so that Texas appeared much earlier in the day and not opposite any other soap. No network soaps were cancelled, and the only new soap that was introduced while I was working on this research was Capitol, introduced in March, 1982.[21]

The continuing relationship between program and audience also means that communicators perceive the core of their audience as loyal. This core is considered carefully in decision making. Whereas the audience is actually very large, and largely anonymous, a core of the audience is more concrete in the process of decision making.

Research on the audience, of course, can be continuous and extensive in the case of soaps, again because of the continuing interaction and on-going production process. While pretests are used for prime-time programming, particularly before a program is initially broadcast, the on-going broadcasting means testing can occur at any time. Also, research can be carried out with audience members of competing shows to determine what the audience finds appealing in other programs. Testing can also reveal what the audience dislikes about the commmunicator's program.

Another factor is that many audience members are very familiar with past story and character development. Their memory, or, better, the communicator's beliefs about their memory, has to be considered. Also, the way audience members perceive their relationship to the program and its makers, and as how they actually relate to the program makers, are important. Audience members for a soap often feel or are led to feel that they can influence a story.

Given a continuing program, audience members can write knowing that in all probability their letters will be read by someone while the show is still being broadcast. Involvement and investment on the viewers' part are what soap makers strive for. Many practices and conventions are utilized to achieve this end. It is also in the general interest of the communicators to have the audience feel it can affect the show. While this influence is true to a limited degree, story direction is often planned for several months in advance, if not further. Decisions are continually made about specific details, particularly to handle contingencies, but larger long-term decisions are less open to change. In part, the audience cannot know the exact nature of the long-term direction and end. One particularly illuminating comment was made by a production executive. As she put it, whereas the degree to which the story could be changed by mail was limited, suppliers liked the audience to feel it can affect the show.

There is a complex interaction as the different sources of images and information play into each other. The major sources of information about the audience's tastes, opinions, and choices are ratings and letters. Shows also receive phone calls, although these are relatively infrequent. They are usually reflections of frustration on the part of the viewer, for example, when a program is interrupted for a news bulletin.

Other sources of feedback are the friends and relatives of production personnel who watch the show. The reactions and comments of production personnel are additional resources used to develop or assess conceptions of programming success or failure. Research on the audience, its demographics, and its likes and dislikes, is also carried out, although this is problematically related to the communicators' view of the audience. Another dimension is the media culture view of the audience created and reflected in the various fan magazines and program digests. All these factors work to create a situation of great complexity.

One important generalization about production is that the audience the production personnel actually consider is often others involved in the production process in the organizational context. Warren Breed's and Gaye Tuchman's studies of news production, for example, indicate to what extent news is an organizational product (Breed 1955; Tuchman 1979). In the case of soap production, this was occasionally made clear when a producer, director, or performer would remark that Procter and Gamble expected to see a certain type of shot.

## RATINGS: THE AUDIENCE AS STATISTIC

The importance of ratings for the communicators is evident in a number of ways. As several people remarked, "You live from Thursday to Thursday." Thursday is the day the Nielsen ratings are available for the past week's programming. Asked if others were interested, two producers agreed that every writer was interested in each week's results as were others, including the actors.

The writer will call every Thursday. He might say, "Hi, it's a nice day. I got the script on the way." Then "Did you get the ratings? Did the ratings come in yet . . . ? The actors may not want to get into specifics but they will come up rather timidly and say, "How are we doing?"

The ratings, mimeographed and distributed from the production office, include basic information about daytime program, the place each show finished, the rating and share of each show, the top ten daytime programs, and a comparison of the ratings of those top ten for the previous week's program and their overall place for that same week. Shares refer to percentage of sets in use of homes watching television at a certain time. Ratings refer to the percentage of the total potential audience at a given time that competing programs reach.

Ratings are very important as a measure of success, but they are limited in what they reveal. Ratings and shares can be correlated with specific programs and are more immediately available than letters, but they still do not tell the communicators what the audience actually experienced, what made it tune in or stayed tuned, what it liked or disliked. The problematic nature of ratings is reflected in a number of statements.

We have no sophisticated way to track what impacts on ratings. It may be as simple as all the kids come home and Mom turns off the television to fix the turkey, therefore the ratings drop. It can be that all the kids come home and turn on the independent station. We really don't know.

Another producer emphasized the competitive context of the ratings. I had mentioned that it was impossible for a program to know what did or did not pull the ratings.

What you really don't know is, is it something you have done right, or is it something the competition has done wrong. That's a factor. We keep hearing from people in focus groups, too, that General Hospital has now peaked and the audience is kind of bored with what they are doing. They can't top themselves . . . so we have a better chance. But the ratings don't tell you where you get the audience from. Are you gaining? If they do something wrong, it's good for our side.

The headwriter of Edge of Night commented on the ratings as feedback, in this case citing a sudden decline.

[If] your rating plunges suddenly if you've got a story nobody cares about, that'll tell you something . . . that's feedback for sure.

The interpretation of the ratings involves the consideration of a number of factors depending on the competitive context, goals of the program, and changing patterns of demographics. One important way they are used is to judge the success of a story that is peaking.

M.I.: What do you do with that information (the ratings), so you are a little up or a little down?

Headwriter: A little doesn't mean a lot. A lot if you really are expecting a story to really pull the numbers, one that is on its peak, and the numbers don't correspond then you know that story is not working.

A good example of a story expected to pull the numbers that did not involved the "Carrie Story" in which Carrie is shown to have a multiple personality and be capable of horrible acts.

There are two ways of judging whether a story works. One is ratings, the other is creatively. The Carrie story is very interesting. Jane Elliott is a wonderful actress, and Doug wrote a nice story. However, in terms of ratings, it obviously didn't work because the numbers either held or slid a little and only went up in the last week of the storyline when it looked like Carrie might kill Ross. If people had cared it would have gone up right away as it did on General Hospital when they were doing Joe and Heather and Heather came out of the hospital with a gun.

Story is also written competitively to peak at the same time that other programs are peaking as was the case when Luke's and Laura's wedding was to occur on General Hospital. In that context, ratings would be used to determine how well Guiding Light did in an effort to counter what they knew a very popular competing program was doing. The competitive context also affects how ratings are viewed and used during the sweeps weeks when the results are used to calculate local advertising rates.

The demographics of the audience and audience habits, as well as the time of the year, also are considered carefully. The composition and size of the audience changes seasonally and with holidays. As the writer indicates, the goals of the program, the timing of the higher ratings, and information from letters are used to provide an interpretive context.

M.I.: The ratings correlate strongly with a good storyline?

Headwriter: Or other things. Our two strongest weeks this winter were the Thanksgiving and the Christmas week holiday. They were our strongest weeks, which means we have a very young following when the kids come home and take over the sets; our numbers go very high. You don't get numbers from college dorms, none of them have Nielsen boxes and especially in the student union where you've got 150 kids glued to a set and nobody is registering those numbers. When they come home then they register. Our numbers went to number two during Thanksgiving week, which is a week the show has been traditionally low. We went to number three, I think, during Christmas and New Year's week.

M.I.: Did that tell you that some of the younger storylines were beginning to work?

H: I had purposely focused on the kids.

M.I.: Was it intuitive?

H: No, the mail was all getting younger. The reaction to the younger stories was growing much stronger in the mails.

As is evident, ratings and letters are used to make sense of each other. I consider the letters next.

LETTERS: THE AUDIENCE AS VIEWER

Letters are primarily received by CBS, the shows, or Procter and Gamble, and tend to be addressed to the executive producer, headwriter, or performers. Far fewer letters are sent to directors or other personnel. The letters are collected and analyzed; the content is summarized and copies of the summaries are sent to various individuals. Some of those individuals receive copies of the letters. The letters are answered by Proctor and Gamble's Consumer Services Department, using information provided by the production staff, as a way of establishing or maintaining a good relationship between program, sponsor and viewer/consumer.

Often two or three months pass between the time the letters are postmarked and the time letters are received by appropriate personnel. Because the length of time varies and because there are delays between the times letters are received, summarized, copied, and sent on, letters are limited in their usefulness. Ratings offer a much quicker and more consistent form of feedback. Also, ratings can be more closely correlated with specific programming content. Although again, how each is used--both programming and ratings --to make sense of the other, is not self-evident and is, in fact, problematic.

The summaries tended to distribute the mail into a number of categories, all of which are tabulated--general comments, comments on storylines, comments on character relationships, comments on cast, and the numbers of letters to each performer. The general comments category includes letters that evaluate the show, location shooting, or general scenes, make judgments about the morality or lack of morality portrayed, request general directions for the show to move in, or call attention to seemingly unrealistic or inaccurate details. Comments on storylines summarize whether and why the viewers like or dislike the storylines and whether they like the writers. There are comments on specific storylines and requests (or demands) that storylines and relationships take a certain direction. Another category of letters about the characters expresses whether the writer likes or dislikes a particular character. There is also a tabulation of the total number of letters each performer gets during the period covered. In the following discussion, I present the various categories of letters and how each is used in the general assessment of cast, characters, storyline, and general quality of the show.

Letters to performers are opened and read in order to be tabulated so that threatening or upsetting letters can be intercepted. Evil characters tend to receive such letters, but the number of such letters is a very, very small percentage of the total to performers. Some personnel observed that far fewer threatening letters are received now as compared to the number received several years ago.

Approximately two-thirds of the letters to performers, even if they play characters the audience "loves to hate," primarily praise the performer. Many of these letters, along with others, request photographs and/or autographs, sometimes a personal letter or call. An occasional letter asks about careers in acting or would relate how the letter writer was influenced by the performer/character.

Women by far write more letters than men, probably an even greater percentage than the percentage in the audience in general. Soaps are designed to attract and hold a female audience, and their involvement in the programs, as reflected in the letters, can be read as indicative of themes, I think, that are important to other female viewers.

What is most important to the program makers is that the viewers are emotionally involved with a character, concerned about the outcome of a storyline and its impact on the characters. In a sense, it does not matter if a viewer strongly dislikes or likes a character. There are characters the audience intensely dislikes, and there are those that evoke extremely positive feelings. What the producers use as a sign that a character/performer is not working is if a character/performer gets very little mail. A major concern is that the audience react to a performer. The headwriter commented on the use of letters:

[If] someone doesn't pull letters--whether it is criticism, or not criticism--something is not working.

An example was the significant difference in how two major characters pulled letters. In the February 1982 tabulation there was quite a difference between the number of letters John Schipp (Kelly) received and the number Jennifer Cooke (Morgan) received. Jennifer Cooke was a replacement for another actress who previously played the part.

John Schipp is pulling 222 letters; that's the most. Then comes Jane Elliott; then, I guess comes Nola, Lisa Brown, Michael Tylo. All the others are below that. But those are the stories we are pushing. That tells us that John Schipp with 222 is really fantastic. But look at Jennifer Cooke: 61. She's playing with John Schipp so we know that isn't working as well as we'd like it to work.

In this case, the general interpretation was that, given the response to John Schipp in the same story and the audience reaction to the previous performer, Jennifer Cooke's performances could or should be improved. Again, the headwriter provides some insight into the general use of letters.

M.I.: What kinds of letters do you pay attention to, something working or not working?

Headwriter: Letters that set a trend. Where
you can see a whole trend of audience boredom,
disinterest in a story . . . you can read between the lines that they don't care about
this character, or this character getting together with that character. Even with those
letters you have to give your story time. You
can't abort something because they are not
identifying with it right away.

M.I.: You need a period of time in which to
let people identify and involve themselves
with. How are the letters phrased that show
there is little involvement?

H: Why are you spending so much time with so
and so. They don't interest me. I don't
care about them.

M.I.: If there is a pattern, a good number
of those . . . you use the letters. . . .

H: As a kind of a pulse beat. The lack of
response to a performer can be the most telling. If you have a character there in a forward story, and they're supposed to be a sex
symbol or a turn on and there is no response
in the mails, it is not working. Either the
actor is not working, the character is not
working, or the combination of both is not
working.

Mail about some characters will urge the program makers
to get rid of the characters. How such letters are weighed
comes across in a statement by a producer.

I'll tell you. The weighing of what is written is a most difficult part of the job because negative responses in themselves are not
necessarily deemed negative responses. The
fact that we are getting a response is not
negative. People are writing to us and telling us they hate Nola; what they are saying
really is they hate what Nola is doing. And
they may threaten us, "We are not going to
watch." But the reason they are watching is
to see how Nola is going to get it back. If

we turned it around and made her a good person all of a sudden there wouldn't be any interest in the show and certainly not in the story we are trying to tell. You have to somehow divorce yourself from what is really being said and try to understand what is going on behind the mind of the person who is writing the letter. Not everybody who writes is the most stable of personalities and you have to take that into consideration. (How can I say it kindly?) It's true they are the audience but are we necessarily going to listen to the opinion of somebody who is ranting and raving about something? We can't allow those letters to have much potency.

One example of the influence of the audience in relation to character development was recounted by the executive producer of Guiding Light. Asked which letters had an impact, he stated, "Letters that surprise you," and gave the following example.

Rita (a character who had been continually unfaithful to her husband) had a past in Texas. Someone was killed and a finger was pointed at Rita. She didn't really do it. What happened was we were trying to clean up Rita a little bit--she was getting to be a whore really. We tried to clean her up. The letters, they hated her. They said, "How can you tell us she is so good when she killed that man in Texas? She lied about this!" That wasn't what we said at all; we said she didn't kill this person. But they didn't want to believe this, they wanted to believe she did (kill this person). We got so much mail with nobody believing what we were trying to do with this character we ended up throwing our hands in the air saying it was useless to try to clean up this woman because they don't see her that way. So we went with it.

Communicators have internalized an image of the audience "out there," and in the story creation process, which involves a number of individuals evaluating and making suggestions for the writer's proposed story they consider possible audience responses. This sense of the audience and the concern for audience reaction lead to an internalized sense of what works. It also means that letters that surprise the communicators tend to be considered more carefully, a theme reflected in another producer's comments below.

It is also clear that greater attention is paid to letters that are not extreme, that are carefully and logically argued, and/or that come from legitimate organizations. The following quotation from a producer reflects each of these themes. When asked if there were certain ways letters were phrased that led him to attend to them more than others, he commented:

It's kind of gut level reaction. The ones I look for have neat handwriting and use syllables of more than two occasionally. If they are literate and you get the feeling these people are genuinely outraged by something that under normal circumstances they would have never written to you, and you would have never heard from them, but they happened to tune in and they saw something they felt irresponsible or insulting of their intelligence they felt they had to say something about or something was flagrantly immoral in their estimation. These are the people that make up what Nixon unfortunately called the silent majority--I tend to believe that there is a silent majority. I don't think most people are demonstrators, yet most people have a point of view and their thresholds of annoyance are stretched quite wide. You have a very good operating room within their parameters--when you go beyond that, you are going to hear from one or two of them. Those one or two may represent an enormous amount of our audience. Those are the people who make up the bulk of our audience and those are the people we want to reach. When you get something coherently and intelligently written, something you may not have thought of--for example, one of the things we mentioned about the second rape of Rita. Wow, for her not to have turned that in, dead irresponsible and that's why we made her come forward during Holly's trial. That's how that was generated, because for her to keep it quiet, whether or not she is a bad girl or a good girl, is not the point. The point is that there are a lot of responsible organizations that are trying to get women to say, "Hey, whether I slept with the guy or not, prior to this, the point is he came in and took, therefore, it wasn't a sexual act, it was an act of violence. I was violated, I was degraded. For that reason, I want to come forward. That act cannot continue to happen." We didn't realize it until we started getting letters from various women's organizations. We didn't feel anyone would take Rita seriously enough. What they are saying, "She may be a hooker in the street, but if the guy didn't pay it and she didn't ask him, then it is rape. She has her rights, too."

The interpretation of a letter and the response to it are related to the perception of the letter writer. Extreme or illegible letters are viewed quite differently from better written and more logically argued ones. As the producer argues or assumes, given a large audience with a range of tolerance, when an audience member writes, and particularly when a number of individuals write forcefully, their comments must be considered.

The headwriter of Edge of Night commented on the limited use of letters, their help in identifying particularly appealing characters or their help in identifying a story that they object strongly to.

The audience doesn't give you any ideas, that's for sure. You don't get any ideas about what the story should be about or who they should be about, although you might see from the audience about a character they are crazy about, then you might want to emphasize the role. The only time you get feedback in the negative sense is when there is an overwhelmingly negative response.

A good example of negative feedback was provided by a producer of Guiding Light.

We brought Bill Bauer, Ed's father, back on the show, the same actor who had played it years ago, who supposedly had been killed in a plane crash. Now it turned out he had not been on the plane and had been living an illicit life, had another family somewhere. The response from the public was apparently very

negative to this story. "How dare we do that
to Bert." It just wasn't a good thing to be
doing. Evidently the response was so strong
and articulated by people who should be listened to by the tone of their letters that
they decided to take action on that and they
got him out of the story as quickly as they
could.

Negative letters have an impact also if they call attention to improbably character behavior. One producer made the
following comment:

If people are reacting negatively to the way
a story is developing based on character history, those are paid attention to. We'll try
to give them a reason. We'll put into a
script in the future some reasoning to allow
the story to go on. We'll realize we are
pulling a fast one on them and can't get away
with it.

One interesting category of letters includes protests
about performers leaving a show. Many letter writers tend
to assume that performers do not choose to leave a show.
Quite often information appears in soap "buff" magazines
about why a particular performer might be leaving a program.
Many soap performers leave soaps to try to find work in film
or prime-time television or in legitimate theatre. The show,
however, generally is blamed. A producer vented his frustration in one comment.

We always get blamed. I've got more letters
that say, "How could you do this? How could
you be so stupid?" They think it is a decision we came to. It doesn't seem to enter
their heads that an actor might want to do
something else. [Emphasis mine]

Some audience members probably do not want to consider
this factor in casting changes. Given a close association
between performer/character and the viewers' intimate involvement in a character's life, an actor leaving voluntar-
ily would violate their assumptions that are part of their
"suspension of disbelief."
Letters, then, are important to the program makers. They
help identify appealing characters/performers or storylines.
They also call attention to inaccuracy, implausible character

behavior, or unacceptable stories. Again, letters and ratings are used to make sense of each other.

## LETTERS: THE AUDIENCE AS SOCIAL BEING

Dear Writers,
My best friend and I would really like to see Morgan and Kelly get married. If anyone deserves happiness they do. I think it would just be awful if Nola got her way and got Kelly. It would really disappoint alot of people if that happened. I hope Kelly and Morgan get married and stay that way, for good. Also, give Andy what he deserves, a rotten life. 20 years in prison. If everything works out, we would be very happy. By the time this letter gets to you we hope everything is worked out. But we are sending this in case all these problems aren't solved.
Watchers forever,
Shelley and Susan.

P.S. Heck, at least let Kelly and Morgan make love. She wants to so bad. PLEASE!!! And man, is Kelly cute. Do Kelly and Morgan have something going in real life?

This letter invites a sense of wonder and amusement. Clearly written by two young women, the letter conveys their concerns, the outcomes they would like to see, their curiosity. Letters such as this also reflect the problematic distinction between the realities of the program and real life, between characters and performers.

I was particularly taken by this letter as the writers openly communicate their wishes for the characters in the story. They recognize the writer as the manipulator of the characters' fates and know that the problems may be worked out, but still feel they had to make an effort that they hoped would bring about a solution to the problem. And then in a postscript, their wishes become even more intense and focused as they <u>speak for Morgan herself</u>. "Heck, at least let Kelly and Morgan make love. She wants to so bad. PLEASE!!!" They state their view of Kelly, the same Kelly they know Morgan wants to make love to. Finally, in the final question, reflecting the ambiguity of their framing of the performance, they ask about the relationship of the characters (performers?) in "real life."

The letter, with its intensity, intimacy, and shifting frames, provides a good opening for the various letters copied here. I have not been able to reproduce the look and feel of the letters, which does affect how the program makers interpret or use them. Entire letters are included, with errors intentionally retained. Again, their length, complexity, intensity, and passion are good indicators of the audience as social being.

One of the important themes in many letters is the desire to see a domestic, romantic, and moral world "out there." The following letter was one of many that the program received when a veteran performer left the show. I include several letters with the same concern later in this section. This letter writer articulates the desire to see both an ideal moral order and romantically involved happy couples. After expressing that we "all need to feel and know that there is still moral, average, day-to-day living out there," she concludes with the comment that Ed and Eve would be a "good match."

As a "good guy," the character/performer had come to be important for many viewers. There is a clear sense of the typifications involved in the character's history and identity in the letter, particularly as a member of the Bauer family.

Gentlemen:
I and many of my friends and relatives are deeply disappointed to hear that Mark Hulswit, who plays the part of "Ed Bauer" in the "Guiding Light" day-time serial is thinking of leaving.
He's a tremendous actor and one of our favorite characters. The program just won't seem to be the same.
Quite honestly, the traditional Bauer Family is still what makes the show. You may not think so, but most of us like the more "down-to-earth" story and characters than the all too many added "way-out" concepts. We all need to feel and know that there is still normal, average, day-to-day living out there and the fact that the Bauer Family and particularly Ed does not go along nor will or ever wants to be anything more than a good family man, good doctor and contribute to society what is badly needed today is a comfortable feeling. There is already enough sadistic novels, television plays, news and

"what have you" to make you want to run and
hide.
Please, Mr. Mart Hulswit reconsider.
Good luck to you whatever you decide.
Sincerely,
"A Pittsburgh Viewer"
(of many, many years)
P.S.
Don't you think "Ed" and "Eve" would be a
good match?!!

The desire to see or find in the program an affirmation
of a moral and meaningful social world is also evident in
the following letter. Again, it is unclear whether the letter writer is referring to the performers or the characters.
I think the writer has a need to believe that the performers
treat each other well even though the scripts might call for
the performers/characters to mistreat each other. The underlying wish to believe in the fundamental rightness of a social world that is moral and harmonious comes across in many
letters.

To Everyone on the Guiding Light:
It's wonderful to see what all of you are doing for yourselves and for each other. It
really is a Day Care Center. It takes a lot
of courage to admit and correct mistakes.
Now all of you are showing us the way to be-
have toward others. I know and feel that
whatever happens to the characters in the
script the people are acting with love and
concern and seeing the other guys point of
view.
Much happiness to Elvera and Chris and to
everyone there.

One major category of mail, typically to the writer or
the executive producer, concerns how the letter writer would
like relationships between the characters to work out. One
of the characteristics of such letters is that often they
attempt to give some legitimacy to their position and per-
suade or, at times, attempt to coerce the program's writer
or executive producer. One letter that made a personal appeal, however, stood out. It also, I think, reflected the
uses and meaningfulness of soap magazines to the audience.
Such magazines seem to help the audience know the show better, know the performers "in" the characters they know well.
The letter began:

Dear Writer:
I saw your picture in the February or March
issue of Soap Opera or Daytime T.V. You look
like an understanding man so why can't you
get Ed and Rita back together? I think they
make the show. Let them go to Jamaica together and discover themselves again. This deal
about Rita and Allen is crazy. If that happens I won't watch the show. I think Ed and
Rita are good together. Please get them back
[together]. Also it would be good to get Mike
and Elizabeth together again. They are a
great twosome. The rest of the show I don't
care about and I can't stand Andy or Vanessa.
They are really bad. Please get my 2 couples
back together again. Thank you.

Another letter is particularly interesting because the
writer clearly distances herself discussing storyline and
appeals to the writer's sense of professional craft and
pride. A major theme, again, is the desire to see a couple
reunited (Hope and Alan) in a relationship idealized as
changing Alan and giving him happiness.

Dear Writer:
I am a devoted fan of daytime drama. My favorite actress is Elvera Roussel, she brings
a ray of light to the sensitive role of Hope
Bauer Spaulding. I sometimes wish that the
writers would be more innovative and carry
the story lines in different directions. As
of now, every story tends to repeat itself.
Case in point: Here we have what is the most
piognant [sic] story line with Alan and Hope,
that could bring us months of good entertainment, filled with many compelling stories.
What more could one ask for? When you have
the daughter of Mike Bauer, who is also the
granddaughter of Bert Bauer married to Alan
Spaulding, I love the whole concept.
I would like for Hope to give Alan a baby son.
Why not? Alan does love his young bride. She
gives him a chance to relive his youth through
Hope. I don't think Alan was very happy as a
young man, he was rich and spoiled but not
happy.
Please try and to preserve and keep this very

human drama with Hope and Alan going by let-
ting them somehow stay married and together.
It is such a thrilling Storyline.
Fan of Elvera Roussel

Another letter is even more transparent in its desire to
see perfect couples reunited or united.

Dear Guilding Light:
I am very worried about Ben and Amanda. I am
afraid they are not going to get together.
It would ruin the whole story. I just don't
want Ben and Eve together because I think Ben
loves Amanda and Amanda loves Ben. And I
think Eve loves Ross and Ross loves Eve. Just
leave Benassa out of it. I don't care who she
gets together with just as lone [sic] that it
isn't Ross!
Please try.

While some viewers write to express their frustration
that a "bad" character has not been revealed and/or punished,
others can come to feel that an evil character, in this case
Alan Spaulding, should not be punished. He has been redeemed
through the "love of a good woman" and his pursuer, Mike
Bauer, is viewed as petty in his single-minded effort to
have Alan caught and punished.

Dear Writer:
Why does Mike have to harp at Alan about Roger
Thorpe-Dr. Moreno constantly? He sounds like
a broken record. Here's Alan happy as a lark
and Mike is still acting like a moron. Roger
Thorpe is dead, the past is gone, and everything that happened then and there is irrele-
vant to the way Alan is now. I like the direction Alan's character is taking; that of a
devoted husband and father. If you didn't
make his shady past so important or Mike's
pigheadedness so evident the story would be
much better. As far as I'm concerned Mike is
the villian for not being able to see beyond
his own little pettiness . . .
Sincerely,

The following letter conveys a sense of how important
romance--ideal couples living happily ever after after experiences of "hard times"--is to many viewers. It is signed,

as some letters are, to give the impression that the viewpoint in the letter reflects that of a large number of viewers.  Also, the writer of the letter clearly recognizes that
the story is a story and that the writer of the show is responsible.

Dear Writer:
We are really <u>furious</u> with you.  Why did you
write Elizabeth out of the show.  We wanted
Elizabeth and Mike to marry and live happily
ever after.  Mike and Elizabeth have had
nothing but hard times since she came on the
Guilding [sic] Light and you know it's about
time they they lived happily ever after.  You
have made us so mad until we have started
watching <u>Another World</u> on Channel 5.
Southern Viewers

     Some letter writers will suggest storylines if they think
the storyline will bring back or keep a character/performer
they like.  The following letter suggests that the device of
a character having a "long lost" twin brother be used to
bring back a particular actor.

Dear Sirs:
As a truly devoted fan of Michael Zaslow who
played Roger Thorpe on your show I feel the
show has lost something since he "died".  I
have an idea you might like.  Here it is.
Roger had a twin brother who even Roger didn't
know about, only his father did.  The brother
was put in a sanitarium at an early age.  He
comes back for revenge on those who had anything to do with his brother's death.  I hope
you like my idea.  Please reply.

     One of the most successful characters is Nola.  She is
clearly a character that "people love to hate."  Letters to
the show express outrage at her behavior and frustration that
she is not revealed and punished for who she is and what she
has done.  Nola was selfish, deceitful, and continually lied.
What was particularly infuriating to many letter writers was
that other characters were not aware of her motives and lying.  Some characters, because of their naïveté, or what the
letter writers called "stupidity," were singled out for criticism in letters.  The following conveys the emotion, as well
as a sense of humor, behind a letter.

It's hard to believe that you can think anyone
can believe a character as dumb as Nola can
go on thriving on lies a moron should have
caught up with.
Her dirty tricks make Kelly act like a doctor
who wouldn't know the difference between as-
pirin and arsenic--if he ever managed to finish school and be one.
The Nola character just doesn't do anything
for the program--except drag it down. Hope
you're "listening".

The frustration of seeing Nola's involvement and success
in keeping the couple of Morgan and Kelly apart, and the desire on the part of the letter writer for life to be beautiful for Morgan and Kelly, comes out strongly in the following:

I (and many others to whom I have spoken) have
waited patiently for the relationship of "Morgan and Kelly" to make some kind of progress--
in any manner. Your persistence in separating
them is most frustrating, to say the least.
It is distressing and nauseating (in the
strongest sense of the words) to watch "Nola"
intervene at every turn.
You have indeed proven the old adage: "Hope
springs eternally--although it doesn't last
long". Could you possibly give a few "faith-
ful viewers" (and the cast) a chance to believe life can be beautiful?
Others in the cast have received a few moments
of happiness, couldn't you do likewise for the
"younger set"? What "yardstick" are you using for the "light that guides you"? Young
people (I believe) need to feel that life need
not be filled constantly with turmoil.
I have reached the depths of despair watching
"Nola" create so much misery. Let's have a
little happiness for "Kelly and Morgan" instead of tears.

As I noted earlier, letter writers will attempt to distinguish themselves from other viewers, other women. The
characterization of the typical soap watcher apparently is
not a flattering one. Interestingly, this writer also men-
tions that she reads soap opera magazines and finds support
for her position there. The important issue of whether the

prolongation of a conflict is producing boredom is discussed. Also, there is a parting threat as the writer signs the let-ter "ex viewer."

Dear Executive Producer:
I have never written a letter concerning a
soap opera, and have always thought the women
that did were silly. But I just had to do it
this once. I have watched the Guiding Light
for many years and have always thought it to
be the best daytime serial on T.V. But I have
been very disappointed lately. The show has
become very monatonous. I realize you have
to stretch a story out to keep the viewer in-
terested--But the story line about Morgan,
Kelly, and Nola has been run into the ground.
Its been the same thing, week after week,
month after month. As much as I have always
liked the show, I'm not even interested in
watching it anymore. And a lot of people
agree with me because I have read their comments in Soap Opera magazines. It's not even
realistic to believe that anyone could be as
naive as Morgan. And you know someone would
figure out Nola by now. I realize it's just
a Soap Opera, but really--if you want to keep
viewers you are going about it the wrong way.
When the Guiding Light comes on I take a nap.
If you were to ask other viewers their
opinion, I think you would find I'm not the
only one who feels this way about the show.
An ex viewer

The following letter is extremely long. The detail and
its length convey a very deep interest in the program. It
also moves from comments about characters and storyline to
suggestions for future story using an event from the writer's
own life. Her characterizations are also interesting as they
reflect a chatty interest in the lives of the characters and
a concern for their futures.

To the writers of the "Guiding Light",
As a long time viewer of this show, I have
some comments and suggestions about the story
line and many of the characters and actors.
The characters of Alan, Nola, Diane, Rita,
Banessa and Andy are up to no good. They all
deserve to be hurt or punished in their own

individual way for their shrewd tactics toward
others in the story.

In the story line the writers may have other
plans for Nola. The viewers are aware of Nola
and her never ending lies and manipulation to
ones she makes fools of. Never giving up she
plans all sorts of trouble to them just to win
Kelly for herself. It would be something if
her planned pregnancy didn't work. She would
be lost if she couldn't use people, like
Kelly, Morgan, Tim and Floyd. But her lie to
Dr. Sedwick about Morgan being pregnant by Tim
when she's actually talking about herself,
hoping she's pregnant, was astounding. She
is a very despicable dame who wants to join
the upper class and get a free ride to obtain
it to marry student doctor Kelly and live a
life of luxury in a mansion. She thrives on
her dream world. She seduced Kelly to bed
twice to make sure her plan worked to get
pregnant. Her lies will be known to ones she
has hurt in due time. At least Hillary and
Katie know she is a big liar. It was fun to
see these nurses have run-in with Nola. Maybe
one of them should have pushed Nola's nose in
or better yet, let Kelly do it someday. Nola
has no real friends yet she tells Morgan that
she is her best friend. Innocent Morgan be-
lieves her. Marriage to Kelly could ruin his
whole life, and getting pregnant is the only
way Nola can get him. It would be very different if they marry and live on "poverty
street", making Nola worse off than she was
when she was single. Providing Nola gets
pregnant and marries Kelly, it would be fun
and interesting to see her have a bad misfor-
tune as she needs to be taught a lesson the
hard way. I am suggesting a miscarriage of a
different nature instead of the recent ones
caused by personal and shocking news like
Amanda and Rita. I had a personal experience
some years ago with what is called an ECTOPI-
CAL PREGNANCY. Writers may not have heard of
it as it isn't very common but can happen.
The Fallopian tube on my right side became
ruptured as the egg was improperly developed
and required surgical removal of the tube.
My personal experience when like this. Not

feeling good in a few short weeks of pregnancy, I arose one early dark morning, got dizzy and felt my way to the bathroom by clasping my hands on the wall. I hit the edge of the bathroom sink, cut my chin and passed out on bathroom floor. My husband was home and rushed in to pick me up. After awaking, I had very bad chills (internal bleeding, I believe). I was rushed to the hospital by ambulance and covered with heavy blankets on trip there. After the tube was removed I spent time in recovery room and while there my blood pressure dropped very low and I was sent back into surgery for the second time in one day for removal of the ovary. I came close to not making it. But with getting blood donors and receiving blood I had lost, I finally recovered and very thankful. My obstretician explained the ruptured tube was just like a flat tire meaning it was like a tire going flat. My OB doctor also told me that "I scared the hell out of him". A person whose had this sort of miscarriage can have other children since there is the left tube and ovary. I had two children before this happened.

You may wonder why I am suggesting this. I don't think many people have much knowledge of this sort of miscarriage as I wasn't until I suffered this problem. I just think viewers, especially women might find this different and most interesting. To my knowledge, it hasn't been portrayed on television. If true, your show would add a first, and I just feel the actress could play the part very well, as the character of Nola. I am aware that soaps get medical information and I am sure than an obstetricion or a gynecologist can be of a great help on this matter.

The Bauer family are lovable people. The cast is great. I especially like the actress who is beautiful that plays Hope. I think this actress plays Hope better than previous ones. It is great that Ed and Mike have a half-sister such as Hillary. It is a joy to see many more young people on the show. On soaps today with the liberated morals regarding sex and tones of women's lib, show seductive women acting the aggressor and boldness and making certain characters of men look like they are the weaker sex when they coo and lure the men to bed with them. It appears soaps like for viewers to see who goes to bed with who. A noteable actress named Katherine Hepburn stated recently in our local newspaper saying she deplores the absence of real love portrayal in films and TV today. That it amounts to just sex today. Just plain sex and that's old stuff. There is nothing new or fantastic about it as its been going on for a long time. But now we have it washed with the rest of the dirty linen--in public.

The character of Rita is a spoiled beauty, an opportunist and a conniving seductive gal. Her marriage to Ed has been wrong from the start. Ed has been generous with Rita giving her a fine large home. She got restless and dissatisfied, accused Ed of not giving her enough attention. So, she became charmed by Alan, his wealth and power, enjoys parties and in that wants her own way. She thinks Mike should stop any investigation about Alan for Hope's sake and forget the whole matter without regard for thought or act on Mike's principles as a lawyer. Now she and Alan have betrayed Hope and Ed in Jamaica. The affair there with Alan left her with wonderful memories forever it seems--her dreamy vacation and not caring much for ones she has hurt--Ed and Hope, since she wants to be the Rita she wants to be and not the Rita others think should be, according to her. As a viewer, I got a real charge out of Rita when she learned Hope coming there, forcing poor little ole Rita to end her dream vacation. She was disappointed, irked or pouty, showing her spoiledness and doesn't like it when people or things get in her way. She and Vanessa are a lot alike in character, although Rita hasn't had wealth all her life like Vanessa. Let's hope she and Ed dissolve their rocky marriage with divorce. Glad Mike snooped and found Rita's bag and compact left behind. Hope Holly returns soon--like the actress who plays Holly.

Alan is destroying himself and his business, along with Diane's never ending help in order to avoid all the ugly disgrace. Alan's overly mean treatment toward Elizabeth, poisoning his son, Philip's mind to hating Mike because of Elizabeth and the fact he has now betrayed all his wives with other women and hiding a doctor in Jamaica surely makes him a true villain. Hopefully, Mike's investigation ends soon.

Hope is the sweet girl who deserves life's best. It's sad she is pregnant. She is a strong girl and will be OK even having to divorce Alan. One wonders, will Alan go to prison or get killed off? It will be most interesting.

Morgan is a sweet girl. Too bad she and Kelly's romance ended in such disaster. She should tell Tim how she really feels about Kelly whether she and Kelly rekindle their romance or not. His (Tim) drinking stops her.

Vanessa is the wealthy seductive, possessive and arrogant gal with Ross, and runs to daddy when things aren't going well. The way she carresses Ross's face and coos him is something. Diane does same with Joe Bradley. Will be interesting when Mike learns of Diane's deep involvement with helping Alan.

Andy is headed for big trouble. His mother, Barbara will be very hurt someday, and Holly too. The way he uses Katie, his roughness and temper is destructive.

The Jamaica scenery was beautiful. Wish we could have seen more rooms in the villa than just the bedrooms. It is a dreamy place to spend a vacation. One more thing. Rita's gowns were gorgeous. She must have thought she was a lonely queen or princess until Alan showed up.

Hopefully, I may have the opportunity to get some response about my suggesting the ectopical pregnancy--from writers, sponsors or whoever. Thought you may be interested in a viewer's suggestion.

The Nola-Kelly-Morgan story was very important to the program and viewers. The following letter writer's desire to see Nola punished is phrased as a desire to get her "off the show." It is problematic if this is the case because apparently many viewers like to see the evil person punished. Also, they "love to hate" certain characters. In some cases, the resolution of a storyline, as temporary as it may be, whereby the good characters win or are brought together, brings a great deal of satisfaction. This is often emphasized in letters. Others, however, emphasize punishment or some form of suffering for the evil character. This occurs if the evil character is murdered or disappears too quickly. A staff member who frequently received the phone calls to the program noted that viewers would call in upset if an evil character did not suffer enough!

The moral attitudes are interesting. Most of the people are saying we want to get rid of Nola are not so much saying get rid of her but punish her. They feel they have a right to see these characters punished. My big joke at the time was [to say] they want to see Nola in hell--as if they get some perverse release out of all of this.
  We got a phone caller. They thought she [Nola] was going to leave town. They were so upset. Another character they thought was just going to die and be gone that way. Here they are getting their wish in getting rid of the character, but not the way they want to get rid of her. When Lucille Wexler died, they were upset she died so suddenly. They wanted to see her suffer. With Nola Reardon they have really gotten their wish seeing her suffer repeatedly for what she did last summer.

  The following is an example of a letter writer demanding the end of Nola.

Gentlemen:
Believe me, if you let Nola get away with this very stupid escapade, many of us plan to forever stop watching the so-called award winning show: The Guiding Light. There is no one with the smarts of Kelly who could go along with this thing so blindly. Now come on--let us see Nola put where she belongs, and that is off the show. Can't stand her, and you have used her long enough to disrupt everybody's life, and let us go on to better

things for Katie also--you run these things
on much too long with the likes of an Andy.
Sincerely,

The Nola-Kelly-Morgan story dramatically peaked at one
point in July. In the program that aired July 27, Kelly
"told Nola off," and for many viewers it was an emotionally
significant and satisfying program. A large number of letters were sent to the show; many related the pleasure of
seeing Nola "revealed" to the overall satisfaction that the
program gives them. Viewers strongly expected/hoped to see
Nola revealed and Kelly and Morgan united. They are virtually grateful that the makers of the program gave them that
satisfaction.

Producers & Writers of Guiding Light:
Thank you so much for making me so happy in
last Fri. July 24th and again today July 27th
been waiting for Kelly to catch up with Nola
for so long. How I love Fri. & today's shows.
Thank you, thank you. Made me so happy I
cried, seeing Nola get what she needed for so
long. And I hope Floyd don't have to marry
Nola, Hope she has to have that baby alone.
But I am so happy what ever goes on the show
now--I relaize you have to have someone to
cause trouble. Thanks again for making my
day much greater. Kelly & Morgan getting back
together again. Want to see more about Hope
& Allen now. O.K.
Sincerely,

Gentlemen:
Here I am actually "hooked" on a program, to
the extent of not even accepting an invitation
if it means not being able to see my program!
In fact, I buy everything but the diapers that
are advertised!
The reason I am writing is to tell you how I
feel about some of your cast.
The little lady that plays Nola Reardon is a
darling, beautiful child--and certainly should
go places. While she plays a difficult part,
she actually makes you live the story with
her.
Puhlease--don't let her do any more damage.
Tell your writers to let her mend her ways.

Bad girls do, you know, and find happy solu-
tions in their lives.
This weekend past was a very hectic one--so
realistic for me, that I had to take extra
heart pills to calm down (I'm a heart patient)
when I thought Nola was going to wreck Kelly's
life. Your writers were great on that issue--
except I doubt if Bea would have, in reality,
gone to Kelly. In my mind, Kelly would have
asked the doctor how long Nola was pregnant,
and found out that way. Nola needs her mother now. Kelly sounded like a nut when he
spoke to the doctor--not like a medical
student.
I love him, he's like my son. He didn't follow thru.
The story is great--I love it and the actors
and actresses are wonderful.
Sincerely,

One appreciative letter was extremely brief.

Bravo! How very well done that was!
Sincerely,

Dear Writers of The Guiding Light,
Im serously grateful for the turn out of the
show concerning Noala Reardon (Lisa Brown) and
Kelly Nelson and Morgan Richards has made me
very very happy. But as everyone knows she
hasn't yet given up. I know she will keep on
trying but until then I will continue to enjoy
the show and will immedetly tell everyone
about the show soon you will have many viewers I promise (I hope)
Sincerley,
A very happy viewer

Dear Writers,
Thank you for allowing a happy ending between
Kelly Nelson and Morgan Richards on the Guiding Light. I've been following the show off
and on for about 5 years. Sometimes I would
get so disgusted with the sadness that I would
stop watching for several months. Finally
something nice happened and it was wonderful.
Please let more happy endings develop--I, for
one, would like to see more of them.

The degree to which viewers expect a particular performer to play a part and the degree to which they protest changes was demonstrated by a flood of letters after Mart Hulswit was replaced by another performer.

Dear Sir:
Yesterday I was notified that after 12-1/1 years of dedicated service as Dr. Ed Bauer, Mart Hulswit is being fired or let go. This action is being taken to so-call <u>better</u> the show and compete with ABC. No competition, CBS is the best. GL is already hurting because of several characters leaving show, Rita, Vanessa, Ben and Diane. And now to let Mart go! What a mistake. I am very angry and you will get letters from many such people--It will hurt GL a lot more to lose as many as 1000 viewers if this takes place. And that is what's going to happen. Please reconsider --Ed is a part of GL and anyone else in his place couldn't do the show justice. Spice up his role--get more action. When Ed had Roger Thorpe on, it was super good. Think of something else.

To the Producers:
I recently heard that the part of "Ed Bauer" was being recast, and I am writing to let you know that neither I nor any of my friends who watch the show are pleased with the idea. While Mart Hulswit is no Robert Redford, he has nevertheless made the character of "Ed Bauer" very real and has brought a quality to that character that I believe no other actor could duplicate.
The simple fact is that Mart Hulswit is "Ed Bauer". You don't need to replace him with some other gorgeous actor to compete with General Hospital. If looks were the only thing that attracted viewers, then many hit shows wouldn't have been hits. So, don't go looking for someone you already have. I know many other viewers feel this same way, and I hope they also write to let you know.
Sincerely yours,

To Procter & Gamble:
I have been a long-time fan of <u>Guiding Light</u>

and a user of Procter & Gamble products.
I am very distressed by the action of Procter
& Gamble, the writers, and producers of Guiding Light.
I cannot quite believe you have replaced Mart
Hulswitt as Ed Bauer. He was my favorite actor on the show. He portrayed Ed as a very
natural, sensitive, handsome, sexy, intelligent man. If he is replaced, and I'm sure the
powers that be at Procter & Gamble have made
up their corporate, collective mind, I intend
to replace all Procter & Gamble products.
Your products can be replaced but Mart
Hulswitt cannot.
I am 35, a graduate of the University of Pennsylvania and will be an ex-consumer of Procter & Gamble products.
Sincerely yours,

Another series of letters was from viewers who were quite
upset with the direction they perceived the show to be
taking. Some referred to an earlier time when the show was
more appealing. Many viewers were particularly upset with
the increasing domination of the program by young characters
(late teens, mid-twenties) in the featured stories. Others
were upset by what they considered to be a moral decline in
the programming. Coupled with the outrage is a threat to
boycott the products of sponsors. The first two letters
were both addressed to CBS and refer to what the viewers see
as a pattern affecting both Guiding Light and As the World
Turns, two Procter and Gamble shows aired, at that time, back
to back.

Sir:
What in heavens name has happened to the
writers of two daytime shows namely, As the
World Turns and The Guiding Light? They have
become trash programs—the writers seem to be
hung up on sex. I have watched and enjoyed
them for many years but I just can't imagine
how you think that seeing Alan Spaulding and
Rita Bauer in bed making love several times
on one show is good TV? What makes it even
more distasteful is the fact they are married
to other spouses on the show.
Is it any wonder our young people think sex
no matter what is O.K.? I can tell you one
thing if this continues we are beginning a

campaign to let the sponsors know how we feel
and will boycott their products and advertise
our reasons.
In the past the Hughes family gave us many
hours of entertainment and now you want that
changed. We are dead serious about our campaign.

THE GUIDING LIGHT
New York, N.Y.
I have written many letters to you complaining about the profanity and the low moral tone
of this show.
It is common practice on this show to present
to the viewer profanity (excessive) suggested
sexual intercourse—men commonly shown in
women's apartments—in bed with them—without
of course the benefit of marriage. I would
like to point out that bedroom scenes are
completely unnecessary and are highly offensive to decent people. If men are not actually in bed with a women they are shown running around the women's apartment or lolling
around on a davenport half dressed. Many
times after a new person is put in a show after only a couple of days aquaintance the
first thing the say to a member of the opposite sex is "I want to make love to you". If
course what is meant is they want to make sex.
The reason for this letter is to point out to
you that my complaints have fallen on deaf
ears and I plan to support "THE COALITION FOR
BETTER T.V." This of course starts up in
March.

Writers will make reference to the program in its earlier days, primarily to criticize what the viewer considers its
growing immorality. The ghost of Papa Bauer appears in this
one.

Dear Writers of The Guiding Light,
We must tell you how disgusting this story is
since there are so many bedroom scenes. Oh,
that Papa Bauer were still living. It was so
clean then. The only reason we watch it now
is to see if Allen ever gets what he has coming.

Thank you.
Mr. & Mrs.

Occasionally letters express extreme feelings of revulsion and disgust. The following letter is in stark contrast to the others reproduced and gives some sense of the range of responses to the same show that the producers contend with. Such a letter, however, would be viewed as extreme and disregarded.

Dear Sir:
I have neglected writing for quite some time to let you know what I think of quite a few of your rotten programs. They are gutter quality. Every day there is nothing but sex, nude bodies and most of the time in bed. The impression that if a man asks a female out to dinner that he is to go to her place or to his for his pay for the dinner. Now I say male and female because it would be a disgrace to a man or a woman if such a gutter rat was man or woman. Now the Roger Thorpe and John Dixon in those two programs are to obnoxious to be allowed on a program for any length of time and the writers of those programs should be prosecuted for writing such. And let me tell you those programs and those two people make many people thru the country get murder in their minds. Those 2 should be castrated like farmers do their male hogs and then make them eat 'em. There are a couple females should be (Reta Bauer hussy) turpentined like people used to do years ago to strange dogs.
Now if you people running the network had the decency yourselves you wouldn't allow such things be broadcast and if you believe there is a God and you pay for all the wrongs you do of which you are contributing to delinquency of children and some adults (for some adults don't have sense enough to stand up for whats right and decent) God help your mind and Soul before you die because you will surely burn in Hell for what you are doing.
Please pass this on to the writers for their minds must wallow in the filthy gutter all the time to write such trash. The disgusting kissing that so much of it goes on in each program. Thats immoral, indecent, they don't

kiss. They just suck each others lips. And
Oh Dear what a Hell those writers will be in
and the people that plays the parts surely
wants money badly to play such a part. A <u>male</u>
that kisses that opens his mouth and puts his
dirty lips over hers should be <u>shot</u>.
The whole business is a stinking rotten dirty
business. Gutter business. The television
could do wonders of good for the world and for
influencing young people in the right way.
Educate them and have honorable citizens a
decent respectable loving people. But no,
they'd rather have them rotten disrespectful,
in fear and trouble. I do hear more and more
disgust for T.V. programs, more people saying
they turn them off. Don't watch or listen.
I hope someday soon they (people) march together and demand a change or force all the
networks to stop their filthy program. And I
hope if it isn't stopped by people protesting
that God takes a hand and destroys the whole
business. My! My! how the air is polluted day
and night with the filthy songs, loud bang
bang of what they call music and the dirty
language and almost nude bodies.
Many of the things sponsors pay for their ads
on T.V. are as bad as the programs. The
looks, the sound of their voices are so disgusting that if the product was any good people wouldn't use it after seeing and hearing
them. I hope I have conveyed to you my views
of your part in this and please tell the writers of these programs they are sick, sick,
sick and God knows they need help.
I watched the three men from each networks on
a few times and they were disgusting. They
said people didnt' like the rough stuff westerns so they would slap the people with lots
and lots of sex and they don't understand that
many many people enjoy a good clean funny program.
I hope many people write and let you know how
you are polluting peoples minds especially the
young. Setting a very poor example.
Words can't express how obnoxious you all are.
Hope you wake up and revive your conscience.
Read this and weep.

On the other hand, viewers may be quite sophisticated and analytical. The following letter disapproves of the centrality of younger, new characters. The letter writer indicates she is aware that people age 30 or over "comprise the bulk of the soap opera audience for Guiding Light" and that the shift to younger characters and storylines is designed to garner new fans.

As a long time viewer of the Guiding Light, I hope you will give my letter careful consideration. I have been very upset with the addition of 4 new characters who have been given major storylines on the soap; Kelly, Morgan, Nola and Tim. Their boring conversations, (they say the same things day after day, week after week) very predictable schemes, petty problems and jealousies (including the ridiculous fights between Kelly and Tim and the shouting matches between Kelly and Morgan) have really lowered the program down to the level of the other soaps. I now switch to Texas whenever these 4 characters come on and Texas has to be one of the worst soap operas. Young people do NOT make up steady viewer audience so you are in danger of losing a large segment of support (people like myself) by continuing to let them play such an important part on the show. As a teacher, I can only watch GL during vacations but I have been following the show since the 1st Leslie Bauer was on and before the Norris family came on the scene. For that reason, I feel I can speak with more authority than someone who has been a fan for only a few years. I am in my 30's and know that people my age or older comprise the bulk of your soap opera audience. Currently the Guiding Light has many many strengths over all the other soaps and has retained these strengths over the years. 1. They have <u>many</u> talented people on the show. 2. They have been able to hold on to the actors giving the program needed stability. 3. The actors & actresses are picked for their talent, not their looks. They look like the character they're portraying, except for your new Jackie & Andy Norris. 4. Most of the plots are <u>not</u> ridiculous, except for the 4 mentioned above. 5. They still have the Bauer family. 6. They use more older people on the show than some of the other soaps, making it much more realistic and true to life.

I thought GL did an EXCELLENT selection with the following newer characters: Alan Spaulding, Ross Marler, Dianne Ballard, Katy, Hilary Bauer, Lucille Wexler (now written out), Jennifer Richards and even Floyd for the lighter moments. In addition you have superb talent in Eve McFarren (Janet Grey) and Holly Thorpe, (Maureen Garrett, now leaving the show) and very good performances from Ben McFarren, Bert, Ed & Mike Bauer, Sarah, Barbara, Adam, Roger (now out), Amanda, Steve Jackson and Lainey. As you can see, I have mentioned just about everybody on the show in a complimentary way. I do think it's a waste to not have bigger story lines for Eve and Ben. I hope they will not be lured away because that really will be your loss. I'm terribly disappointed that Maureen Garrett has left the show although I understand her reason for doing so. She is so obviously intelligent and gifted as an actress that I felt she was being wasted anyway after Roger's death, with such a minor part. I remember when Maureen Garrett replaced Lynn Deerfield in the role of Holly. It was the easiest transition, something I never had to get used to. She brought a lot of warmth to her character and I hope her role will be brought back with another fine talent in order to keep the Ed/Holly story line going. Please keep the Bauer family going strong. They have been the strength of the show and must be holding quite an audience over all these years.

In contrast, the new Jackie is a disaster. Cindy Pickett was great but the first time I saw the new Jackie, I laughed--she was so unbelievable. For one thing she doesn't even look old enough to have a son Philip's age and her acting is not convincing. Andy Norris is another poor selection. He just doesn't look like an Andy Norris. Whoever is responsible for hiring these two did not do a good job.

I'm writing this letter because I think the Guiding Light is the BEST SOAP OPERA on the air now and I would like to see it continue in this category and not become similar to other soaps. By increasing the number of young people (Kelly, Morgan, Nola & Time) and letting them take over a portion of the show you have _already_ taken a big step in what I consider a fatal direction. GL already had enough talented people whose roles could easily have been expanded (Dianne, Katy, Hilary, Sarah, Adam, Bert, Ben, Floyd, Barbara, Rita, Stafford family, etc.) so it wasn't necessary to bring in new people. Alan Spaulding and Ross Marler currently have big roles and I think that should continue, along with Ed, Mike, Eve and Ben.

Unfortunately there will never be a soap that can in any way come close to what Another World was a few years ago when Steve, Alice and Rachel were on the show and Harding Lemay was developing the characters psychologically with outstanding scripts acted out by a superb cast. I feel privileged to have been able to watch a show of that calibre on daytime T.V.

Since I have been a fan of the Guiding Light for about 15 years, I hope you will take my suggestions seriously and not try to gain new fans at the _expense_ of long-time steady viewers like myself.

When the program is pre-empted, or interrupted, for whatever reason, there is a very strong reaction. In one case the viewers were particularly incensed because the interruption came at a peak dramatic moment and the newscaster said there was no news regarding the release of the American hostages in Iran.

To Whom It May Concern:
Although we are ardent fans of your network's Emmy-winning afternoon drama, "The Guiding Light", we recognize the importance of certain news events and the necessity of preemption at times. However, we were extremely disturbed at your interruption for a ten minute period of "Guiding Light" on Monday, January 19th, because the "special report" by Dan Rather and Leslie Stahl contained no _new_ developments and because Mr. Rather seemed to be prolonging the report, reaching for questions, instead of giving a brief update and wrapping it up quickly.

The most frustrating aspect of that interruption was the timing—at an extremely dramatic moment during a climactic scene which was the resolution of a story line that had been developed since last spring! Unlike prime time TV, soap episodes are not re-run in the summer, and we cannot see any scenes we miss.
We appreciate your excellent news coverage; in fact, we rarely miss the CBS Evening News. But that was one special report which could easily have waited until 4:00, when a serial drama would not have been interrupted (or you could have still shown the soap in its entirety). If continuous coverage of a news event is indicated, it would be better to preempt the entire soap rather than prevent the viewers from following the story. I can guarantee that the vast majority of viewers you reached (I assume it is the viewers you attempt to serve here) with that report were as upset as we were at its timing and lack of any vital or new information, and in that particular case would have much preferred to remain "uninformed" for another hour. I can't help but wonder if you would have interrupted "Dallas" as readily with that same report!
We are interested in the news, the hostages, and being informed of major events. But please keep in mind that it is possible to fulfill your obligation as a responsible news source without making your viewers too angry to hear a word of the report, as some friends told us was the case with them. Please consider messages at the bottom of the screen (the way local stations give weather bulletins without interrupting programming), brief news bulletins with details to be given later, or presenting the soap in its entirety despite the interruption.
Thank you for your time and attention.

Dear Sir:
I have watched "Guiding Light" now for months. When the plot all came to a climax on Jan. 19th, you interuppted the most important scene to put Dan Rather on with unimportant news concerning the hostages. Now I never will know what happened in the courtroom scene to

Jennifer. When you returned to program it had
all happened already and I was appalled to
think you'd do this to the public. Especially
after waiting months for it all to come to a
head.

Occasionally letters ask for information about a paint-
ing, hat, or other object that a viewer has seen on the program and would like to buy or have.

Dear Sir:
I am writing to ask for any information you
can provide about a dress worn by one of your
characters in a recent episode--the dress worn
by Eve McFarren for Lanie's wedding.
I would like to know the designer and whether
it is available in stores. Also I would like
a photograph of the dress if there is any way
that is possible.
Thank you.
Sincerely,

At times writers will comment on how the show has helped
them with a problem. This writer compares her problems to
those of Morgan. This letter is also indicative of the letters that ask if the writer can appear on the show or visit
the show.

Dear Guiding Light,
Hi. My name is ---, 14 yrs. old, freshman and
very eager. The reason that I am writing you
is because I am interested in being on your
show.
I watch Guiding Light every day. I never miss
it. The show is so wonderful, well what I
mean is that it helps me through a lot of problems I have.
My life hasn't been to happy lately. I've
been having a few problems that are similar
to Morgans. (Tim, Kelley, Nola) It has done
so much for me. And now my problems have been
helped, because Morgan has done an awful lot
for me just by her working through all of the
problems she's had.
I thank you very much for taking time to read
my letter. I love the show and everyone on
it. But once again, 'thank you!'
Whenever you need someone, even a very, very

short part, please let me know!?! I know I
could do a very good job. And I know I will
please you very much! Thank you, again.
Yours truly,

P.S. I have my parents permission to be on the
Guiding Light!

The following letter I think reflects the tendency for
viewers to develop a frame of reference based upon other
media experiences. Specifically, the writer here notes the
similarities between how working-class life is presented in
the program and in Tennessee Williams's work.

Dear guiding Light:
The scenes with Nola and her mother and broth-
er are starting to look like something out of
Tennessee Williams.
That's a real interesting little slice of
life, there. It's a nice contrast to the
middle-class-ness of the Bauer family.
Sincerely,

New viewers will request information on past story and
relationships so that they can better understand and enjoy
the program. Various soap opera magazines also convey information in response to questions from their readers.

Dear Sirs:
I have a request that at once is simple and
involved. I just began to watch "Guiding
Light" a couple months ago and I am still
struggling to determine who everyone is and
what connections each character has to the
others on the show. My request is for you to
unravel that for me. Could you please send
me a brief synopsis of each of the top 15 to
20 characters, identifying their family connections, their marriages, and their feelings
toward any other character (if it is especially relevant). I would greatly appreciate this
list and it would improve my enjoyment of the
story which has already begun to captivate me.
Thank you for your time.
Sincerely,

Some writers will call what they consider various errors
to the attention of the producers. These comments often have

to do with what the viewer finds improbable and distracting. The following letter cites annoying mannerisms of performers and a performer's (character's) behavior that seems unrealistic.

Gentlemen,
We enjoy your program each day. Several of us have noticed that "Morgan" and a few others are constantly fidgeting with their fingers. It really looks amateur. Also, she never carries a purse when she is shopping. Keep up the good program.

A small number of letters addressed to the show or its producers will request photographs. The largest percentage of letters to performers similarly include praise and a request for a photograph. The letters convey a sense of the enjoyment and importance of the program to the viewer.

Dear Producer,
My name is --- and I am 14 years old. Everyday Monday through Friday at 2:00 p.m. I always watch your program Guiding Light. I would like to ask if possible if I can have a picture or poster of the entire cast of the Guiding Light. I would like to hang it up in my room, because I will soon be going back to school and I won't be able to see the program. I would sincerely appreciate all your cooperation.
A sincere fan.

Dear Sirs:
I enjoy Guiding Light very much. But my most favorite people are Kelly and Hillory, and Morgan. If you don't mind I would like a signed picture of them each. I will be glad to pay for them. I like Kelly so much that I cried when him and Noahla where going to leave Springfield and get married. If you need anyone I will be here.
Your biggest Fan,
P.S. I am only 12 but I will be 13 on December 6.
PPS Sorry if I misspelled some names. And I would really like them pictures.

Dear Sir,
I would like to have a picture of Kelly and a
picture of Morgan. I just love Kelly he is
so good looking you can tell Kelly I said he
was good looking. My name is --- I wish he
would come to Altoona I would like to meet
him. So please send me a picture of Kelly and
Morgan and thank you very. Hear is my address. So I will be waiting for and answer
and the pictures soon. Write right away.
Have Kelly sign his picture for me. Well I
am going to close for now. Send me thoes
pictures and thank you very much.
From,

Dear Sir:
I'm not writing this letter for myself but for
my mother who is an invalid. As you can imagine, she spends most of her time watching TV
and her favorite show is "The Guiding Light".
I wonder if it would be possible if she could
receive a photo of the cast members of that
show. This would be a great thrill for her.
Thank you so much for your kind help.

The theme of viewers experiencing the characters as
friends is reflected in the following letter which begins
with a recognition of Hillary as a part on the show but ends
with a wish for the character.

Gentlemen:
We think Hillarey is so sincere in her part
on the TV program, "Guiding Light".
Hillarey makes one feel so close to her, light
a true and trusted friend.
She put Kelly and Morgan's happiness ahead of
her own and was instrumental in bringing them
together again.
We really like Hillarey and wish her the very
best!
Yours truly,

Dear Guiding Light Gang;
Hello! How are you all doing? Fine, I hope.
Me, I'm okay. My name is --- and I live in
Boonton, New Jersey.
I just wanted to say that you are all doing
such a *GREAT* job on the show. The show al-

ways leaves you hanging in suspense, just when
you were waiting for it all to happen, and
then it doesn't.
Watching the show makes me feel as if I already know you all, but I know on the show you
are just acting and you all are not really
like that at all in real life.
Well, keep up the *GREAT* work.  (Remember,
I'll be watching!)
Love always,

(Thanks for the #1 show in my life)

By far the largest percentage of letters are from women.
In fact, they appear to represent an even greater percentage
than that which characterizes the audience in general.  The
primary concerns are to see romantic couples united or reunited and to have their happiness last.  Conversely, they
often feel strongly about an evil character and wish the
character off the show, revealed, or punished.  Quite often
the evil character, such as Nola, stands in the way of the
ideal romance.
     There is good reason for assuming that the audience has
very strong expectations about what should and will occur,
but will also enjoy surprises, if these surprises do not violate fundamental expectations.  As Dolf Zillmann notes:

[Apparently] pleasant excitement can result
only from the anticipation of desired outcomes
when the anticipation is not tempered by a
substantial likelihood of alternative undesir-
able, even dreaded outcomes.  (1980: 134)

In fact, Zillmann emphasizes resolution of the conflict or
threatening situation as opposed to the emphasis on uncertainty that characterizes much writing on suspense.  What in
fact can be or is a negative experience, characterized by
fear and apprehension, should not be considered apart from
the resolution of suspense.  In fact "suspense and its resolution form a meaningful entity that must be kept intact for
the explanation of the popularity of suspenseful drama"
(Zillmann 1980:157-58).
     With soaps, there is also the fact and knowledge on the
part of the viewer, that the show will go on and that further complications will result, generating tension over the
well-being of liked protagonists such as Kelly and Morgan.
     The viewer, as is reflected in the letters, has a privi-
leged view of what is occurring, and their concern for a

liked protagonist, particularly for one who is the object of
some intrigue, will be reflected in their effort to, in effect, write the story. The viewer knows more than the protagonist and wants to use that information. At times characters in the story become implausible because they should
know what the viewer does. Letter writers will then criticize the characters for their stupidity, as in the criticisms
of characters who were not able to see through Nola's
schemes.

While some viewers emphasize the well-being of liked
protagonists, others emphasize the punishment of disliked
characters. I copied one letter from a couple who stated
they watched only to see Andy revealed for the evil person
he was. Again, knowing who the evil person is generates a
desire to manipulate the fate of the characters. The letter
writing and the threats of not watching the show or boycott-
ing the sponsors' products are all efforts to make the story
take a desired direction.

While viewers (and letter writers) expect the evil character will get caught and be revealed, for some the satisfaction lies in guessing how he will get caught. Here there
seems more of a distance and appreciation of the way the
story progresses. Some writers very much appreciate the
story on the level of a problem being solved. When Kelly and
Morgan are united and Kelly tells Nola off, one writer simply
says, "Bravo! How very well done that was."

The letters create or convey a sense of the audience
quite different from the statistical or impersonal artifact
of the rating process. The satisfactions and frustrations
of the audience member as a social being are many. In a
fundamental way, the program creates and stimulates a sense
of how life could and should be. As one letter writer
stated:

We all need to feel and know that there is
still normal, average, day-to-day living out
there. [Emphasis mine]

Ultimately, the interaction through ratings and letters
provides a continuing form of feedback, although it is problematically related to audience tastes and current program
content. Letters, in a sense, tell suppliers when story,
character, or performer are not attracting or developing
long-term interest and are often used to corroborate what
suppliers suspect about the appeal of the programming. The
pressure to carefully and continually monitor success is reflected in the attention paid to the ratings, which are correlated with suppliers' perceptions or expectations about how

the programming should affect--"pull"--the ratings. The speed and degree of changes that are made vary and depend upon a number of factors, including performer guarantees and the stage of the storytelling, as was the case in the "Carrie Story."

The orientation of the people working on soaps and the sources of rewards, including social acceptance and approval, involve more than satisfying the audience as measured by the ratings. Satisfaction is taken in telling interesting stories well and in reaching large audiences, in accomplishing organizational goals by getting a program produced quickly and efficiently, and in being nominated for and receiving awards. Awards are viewed, in the case of television's awards for daytime programming, as recognition by peers and, therefore, as particularly satisfying, but a temporary consideration.

Ultimately, the shaping values of competition and entertainment, as extensions of the economic interests supporting the system, justify the decisions that are made. Entertainment success is measured by ratings. Even if a program has a very large audience, the competitive pressures limit any commitment to any enduring creativity that does not pull the ratings. The search for novelty, in conjunction with the use of and articulation with reality trends, the ways these trends themselves change and shift, and the close continual monitoring of ratings success, generates considerable pressure to alter story to fit the pressures and "hype" the ratings. Letters play a more indirect or long-term role and are used, in conjunction with all the other sources of information, particularly to measure the appeal of a performer.

# 9
## *Guiding Light* as a
## Socially Constructed
## Reality

In general, then, the determining context for
cultural production is always that of their
market. In seeking to maximize this market,
products must draw on the most widely legitimated central core values while rejecting the
dissenting voice or the incompatable objection
to a ruling myth. The need for easily understood, popular, formulated, undisturbing, as-
similable fictional material is at once a commercial imperative and an aesthetic recipe.
(Murdock and Golding 1979:40)

Soap time is for and of pleasure, the time of
consumption, of a collectivized and commercially induced American Dream. (Porter 1979:
96)

Exploring the relationships between the world in a soap frame
and the conditions and processes that generate the symbolic
world reveals a complex process linking market situation,
organization goals, work practices, and performances. The
primary dynamic affecting the process and performances is the
competition for large demographically ideal audiences/markets
of women 18 to 49. As a symbolic form virtually created to
produce an audience, Guiding Light reflects the dominance of
marketing and the commercial process that makes it available.
ABC's recent success in attracting larger and younger
audiences, creating a brand loyalty to the ABC soaps, and
promoting and establishing General Hospital as the most popular soap opera led to changes in the Procter and Gamble
soaps, specifically in the case at hand, Guiding Light.
ABC's success changed the perceptions of what soaps could be
and should be like and intensified the latent conflicts of
interest between CBS and Procter and Gamble. Whereas CBS and
Procter and Gamble once dominated soap programming, this was
no longer the case.

The pressure and changes instituted to make Guiding Light more successful in competition with General Hospital affected virtually every aspect of the production process. They had an impact on the resources made available to the production, the relationship between CBS and Procter and Gamble, the authority structure and organization of the work process, the technology employed, work practices and related storytelling, visual, audio, and musical conventions, the stories deemed tellable and sellable, the perceptions of the audience, and the look of the show. All are interrelated and attest to the complex process linking the commercial goals of the communication/production process and the performances.

As several production personnel noted or admitted, demographic concerns and the competitive process were making Guiding Light more like its primary competitor, General Hospital. CBS was trying to affect Procter and Gamble's productions to make them more like ABC's. Sonny Fox identifies the underlying dynamic.

> The demographics, the figures in terms of the poulation breakdown and the habits and patterns of viewing, are the things that really are what shapes a network, and the reason that all three networks are more like each other than unlike—because the parameters that they deal with are the same. (Fox quoted in Klein 1979:36)

The general pattern is for the least successful network to be the most innovative and if successful, be imitated or matched in a year. Soap operas belong on Hirsch's list:

> In terms of program innovations, the tendency has been for the network with the lowest rating (formerly ABC) to differentiate its products from the others by introducing new concepts (Monday night football, higher levels of violence, tough documentaries); successful innovations, like price increases, have then been "matched" or imitated within a year by the remaining networks. (1980:86)

While soaps have not attracted much popular or academic attention until recently, they are commercially quite important. They are important to program manufacturers, distributors, and advertisers. They attract ideal female audiences/ markets for home and family care products; they ideally create loyal audiences/consumers for programs, commercials, products, and networks; they facilitate advertising campaign planning; and they are extremely profitable given their low production costs in relation to the revenues they bring in. That Procter and Gamble owned six soaps (now five) including Guiding Light, whereas the dominant commercial television pattern is for advertisers to buy "spots" from networks testifies to their attractiveness. For a manufacturer of home and family care products, soaps are an effective and highly economical way to deliver product messages to women in the home, where their products are largely used. The domestic romance of a soap is an ideal domain built around commercials that romanticize domesticity. Procter and Gamble's primary interest is what it costs to reach potential markets. The bottom line is the "cost per thousand viewers"--the lower the cost the better.

CBS as a distributor of programming has interests different from Procter and Gamble's. They are primarily concerned with selling markets to advertisers. Selling these markets is very much affected by the ratings of programs, which function as domains for commercials. The higher the ratings, and the greater the success in reaching a targeted audience/market, the more they are able to charge for advertising time. In addition, if they owned their own soap programming, they would profit even more and be able to control program content directly. When the Procter and Gamble soaps on CBS were the most popular, the arrangements worked out between CBS and Procter and Gamble were more satisfactory to CBS. ABC's profits from soap programs they directly owned had changed CBS's approach to the relationship.

The performances generated by the work process were changed in a number of ways. A useful shorthand term, which emphasizes the commercial interest in "product differentiation," is the term "look" of the show. On the one hand, Guiding Light was to be changed to remove negative characteristics of traditional soaps but, on the other hand, remain distinctive and appealing as it adopted many of the qualities perceived as responsible for the success of the ABC soaps.

The show's look was changed by: (1) increasing the percentage of younger characters, (2) telling "youthful stories" appropriate to the age group, (3) having fewer storylines, (4) increasing pace in delivery, cutting, and story movement, (5) adding elements of overt fantasy to the "realism" of everyday life, (6) shooting on location, (7) increasing "production values" such as more expensive sets and costumes and (8) giving an overall lighter, more upbeat air to programming. At the same time, many traditional practices remained, including the primacy of romance and a domesticated world. The mix of traditional and newer elements, and the overall nature of the symbolic world, is best understood by examining the nature of the work process mediating or linking market conditions and performances.

Procter and Gamble relies upon an advertising agency for administrative contol and, to a lesser extent, creative control. The distinction between managerial and creative control can be misleading given the commercial nature of the process. Compton Advertising hires the creative staff and production staff, while the technical staff is hired by CBS. Important changes were made in the authority structure overseeing the production process. Procter and Gamble recently assigned one supervising producer to Guiding Light to oversee the programming more directly and also increased the authority of the executive producer. These changes partially reflect the complexity of more elaborate hour-length programming, but also are a response to the increased pressure from CBS. Direct network involvement and the possibility of headwriters and network executives taking the programming in a direction that was unacceptable to Procter and Gamble were countered by investing more authority in the role of executive producer.

Procter and Gamble had previously dominated soap programming through their successes and the extent of their involvement in soap production. One area that has always been problematic is the role of the headwriter. There has been a surplus of creative/technical/managerial personnel, but it has not been matched by a surplus of capable and willing writers. As a result, Procter and Gamble has purchased shows from writers, established programs to develop writers, led writers to believe they could tell the stories they wanted to tell and then not supported them (LeMay 1981), and, in general, "put them on a pedestal." One consequence of the new authority structure was that the headwriter left Guiding Light in September 1982, when his contract was up, after a dispute with the executive producer.

Performances are directly controlled by the involvement of the supervising and executive producer in all phases of the production process from story creation and selection to final performances. The executive producer is more directly involved in the daily decision-making process, while the line producer monitors every episode and attempts to avert potential problems given his or her close scrutiny of the individual episodes and their realization. Control also derives from a general tendency to hire from within the production process and reward loyal employees by moving them from program to program, even if a particular individual is not associated with successful programming.

The stories that are chosen to be told and how they are told are strongly influenced by commercial organizational goals. The need to reduce uncertainty and produce a great quantity of material leads to a reliance on formulas, performers and personnel with proven track records, and a general perception of what has been or is currently successful as a model to be copied to some degree. Ultimately designed to create involvement, what works is employed to that end so that stories and popular performers are used for as long as possible. Stories are retold and performers/characters are literally resurrected. A basic justification articulated by production personnel is that there are only a limited number of stories and the basic challenge is telling the same story in new and interesting ways. A limitation on the reuse and the length of a time a story could be told or retold was potential viewer boredom and the danger of violating the moral expectations of viewers. The knowledge that viewers have of past programming also limits how quickly and radically story and character behavior can be changed. The degree to which character behavior was consistent was a matter of some pride and an indication of integrity for people working in daytime television.

The general tendency to tell realistic stories leads to the use of both common sense and news accounts (constructions) of social life. Stories are to be about characters people care about, understandable, believable, and contemporary, resonate with nonfiction accounts of the real world, but also be balanced and avoid controversial issues that would split the audience. Risk is minimized by avoiding offensive stories, scenes, and language, which limits the stories told and how they are told. The requirements of a serial format, the generation of a continuous stream of potential experience, and the pursuit of ratings, combined with reducing uncertainty and minimizing risk severely restrict storytelling on soaps.

The complexity of the process and the general pressure to complete the job within a schedule leads to a concern with preventing potential problems. Given the pressure to meet organizational requirements, particularly deadlines, workers from prop people to performers were oriented to getting the job done and making the process flow smoothly. Actors, for example, might object to a storyline for their character, but they took their complaints to a producer before an episode was taped. Similarly, directors and actors would invest in their work by discussing the realization of an episode before its taping. Potential conflicts with Program Practices are ideally identified before a story is told or an episode taped. When Guiding Light taped episodes on location in St. Croix, the director received a list of suggestions on how not to shoot scenes before he left for St. Croix. In this way the material taped on location would more likely be acceptable to Program Practices. Professional ideologies develop that emphasize meeting organizational imperatives, which are, in turn, dictated by the economic goals of the process. In this way, work is fitted to the structure and relationships undergirding the communication process.

The pressure to get the job done reinforces the tendency toward a concern with form over content, which is also reflected in the emphasis on the look of the show. This is not to say that people did not invest in their work or that they were unaware of the commercial imperatives affecting the production process. Virtually everyone resented the pace at which the episodes were taped and the routine nature of the work. The limited creative participation of directors and actors was particularly frustrating to them. Because story is a relatively secret strategic resource that can be changed at any time, and that is beyond the control of the directors and performers, there are limits to their ability to invest in and shape their work. The breakneck production pace and the constant monitoring of their work were also sources of constant pressure and frustration.

The hour-length format and the more elaborate storytelling has increased many pressures of work and also made it more fragmented. Increased budgets are tied to making more competitive and profitable products. The lengthening of the programs, the increase in their pace—more scene changes, faster presentation of lines, quicker cuts—and their more spectacular and glamorous production (increased production values) all contributed to the increased pace of the work process. The technological developments of videotape and computerized editing were largely used to realize those values and reflected the economic interests making the programming available.

Soap production is particularly interesting as a type of commercial television fare because of the opportunity to use feedback from the audience. Audience research, letters, and ratings are combined with past experience and the immediate reactions of personnel involved in the production. But even here, the demographic and ratings concerns are primary determinants in the decision-making process. Producers, directors, performers—all paid attention to the reactions in the studio and to the reactions of family and friends—but these sources could be contradicted by what the ratings indicated. While the "Carrie Story" was viewed as creatively successful, it did not pull the ratings as expected and was played out.

A great deal of uncertainty surrounds the communication process; and perceptions, decisions, and legitimations reflect this characteristic. The uncertainty was part of the drama and a source of excitement for some who were involved in the process. Past experience, professional judgment, and a reading of competitive patterns and trends all contributed to what they thought would work. Generally, letters confirm what is already believed, and those that are surprising, register trends, or call attention to errors and areas of potential risk are weighted more heavily. Letters seemed to be of greater importance in assessing the success of performers in appealing to the audience. Not much attention was paid to audience research other than ratings and summary statements of audience demographics. Two producers, in fact, asked me to explain the Nielsen summaries I had acquired. Audience research seems most important to higher level decision makers, and may shape perceptions (and justifications) at the production level only later. Both CBS and Procter and Gamble carry out extensive research, but how it is used remains problematic. Again, the important factor is how the research shapes decision makers' perceptions. The primary goal of gaining younger and larger audiences with faster, upbeat stories and the perception that the current soap audiences were more easily bored and somewhat less loyal were important determinants and justifications for current practices and recently introduced changes.

The competition for audiences as markets also reflected the changing tastes of the audience, its experience with other forms of entertainment, and its seemingly increased expectations. Program suppliers' perceptions were shaped by, or reflected a view of the audience as more sophisticated. Cultural competition across a range of media forms appears to increasingly "up" audience expectations or suppliers' views of what they have to do to garner the audience. The pursuit of profit through more appealing/expensive products generates increasing production values/audience expectations.

The production process generates a repetitive, pervasive, limited potential for experience and a limited view of social relationships and process. But there are also attempts to encompass and, in a sense, neutralize potential conflict with differing and different groups in society. The production process takes account of contending or contradictory forces at a number of points. The larger social world is reflected or embodied in the organization or occupational world and the specific practices involved in the story selection, creation, and realization. Some groups or interests have a larger say than others, but there may be, and are, contending or differing groups and practices affecting the process of production and in the process of production. This helps call our attention to the processes of change and variation in soaps and to the complexity of the relationships of a symbolic form to social forces and practices.

The Guiding Light production process generated a symbolic world emphasizing romance. Commercials and programming combine to create complementary symbolic worlds. "Domestic romance" and "romanticized domesticity" reinforce each other or certainly do not call each other into question. Love/sex and money/power are basic ideals if they are pursued or used appropriately. Social dominance and social inequality are accepted and glamorized but only if they are not used selfishly or vindictively. Domestic experience and psychological motivations/explanations are used to justify behavior in a symbolic world that is largely upper-middle class.

The conflict between individuality and sociality is the fundamental issue explored in Guiding Light. As a form of realistic melodrama, the backdrop to the performances is the centrality of competitive individualism in recent Western society (Palmer 1978). Beginning from a premise that individuality and sociality are inherently in conflict, the program explores the tensions and resolutions of the conflict in the context of domestic units. The larger social order is taken for granted so that the class structure, state, and corporate power are embodied in people who appropriately or inappropriately reflect the ideal resolution to the conflict. That is an Amanda, who makes corporate decisions out of resentment, or a Mark, who aspires to power and wealth vindictively, has failed to appropriately weld the contradiction. Afternoon serials focus primarily on the relationships between husbands and wives, friends and lovers, with parent/children relationships secondary and only explored when children are virtual adults (Skill 1983). Topics such as child beating, wife beating, incest, and homosexuality are largely taboo because they basically tear too deeply at the ideal resolution of the conflict within domestic units, based as they are on heterosexual romance, sex, and familial relationships. Given that, in soaps, community is based on the relationships between family and friends, such dynamics at the same time tear at the fabric of community itself.

This account provides insight into the simultaneous commercial imperative and aesthetic recipe that is Guiding Light. Importantly, it explores the social process generating the constructed reality and its connections, both social and cultural, to the larger society. As an extension of my approach I think it would be illuminating to study further the interplay between fictional and nonfictional "fiction," their sources and uses.

Just as the distinction between fiction and nonfiction can be a limiting one, so can the distinction between mass media/popular culture and education. Both are part of the consciousness industry although we tend to want to keep the two realms separate. Both "provide an important part of the ways a public can conceptualize its own activities—they are a vocabulary of collective consciousness" (Chaney 1979:10). Textbooks, for example, are socially constructed and contribute to the way individuals see the world "out there." Teachers typically assign or draw examples from media accounts of society to structure classroom understanding. Media accounts and textbooks are both used to make sense of each other to construct reality in classrooms. It is a matter of studying both processes of production and of using a variety of symbolic forms to discover how they play into each other. The understanding of the relationships between various symbolic forms, social consciousness, and social process would be greatly furthered by studies of their interrelationships.

The concept, or frame, of ideology is open to all manner of uses and abuses in this context. It is very easy to posit "ideological effects" given an emphasis on relations of production and attendant differences in power. Studies revealing the actual social practices and relationships shaping symbolic forms are easily used to explain the character of consciousness of people. Inferences are made about the effects of the performances or symbolic forms. If the bulk of the traditional "effects" research is suspect because of its emphasis on narrowly defined short-term psychological effects, the counter tendency is to posit large-scale, long-term ideological effects as an extension of a more critical approach, whether explicitly Marxist or not. Given that production studies reveal the power relationships and legitimations of the processes involved, it is particularly tempting to assume what needs to be shown.

A fundamental issue is how an ideological effect is demonstrated. Elliott (1982) and Chaney (1979) both cite Geertz's article, "Deep Play: Notes on the Balinese Cockfight" (1973b) as a persuasive account of the relationships between social form, relationships, and meanings. Importantly, Geertz views symbolism as inherently public or social in its nature. Elliott suggests that one way to demonstrate ideological effects is to focus on meanings and social process over time.

Instead of concentrating on private processes at a particular point in time, one is directed towards the social process over time, the development, application and change of different symbols and their currency in different realms of discourse from the mediated to the interpersonal. (Elliott 1982:614)

As Elliott goes on to state, this suggests the utility of participant observation and ethnographic accounts to capture the relationships between meaning, social relationships, and social process. The research must be approached in a nonreductive way to avoid identifying a simple list of needs that are filled. A fine example of the kind of work that is needed is Gans's description of an Italian-American neighborhood in The Urban Villages (1962). He relates the patterns of television viewing to social contexts and relationships, as well as the general values and beliefs of the people he studied.

While we undoubtedly can profit from careful long-term studies of content, we also need to make use of existing data and ethnographic accounts to explore social history and contemporary social process and experience. The traditional concern with messages and effects should be countered or complemented by an emphasis on symbolic forms and social participation. On the one hand, we need more studies of how and why symbolic forms take the shape they do. On the other, we need to know how and why people use symbolic forms as resources and the kinds of social participation they afford. A fundamental promise is that we can simultaneously develop an understanding of culture as expression and culture as instrumentality.

Once we have grasped the fundamental relation between meanings arrived at by creative interpretation and description, and meanings embodied by conventions and institutions, we are in a position to reconcile the meanings of culture as "creative activity" and "a whole way of life," and this reconciliation is then a real extension of our powers to understand ourselves and our societies. (Williams 1961: 40)

Ideally, we can explore the relationships of symbol system and social action, of culture and society, and go beyond the general and unsupported assertions about their interrelationships that are often made. If all of reality is a social construction and creation, it is imperative to study the ways in which reality is created or constructed and the ways in which symbolic forms and the experience they make available articulate with the full range of activities and meanings of a particular society. Doing so, we can grasp the interrelationships of the organization of behavior and meaning as a complex changing process. It is also through such an approach that I think we will be able to better understand society and culture as both an accomplishment and embodiment, as creation and replication. Such an understanding provides the basis for altering the symbolic worlds and "real world" we participate in or are invited to participate in.

# NOTES

1. Anthropologists have emphasized an "instrumental" sense of the concept of culture. Culture as a way of life or mode of adaptation is differentiated from "expressive" or "symbolic" culture, partly to distinguish an anthropological meaning from the common notion of culture as refinement. The rigid distinction between culture as instrumental and culture as expressive has been a limiting or blocking one (Williams 1976).

The term "popular culture" is particularly problematic since it connotes "culture" as referring to art, refinement, taste, entertainment. I will generally use the phrases mediated culture, or mediated expressive culture, but on occasion make use of the phrase "popular culture."

2. I will use the term "soaps" or "soap" in place of "soap opera" on occasion. A more formal label for the programming—"daytime television serial"—can be found at times in the literature, but I generally avoided using the term since it is unwieldy.

3. Studies of production have traditionally focused on news. American research includes Breed (1965), Tuchman (1969; 1979), Epstein (1973), Gans (1979). American research on nonfictional communicators includes Cantor (1971) and Faulkner (1971). One brief study of the nonfiction production process for prime-time television is by Espinosa (1982).

English studies of news include Schlesinger (1978) and Tracey (1978). An important case study of English documentary production is by Elliott (1972).

4. A recent book by Cantor and Pingree (1983) does have a brief chapter on soap production. MacDonald (1978) discussed the radio soap production process insightfully. Most of the academic literature on soaps focuses on "content" and "effects." An excellent bibliography on soaps by Patricia Tegler is included in Cassata and Skill (1983).

5. Sociovidistics refers to the study of visual communication as a sociocultural process (Chalfen 1974). Much of the theorizing on visual communication has emphasized "textual" analysis, often from the perspectives of art or psychology. Sociovidistics relates the study of visual communication to the study of social and cultural process.

237

6. Peacock, an anthropologist, identifies a number of areas of study or disciplines concerned with the relationships between symbolic forms or consciousness and social structure. It is a subject "wide enough to include studies of myth, ritual, and totemism; analyses of the relations between language and modes of classifying or perceiving; theories of the communicative process; psychoanalytic dissection of fantasies and dreams; works in comparative religion, sociology of knowledge, and the politics of ideology; the philosophy of symbols rooted in the writings of Cassirer; the pioneer efforts of such anthropologists as Benedict, Mead and Kroeber to abstract themes and plots from culture; sociologically oriented writings in literary and art criticism; and studies in folklore, enthnomusicology, and archaeology. The topic is broad enough to cut across conventional disciplines within anthropology and to unite concerns of both the humanities and the social sciences, but it is specific enough to define a certain focus for study, research, and contemplation (if not explanation) of the history and condition of man" (Peacock 1975:vii). I would add the sociology of organizations and occupations to the list.

7. La Guardia (1977) provides a brief history of Guiding Light, an excerpt from an early program and a summary of recent story. Cantor and Pingree (1983) cite a study of Guiding Light based in part upon scripts Irna Phillips donated to the Wisconsin Historical Society, University of Wisconsin - Madison, Madison, Wisconsin. Irna Phillips originated the show and wrote many of the scripts for both radio and television. The Museum of Broadcasting in New York City has a radio program on tape as well as a kinescope of an early television program. Both are available to the public. Readers who would like to consult summaries of the very recent programming should read The Soap Opera Digest.

8. The intensity of the drive to improve ratings led to scheduling and program cancellations during the time of the study and shortly afterward.

9. Ratings are used to determine the costs of commercials and profits of networks and program makers. Demographics are important since sponsors want to reach specific audience members. For soaps, sponsors want to reach women 18-49. For a brief discussion of ratings and audience studies, see Cantor 1980:75-77. Additional information on ratings and demographics of soap operas can be found in Cantor and Pingree (1983).

10. The pressures toward using younger characters/storylines are reflected in Harding LeMay's account of his experiences writing Another World for Procter and Gamble. "Procter and Gamble executives summoned the headwriters of their

six soap operas to a demonstration of graphs, slides, and other documentation which bolstered their demands that we follow the trend established by nighttime television. It was explained with explicit crassness, that high ratings among viewers over forty have little commercial value since middle-aged people purchase fewer tubes of toothpaste, bottles of shampoo, and jars of deoderant than do younger people. Consequently, future stories were to be aimed at a wider market through characters more easily identified with their under thirty contemporaries" (LeMay 1981:200-01).

11. While soaps routinely deal with highly dramatic conflicts and problems, there are some topics that are generally avoided. A story, which might be watched by many people, is viewed as "upsetting" to the audience if it does not pull the ratings at peak moments.

12. Writers of a particular soap will "burn out" after several months but are then rehired to write another soap soon after they have been fired.

13. A soap related industry was developing over the two years covered by the research. Performers made appearances in shopping malls; coffee cups and tee-shirts with program names on them were commercially available; soap performers regularly appeared on television talk and game shows.

14. Dan Schiller suggested the linkage between fiction and nonfiction as they draw from or contribute to "reality trends."

15. The major concern in many situations is that costs be kept down. Reshooting and reediting can be very costly.

16. Many roles are important, and, to the extent that they are carried out well, they are invisible.

17. Beginning performers earn between $400-$500, under-fives about $185, "stars" about $6,500 for an hour's performance. Some star performers earn between $200,000 and $500,000 per year (Brown 1982b:106).

18. In a personal communication, Richard Chalfen noted that the strategy is the same in anthropology--if the people in Hong Kong will never see the program, the "natives" will never read the ethnographic account.

19. Before the reliance on the organ, live musical accompaniment consisting of violin, cello, and piano was used according to one knowledgable informant.

20. Soaps are generally not syndicated for domestic consumption, although they are seen abroad. Guiding Light, for example, is aired in Italy. A study of audience reception of the program would be illuminating, particularly as an exploration of the emergence of an "international" capitalist media culture.

21. A new half-hour soap Loving was introduced in mid-1983 on ABC.

# REFERENCES

Barnouw, Eric. 1979. The Sponsor. N.Y.: Oxford University Press.

Barthes, Roland. 1973. Mythologies. London: Penguin Books.

Becker, Howard. 1974. "Art as Collective Action." American Sociological Review 39:767-76.

Bernstein, Richard J. 1978. The Restructuring of Social and Political Theory. London: Basil Blackwell and Mott.

Bogart, Leo. 1980. "Television News as Entertainment." In The Entertainment Functions of Television, edited by Percy Tannenbaum. Hillsdale, N.J.: Lawrence Erlbaum Associates.

Breed, Warren. 1955. "Social Control in the Newsroom." Social Forces 33:326-35.

Braudy, Leo. 1977. The World in a Frame: What We See in Films. Garden City, N.Y.: Anchor.

Brown, Meredith. 1982a. "The Making of Soap Operas: A Special Report." Soap Opera Digest 7(18):26-32, 92-93.

---. 1982b. "How Soaps Are Made, Part II: The Casting Exposé." Soap Opera Digest 7(19):26-33, 106.

Cantor, Muriel. 1979. "Our Days and Our Nights." Journal of Communication 29:66-72.

---. 1980. Prime-Time Television: Content and Control. Beverly Hills, Calif.: Sage.

---. 1971. The Hollywood T.V. Producer: His Work and Audience. N.Y.: Basic Books.

Cantor, Muriel, and Suzanne Pingree. 1983. The Soap Opera. Beverly Hills, Calif.: Sage.

Carey, James W. 1975. "Communication and Culture." Communication Research 2:173-91.

Cassata, Mary, and Thomas Skill. 1983. Life on Daytime Television. Norwood, N.J.: Ablex.

Cawelti, John. 1976. Adventure, Mystery and Romance. Chicago: University of Chicago Press.

Chalfen, Richard. 1974. "Film as Visual Communication: A Sociovidistic Study in Filmmaking." Ph.D. dissertation, University of Pennsylvania.

———. 1975. "Cinema Naïveté: A Study of Home Moviemaking as Visual Communication." Studies in the Anthropology of Visual Communication 2:87-103.

———. 1978. "Which Way Media Anthropology?" Journal of Communication 28:208-14.

Chaney, David. 1972. Processes of Mass Communication. N.Y.: Herder and Herder.

———. 1979. Fictions and Ceremonies: Representations of Popular Culture. N.Y.: St. Martin's Press.

Curran, James, and M. Schudson, eds. 1982. "Editors Introduction: Production of Culture." Media, Culture and Society 4:1-2.

Elliott, Philip. 1972. The Making of a Television Series. London: Constable.

———. 1979. "Media Organizations and Occupations: An Overview." In Mass Communication and Society, edited by James Curran, M. Gurevitch, and J. Woollacott. Beverly Hills, Calif.: Sage.

———. 1982. "Press Performance as Political Ritual." In Mass Communication Review Yearbook, vol. 3, edited by D. Charles Whitney et al. Beverly Hills, Calif.: Sage.

Enzenberger, Hans Magnus. 1979. "Constituents of a Theory of the Media." In Television the Critical View, edited by Horace Newcomb. N.Y.: Oxford.

Epstein, Edward Jay. 1973. News from Nowhere. N.Y.: Random House.

Espinosa, Paul. 1982. "The Audience in the Text: Ethnographic Observations of a Hollywood Story Conference." _Media, Culture and Society_ 4:77-86.

Faulkner, Robert. 1971. _Hollywood Studio Musicians: Their Work and Careers in the Recording Industry_. Chicago: Aldine.

Fischer, Heinz-Dietrich, and S.F. Melnik, eds. 1979. _Entertainment: A Cross-Cultural Examination_. N.Y.: Hastings House.

Flax, Steven. 1982. "Staying Tuned to Tomorrow." _Forbes_, July 19:66-72.

Forkan, James. 1982. "ABC Soaps Clean Up on Ratings Sheets." _Ad Age_, April 12:1.

Gans, Herbert. 1962. _The Urban Villagers_. N.Y.: Free Press.

———. 1974. _Popular Culture and High Culture_. N.Y.: Basic Books.

———. 1979. _Deciding What's News_. N.Y.: Random House.

———. 1980. "The Audience for Television and in Television Research." In _Television and Social Behavior: Beyond Violence and Children_, edited by Stephen B. Withey and Donald B. Abeles. Hillsdale, N.J.: Lawrence Erlbaum Associates.

Geertz, Clifford. 1973a. _The Interpretation of Cultures_. N.Y.: Basic Books.

———. 1973b. "Deep Play: Notes on the Balinese Cockfight." In _The Interpretation of Cultures_. N.Y.: Basic Books.

———. 1980. "Blurred Genres: The Refiguration of Social Thought." _The American Scholar_ 49:165-79.

Gilbert, Annie. 1979. _All My Afternoons_. N.Y.: A & W Visual Library.

Gitlin, Todd. 1981. "Media Sociology: The Dominant Paradigm." In _Mass Communication Review Yearbook_, vol. 2, edited by G. Cleveland Wilhoit and H. deBock. Beverly Hills, Calif.: Sage.

Goethals, Gregor. 1981. The T.V. Ritual: Worship at the Video Altar. Boston: Beacon Press.

Goffman, Erving. 1974. Frame Analysis. N.Y.: Harper and Row.

Golding, Peter, and Philip Elliott. 1979. Making the News. London: Longmans.

Golding, Peter, and Graham Murdock. 1979. "Ideology and the Mass Media: The Question of Determination." In Ideology and Cultural Production, edited by Michele Barrett et al. N.Y.: St. Martin's Press.

---. 1980. "Theories of Communication and Theories of Society." In Mass Communication Review Yearbook, vol. 1, edited by G. Cleveland Wilhoit and H. deBock. Beverly Hills, Calif.: Sage.

Hall, Stuart. 1980. "Cultural Studies: Two Paradigms." Media Culture and Society 2:57-72.

Hall, Stuart, et al, eds. 1981. Culture, Media Language. London: Hutchinson.

Halloran, James. 1981. "The Context of Mass Communications Research." In Communication and Social Structure, edited by E. G. McAnany, J. Schnitman, and N. Janus. N.Y.: Praeger.

Hirsch, Paul. 1972. "Processing Fads and Fashions: An Organizational Set Analysis of Culture Industry Systems." American Journal of Sociology 77:639-59.

---. 1980. "An Organizational Perspective on Television (Aided and Abetted by Models from Economics, Marketing, and the Humanities.)" In Television and Social Behavior: Beyond Violence and Children, edited by Stephen B. Withey and Donald B. Abeles. Hillsdale, N.J.: Lawrence Erlbaum Associates.

Hoggart, Richard. 1970. Speaking to Each Other. About Society, vol. 1. N.Y.: Oxford University Press.

Hymes, Dell. 1964. "Introduction: Toward Ethnographics of Communication." In The Ethnography of Communication, edited by John Gumperz and Dell Hymes. Special Publication 66(6), pt. 2, American Anthropological Association.

---. 1974. Foundations in Sociolinguistics. Philadelphia: University of Pennsylvania.

Johnson, John J. 1975. Doing Field Research. N.Y.: Free Press.

Klein, Paul. 1979. "Programming." In Inside the Business, edited by Steve Morgenstern. N.Y.: Sterling Publishing.

LaGuardia, Robert. 1977. The Wonderful World of T.V. Soap Operas. Rev. ed. N.Y.: Ballantine.

Leed, Eric. 1980. "'Voice' and 'Print': Master Symbols in the History of Communication." In The Myths of Information, edited by Kathleen Woodward. Madison, Wis.: Coda Press.

LeMay, Harding. 1981. Eight Years in Another World. N.Y.: Atheneum.

Levi-Strauss, Claude. 1963. Structural Anthropology. N.Y.: Basic Books.

Liebow, Elliott. 1967. Tally's Corner. Boston: Little, Brown.

MacCannell, Dean. 1976. The Tourist: A New Theory of the Leisure Class. N.Y.: Schocken.

MacDonald, J. Fred. 1978. Don't Touch That Dial: Radio Programming in American Life from 1920 to 1960. Chicago: Nelson-Hall.

McAnany, E.G., J. Schnitman, and N. Janus, eds. 1981. Communication and Social Structure. N.Y.: Praeger.

McQuail, Dennis. 1969. Toward a Sociology of Mass Communications. N.Y. Collier-Macmillan.

Merton, Robert. 1968 (orig. 1949). Social Theory and Social Structure. N.Y.: Macmillan.

Mies, D. 1982. "The Guiding Light--1948-83." Master's thesis, University of Wisconsin - Madison.

Modleski, Tania. 1979. "The Search for Tomorrow in Today's Soap Operas." Film Quarterly 33:12-21.

Murdock, Graham. 1977. "Fabricating Fictions: Approaches to the Study of Television Drama Production." In Organization and Structure of Fiction Production in Television. Vol. 1, Introductory Reports. Torino: Edizioni Radio Televisione Italiana.

Murdock, Graham, and Peter Golding. 1979. "Capitalism, Communication and Class Relations." In Mass Communication and Society, edited by James Curran, M. Gurevitch, and Janel Woollacott. Beverly Hills, Calif.: Sage.

Murdock, Graham, and J. D. Halloran. 1979. "Contexts of Creativity in Television Drama: An Exploratory Study in Britain." In Entertainment: A Cross-Cultural Examination, edited by H.D. Fischer and S.R. Melnik, pp. 273-85. N.Y.: Hastings House.

Newcomb, Horace. 1974. T.V.: The Most Popular Art. Garden City, N.Y.: Doubleday Anchor.

Newcomb, Horace, ed. 1979. Television: The Critical View. 2nd ed. N.Y.: Oxford University Press.

Nielsen, A.C., Inc. 1981. 2nd November 1981 Report, Nielsen National T.V. Ratings. Nielsen Television Index. N.Y.: A.C. Nielsen Company.

Nisbet, Robert. 1966. The Sociological Tradition. N.Y.: Basic Books.

Palmer, Jerry. 1978. Thrillers: Genesis and Structure of a Popular Genre. London: Arnold.

Peacock, James. 1968. Rites of Modernization: Symbolic and Social Aspects of Indonesian Proletarian Drama. Chicago: University of Chicago Press.

---. 1975. Consciousness and Change: Symbolic Anthropology in Evolutionary Perspective. N.Y.: John Wiley.

Pekurny, Robert. 1982. "Coping with Television Production." In Individuals in Mass Media Organizations, edited by James Ettema and D.C. Whitney. Sage Annual Reviews of Communication Research, vol. 10. Beverly Hills, Calif.: Sage.

Peterson, Richard, ed. 1976. The Production of Culture. Beverly Hills: Sage.

Porter, Dennis. 1979. "Soap Time: Thoughts on a Commodity Art Form." In Television: The Critical View, edited by Horace Newcomb. N.Y.: Oxford University Press.

Riley, Linda. 1977. "Conflict Strategies in the T.V. Soap Opera: A Descriptive Analysis." Master's thesis, Temple University, Philadelphia, Pennsylvania.

Rose, Brian. 1979. "Thickening the Plot." Journal of Communication 29:81-84.

Ruby, Jay, ed. 1982. A Crack in the Mirror: Reflexive Perspectives in Anthropology. Philadelphia: University of Pennsylvania Press.

Schechner, Richard. 1981. "Restoration of Behavior." Studies in Visual Communication 7:2-45.

Schiller, Dan. 1980. "Review of Photographers at Work: A Sociology of Photographic Styles." Studies in Visual Communication 6:87-90.

Schlesinger, Philip. 1978. Putting "Reality" Together. London: Constable.

Schroeder, Fred. 1979. "Video Aesthetics and Serial Art." In Television: The Critical View, edited by Horace Newcomb. N.Y.: Oxford University Press.

Skill, Thomas. 1983. "Television's Families: Real By Day, Ideal By Night." In Life on Daytime Television, edited by M. Cassata and T. Skill. Norwood, N.J.: Ablex.

Smythe, Dallas. 1977. "Communications: Blindspot of Western Marxism." Canadian Journal of Political and Social Theory 1:1-27.

Stedman, Raymond. 1977. The Serials: Suspense and Drama by Installment. 2nd ed. Norman: University of Oklahoma Press.

Steinberg, Cobbett S. 1980. T.V. Facts. N.Y.: Facts on File.

Tannenbaum, Percy H., ed. 1980. The Entertainment Functions of Television. Hillsdale, N.J.: Laurance Erlbaum Associates.

Thomas, Sari. 1982. "Some Problems of the Paradigm in Communication Theory." In Mass Communication Review Yearbook, edited by D. Charles Whitney et al. vol. 3, pp. 79-96. Beverly Hills, Calif.: Sage.

Thurber, James. 1970 (orig. 1945). "Soapland." In The Beast in Me and Other Animals. (N.Y.: Harcourt, Brace and Jovanovich.

Timberg, Bernard. In press. "The Rhetoric of the Camera in Television Soap Opera." The Journal of American Culture.

Tracey, Michael. 1978. The Production of Political Television. Boston: Routledge and Kegan Paul.

Tuchman, Gaye. 1969. "News, The Newsman's Reality." Ph.D. dissertation, Brandeis University.

---. 1973. "The Technology of Objectivity: Doing 'Objective' T.V. News Film." Urban Life and Culture 2:3-26.

---. 1979. Making News. N.Y.: Free Press.

Turner, Victor. 1969. The Ritual Process. Chicago: Aldine.

---. 1977a. "Frame, Flow and Reflection: Ritual and Drama as Public Liminality." In Performance in Postmodern Culture, edited by Michel Benamou and C. Caramello. Madison, Wis.: Coda Press.

---. 1977b. "Process, System and Symbol: A New Anthropological Synthesis." Daedalus 106:61-80

Wilhoit, G. Cleveland, and H. deBock, ed. 1980. Mass Communication Review Yearbook, vol. 1. Beverly Hills, Calif.: Sage.

---. 1981. Mass Communication Review Yearbook, vol. 2. Beverly Hills, Calif.: Sage.

Williams, Raymond. 1966. The Long Revolution. Baltimore, Md.: Penguin.

---. 1973. "Base and Superstructure in Marxist Cultural Theory." New Left Review '82.

---. 1974. "Communications as Cultural Science." Journal of Communication 24(3).

---. 1975. Television: Technology and Cultural Form. N.Y.: Schocken.

———. 1976. Keywords: A Vocabulary of Culture and Society. N.Y.: Oxford University Press.

———. 1977. Marxism and Literature. N.Y.: Oxford University Press.

Woodward, Joan. 1970. "Technology and Organization." In The Sociology of Organizations: Basic Studies, edited by Oscar Frusky and G. Miller. N.Y.: Macmillan.

Worth, Sol. 1966. "Film as a Non-Art: An Approach to the Study of Film." The American Scholar 35:322-34.

———. 1974. "Toward an Anthropological Politics of Symbolic Form." In Reinventing Anthropology, edited by Dell Hymes. N.Y.: Random House.

Worth, Sol, and John Adair. 1972. Through Navajo Eyes: An Exploration in Film Communication and Anthropology. Bloomington: Indiana University Press.

Zettl, Herbert. 1968. Television Production Handbook. 2nd ed. Belmont, Calif.: Wadsworth.

Zillman, Dolf. 1980. "Anatomy of Suspense." In The Entertainment Functions of Television, edited by Percy Tannenbaum. Hillsdale, N.J.: Lawrence Erlbaum Associates.

# Index

ABC, 64, 66; Broadcast Standards and Practices, 104, 115; programming, 68, 69, 70, 104, 115, 124; ratings, 69, 227, 228; soaps owned by, 68, 69, 70
abortion, 112–13
acting style, 51
Action for Children's Television, 102
Adair, John, 8, 248
Adam (character), see Thorpe, Adam
advertisers, 62, 63, 74–76
advertising, 228, 229; commercials, see commercials; costs, 63–64, 67, 89; radio, 80–81
advertising agencies, budgets and, 26
advisers, 99–100, 123
affiliated stations, 63
Alan (character), see Spaulding, Alan
alcoholism, 99, 113
All My Children, 20, 31, 64, 66, 68–71, 101, 103, 165
alternate world in soaps, 49–50, 53, 60; commercials in context of, 76–77
Amanda (character), see McFarren, Amanda
Andy (character), see Nors, Andy
Another World, 26, 66, 92, 134, 238–239
Aquafresh (tooth paste), 76
Ashencraft, Mrs., 81
As the World Turns, 26, 66, 69–70, 71, 95, 107, 211
audiences: casting and, 133; commercials and, 76; competition for, 22, 27, 28, 62, 226; demographic makeup, 30, 31, 62–63, 69, 70, 184, 186, 226, 227; interaction with, 13, 51–52, 54–59, 159–60, 181; letters from, 30, 182–84, 187–225; perceptions about, 9, 181–84; performers and, 21, 130; power of, 181, 183; product, as, 80; research on, 6, 93–94, 183, 184, 186, 231, 232; scriptwriting and, 82–86, 88, 89, 158; size of, 65; spot sales and, 68; stability of, 65, 182–83, 227; studio, 24; writers limited by, 126, 130
audio conventions, 173–74, 227
audio tracks, editing, 162, 163
auditions, 130–31, 132
awards, 225

Baby Fresh (moisturized pads), 76
Ballard, Diane (character), 45, 48; letters about, 202, 206, 210, 216, 217
Barbara (character), see Thorpe, Barbara
Barnouw, Eric, 30, 67, 103, 240
Barthes, Roland, 13, 240
Bauer, Bert (character), 41, 48, 114–15; letters about, 198, 212, 216, 217
Bauer, Bill (character), 193–94
Bauer, Ed (character), 41, 56–57, 90, 124; letters

about, 196, 198, 204, 205, 210–11, 216, 217
Bauer, Hillary (character), 42, 57–58; letters about, 203, 204, 216, 217, 221, 222
Bauer, Leslie (character), 215
Bauer, Mike (character), 41–42, 56, 132; letters about, 198–200, 204–06, 216, 217
Bauer, Rita (character), 42; letters about, 191, 192, 198, 202, 203, 205, 210, 211, 213, 217
Bauer family, 196, 204, 215–16, 220
Bea (character), see Reardon, Bea
Becker, Howard, 240
behaviorist studies, 11
behavior norms, 16, 17
Bell, Bill, 66
Ben (character), see McFarren, Ben
Berkley, Busby, 89, 173
Bernstein, Richard, 7, 240
Bert (character), see Bauer, Bert
B-52s (singing group), 90
blocking scenes, 138
Bogart, Leo, 5, 240
bombs, making of, 108
boom operators, 138
Bounce (fabric softener), 74
Bounty (paper towels), 74
boycotts, 102, 103, 116
Bradley, Joe (character), 45, 206
brand loyalty, 66, 72
Braudy, Leo, 77, 240
Breed, Warren, 184, 237, 240
bridges, 179
Brown, Lisa, 6, 63, 189, 209
Brown, Meredith, 6, 63, 239, 240
budgets: secrecy concerning, 22, 25–27; writers limited by, 125

business activities, portrayal of, 35

"cameo" appearances, 90
camera conventions, 164–73
camerapersons, 25, 138, 155, 164–65
cameras: fixed, 168, 170–71; handheld, 169; steady cam, 169
camera techniques, 78
Cantor, Muriel, 35, 64, 112, 181, 237, 238, 240
Capitol, 66, 70, 183
Carey, James, 1, 8, 10, 11, 241
Carrie (character), see Marler, Carrie
Cassata, Mary, 237, 241
casting, 130–34
Cawelti, John, 61, 83, 241
CBS, 62, 64, 66, 103; leasing of shows, 67, 69–70; Procter and Gamble and, 67–70, 81, 226, 227, 228; programming, 85, 124, 135; Program Practices, 103–05, 109, 112, 113–16, 127; ratings, 69, 72, 92; research, 232
censorship, 103–16, 230–31
Chalfen, Richard, 8, 237, 239, 241
Chamberlain, Henry (character), 40, 47, 48, 56–57
Chamberlain, Vanessa (character), 40, 47, 48, 60; letters about, 198, 199, 202, 205, 206, 210
Chaney, David, 3, 4, 6, 8–9, 49, 82, 241; fiction-nonfiction distinction, 15; ideological effects, 234; perceptions about audience, 181
characters, 230; audience desired and, 85; development, 100, 129, 134; emphasis on, 101; ethnic

background, 38–39, 48;
identification with, 13,
51–52, 54–59, 159–60, 181;
letters concerning, 188,
189, 196–99; plot vs.,
101; Procter and Gamble
emphasis on, 101
Charmin (toilet paper), 75
child abuse, 86, 233
children as characters, 48
close-ups, 140, 141, 167, 168
172–73; final takes, 73,
171–72
Coast (soap), 74
Colby, Derek (character), 44,
45
Colgate-Palmolive Peet, 67
Collins, Judy, 90, 180
Columbia, 66
commercials: audience characteristics and, 31, 63,
227–28; competitors, limitations on, 67; insertion,
24; pace of, 160; primacy
of, 73; programming linked
to, 31, 64; sample list,
73–76; spot, 67–68, 228
communication anthropological
studies, 8–9, 10, 11;
technology, forms of, 1;
television role, 4
communications industry: audience influence by, on,
181–84; power of, 181
communicator-audience interaction, 181–82
competitiveness, 22, 27, 28,
62, 226
Compton Advertising, 67, 229
computerized editing, 161–63,
174, 231
Conboy Productions, John, 66
concensus on values, 226
consciousness industry, 4
consultants, 99–100
continuity, audience affected
by, 51–52
contract players, see performers

controversy, avoidance of,
230, 233
conventions, 158–60; 227;
audio, 173–74, 227;
musical, 174–80, 227;
visual, 161–73, 227
Cooke, Jennifer, 91, 189
Corday Productions, 66
corporations: decision making in, 28, 30, 103–16;
home and family care
products, 62–63; risk
reduction by, 103–16;
scripts and, 82–86;
uncertainty reduction by,
89–102
cost per thousand viewers,
67, 228
costumes, 123, 125–26, 135;
"look" of show and, 87,
88, 228, 231
"crawl," see credits, screen
credits, screen, 95, 98
crews, 24, 25, 26, 123, 126,
138; boredom, 25; salaries
of, 26
Crisco (oil), 74, 75
critical letters, 188, 221,
232
crowd scenes, 167–68
cults, 97–98
cultural products, creation
of, 7–8
cultural studies, British,
8–9
culture, 1–4, 6, 238; expression and instrumentality,
235, 237
Curran, James, 9, 10, 241
current affairs programming,
5
cuts: camera, 78; scripts,
127

Dallas, 65, 92
Dalton, Leslie, 132
Dash (laundry detergent), 74
Dawn (dishwashing liquid), 75
day players, 130–31

Days of Our Lives, 66
dead spots, 179-80
deBock, H., 247
Deerfield, Lynn, 216
demographic make-up of audience, 30, 31, 62-63, 69,
  70, 184, 186, 226, 227
dialogue, 47, 51
dialogue writers, 123, 125
Diane (character), see Ballard, Diane
digests, program, 184
directors, 123, 135, 138-44,
  230, 231; performers and,
  140-43; production
  assistant and, 23; writers
  and, 126, 141-42
disease, portrayal of, 107-08
dissolves, 172
distances, significance of,
  165-67
Dixon, John, 213
Doctors, The, 66
documentaries, 4, 5, 6, 15,
  18, 21
"domains" concept, 30, 67
Downy (fabric softener), 74,
  75, 79
Doxidan (laxative), 75
dramatic programming: extent
  of, 2, 5; fictional nature
  of, 15; soap operas, see
  soap operas; symbols in,
  12-13; types of, 4, 15
dreams, 173, 174, 179
dress rehearsal, 138
Duke (character), 161
Duncan Hines (cake mix), 75
Dynasty, 65

echoes, 174
ectopic pregnancy, 203-04
Ed (character), see Bauer, Ed
Edge of Night, 20-25, 30, 66,
  97-98, 114, 125; budget,
  26; camera work, 165,
  167-68, 169; censorship,
  104, 113, 114, 115; future

story, 27; letters, 193;
  music, 175; ratings, 185;
  taping, 161
editing, 143-44, 161-64, 171;
  computerized, 161-63, 174,
  231; pick up edits, 144,
  171
editors, power of, 163
Elizabeth (character), see
  Marler, Elizabeth
Elliott, Jane, 186, 189
Elliott, Phillip, 4, 16, 89,
  90, 91, 241; advisers
  advocated, 99; ideological
  effects, 234-35; meaning,
  creation of, 8-9; methodology, 16-17; phenomenological approach, 32; uncertainty, on, 89
Enzenberger, Hans Magnus, 4,
  241
Epstein, Edward Jay, 237, 241
Espinosa, Paul, 237, 242
ethnic background of characters in soaps, 38-39, 48
ethnographic behavior, 6, 7,
  8; Chaney on, 9
Evans, Jennifer Richards
  (character), 42, 52, 216,
  219
Evans, Mark (character), 42,
  48, 52, 58, 60, 233
Eve (character), see McFarren, Eve
experiences: limited por-
  trayal of, 34, 53; meanings attached to, 1, 6,
  14, 16; mediated and
  unmediated, 4, 6
experts, consulting, 99-100
extras, 27, 125, 130

"fades," 78
Fairness Doctrine, 112
family life, portrayal of,
  34, 49, 53-54
fan magazines, 184, 197,
  201, 220

fans, see audiences
fantasies of characters, 159, 173, 228
Faulkner, Robert, 121, 237, 242
fiction-nonfiction distinction, 15
filmmaking, studies of, 8
filters, sound, 173
final takes, 78, 171-72
Fischer, Heinz-Dietrich, 242
Flamingo Road, 65
flashbacks, 159, 173, 174, 179
Flax, Steven, 242
Floyd (character), see Parker, Floyd
focus research, 93
Folger's (coffee), 76
Ford Theatre, 170
Forkan, James, 69, 242
fortune telling, 106
Fox, Sonny, 227
frames, defined, 14
Frankfurt school, 7, 11
future story, 22, 27, 156

game shows, 65
Gans, Herbert, 11, 15, 21, 235, 237, 242; on audience research, 94
Garrett, Maureen, 216
Geertz, Clifford, 14, 242
General Hospital: character-plot relationship, 101; competitive position, 84-85, 182, 185, 186, 226, 227; ownership, 66; performers, 90; ratings, 68, 69; scripts, 50, 92; spot costs, 69; writers, 83, 91
Gilbert, Annie, 35, 242
Gitlin, Todd, 10, 11, 242
Goethals, Gregor, 73, 243
Goffman, Erving, 14, 243
"golden age," nostalgia for, 23, 25
Golding, Peter, 13, 226, 243, 245

gothics, sets as showing conventions of, 37
Gray Panthers, 102, 114
Grey, Janet, 216
Guiding Light, 6-7, 22-23; audience, 69, 84, 186; budgets, 25, 26; censorship, 104-16; history, 34-55, 122, 226-27, 238; music theme, 175; ownership, 66, 67, 83; performers, 90; production process, 135-45; ratings, 69, 186; scripts, 28, 83, 84-86, 226-27; setting, 36; spot costs, 69
"Guiding Plight," 147

hairdressers, 123, 126
Hall, Edward, 8, 165
Hall, Stuart, 13, 243
Halloran, James, 5, 10, 243, 245
headwriters, 122-33, 229; conventions used by, 153-60; performers and, 148-52
Hepburn, Katherine, 205
Hillary (character), see Bauer, Hillary
Hirsch, Paul, 89, 227, 243
Hoggart, Richard, 163-64, 243
hilidays: portrayed in soaps, 50; ratings during, 186, 187
Holly (character), see Norris, Holly
home and family care products, 73-76, 227, 228
homosexuality, 86, 233
Hope (character), see Spaulding, Hope Bauer
Hulk, The, 170
Hulswit, Mart, 96, 124, 196, 197, 210-11
Hummert, 81
humor, 85, 97; studio, 146-47
Hymes, Dell, 8, 243

ideal community portrayal, 53
illicit sex, 211–14
image of show, 86–88, 227, 228, 231
immediacy of television, 164
incest, 86, 233
individual development, family concern and, 54, 233
inserts, 171
Ivory (dishwashing liquid), 74

Jackie (character), see Marler, Jackie
Jackson, Steve (character), 45, 48, 114–15, 216
Janus, N., 244
Jennifer (character), see Evans, Jennifer
Joe (character), see Bradley, Joe
Johnson, John J., 244
Jones, Indiana, 51
Jones, Jim, 97, 98
Josh (character), see Lewis, Josh
Justin (character), 43

Katie (character), see Parker, Katie
Kelly (character), see Nelson, Kelly
kidnapping, 108
Kleenex Huggies (diapers), 75
Klein, Paul, 62, 227, 244

La Guardia, Robert, 34, 238, 244
Lainie (character), see Marler, Lainie
layered conversations, 159
leasing of programs, 67
Leed, Eric, 12, 244
legal experts, 99–100
legal procedures, presentation of, 108
legal threats, 102

LeMay, Harding, 51, 217, 229, 238–39, 244
length of programs, 159, 229, 231
letters, 182, 183, 184, 187–225, 231, 232
Lever Brothers, 67
Levi-Strauss, Claude, 244
Lewis, Josh (character), 40, 48
Lewis, Trish (character), 40
libel actions, 114
Liebow, Elliott, 23, 244
line producers, 135, 139, 144–45, 229
live shows, 161, 162
location shooting, 38, 137, 163, 167, 228, 230–31; camera use, 169, 170; costs, 126, 138; crowd scenes, 167–68; letters on, 188
logos, use of, 113–14
loyalty, familial, 54
Lucille (character), see Wexler, Lucille
lunch hours, 28
lupus, 107

McAnany, E. G., 244
MacCannel, Dean, 3, 244
McCord, Quint (character), 41, 47, 50
MacDonald, J. Fred, 237, 244
McFarren, Amanda "Wexler" (character), 43, 48, 55–56, 58, 60, 233; letters concerning, 199, 203, 216
McFarren, Ben (character), 43; letters concerning, 199, 210, 216, 217
McFarren, Eve (character), 43, 197; letters concerning, 199, 216, 217, 219
McIntyre, Sara (character), 45, 48, 216, 217
McQuail, Dennis, 89, 90, 244
makeup staff, 123
Mark (character), see Evans, Mark

Marler, Carrie Todd (character), 44, 57, 58, 186, 225

Marler, Elizabeth (character), 44, 198, 200, 206

Marler, Jackie (character), 43-44, 215, 216

Marler, Justin (character), 43

Marler, Lainie (character) 44, 216

Marler, Ross (character), 44, 56-57, 58; letters concerning, 186, 199, 206, 216, 217

Mary Tyler Moore Show, 134

mass culture, television and, 2, 4

Maureen (character), see Reardon, Maureen

media culture, 3-4

medical experts, 99-100

Melnik, S. F., 242

mental illness, 115

Merton, Robert, 10, 15, 244

methodology of study, 2, 7-11, 16, 20-33

Mies, Debra, 244

Mike (character), see Bauer, Mike

minimizing risk, 102-16

miscarriages, 203, 204

Miss Universe Contest, 66

Modleski, Tania, 86, 244

monitors, 171

Monty, Gloria, 92

moral majority, 103, 111

Morgan (character), see Nelson, Morgan Richards

Murdock, Graham, 5, 13, 226, 243, 244, 245

music, 123, 162

musical catalogues, 175

musical conventions, 174-80, 227

musical directors, 174-75

musical instruments, 175

mysteries, 4

narrative, limits of, 82

Navajo, 8

NBC, 64, 66

Nelson, Kelly (character), 42, 52, 57-58, 161, 180; letters concerning, 180, 189, 195, 201-03, 206-09, 215, 217, 219, 221, 222

Nelson, Morgan Richards (character), 42, 161; letters concerning, 189, 195, 201-03, 206, 208, 209, 215, 217, 219, 221, 222

Nestle Toll House (chocolate chips), 76

networks, 26, 30, 31, 62; ABC, see ABC; CBS, see CBS; censorship by, 103-16; competition among, 227; leasing, 67; loyalty to, 72; market access, 63; NBC, 64, 66; programming, 63, 65, 67; ratings, 68-69; representatives, 126

Newcomb, Horace, 36-37, 245

news: advertising and, 73; story line and, 50, 97

news programs, 4, 5, 6, 15, 21, 27; preemptive, 217-19

Nielsen, A. C., Inc., 245

Nielson, Tom, 180

Nielson Reports, 70, 184, 187, 232

9-Lives (cat food), 76

Nisbet, Robert, 53, 245

Nixon, Agnes, 68, 102, 103

Nola (character), see Reardon Nola

Norris, Andy (character), 45; letters concerning, 195, 202, 206, 208, 215, 216, 224

Norris, Holly (character), 45; letters concerning, 192, 205, 206, 216

occupations, sets as indicating, 37

One Life to Live, 64, 66, 68-
  69, 101, 103
opinion research, 15
organs, 174-75, 179
overtime, 137
Oxydol (detergent), 75, 79

pace of show, 159-61, 228,
  231
Palmer, Jerry, 233, 245
paraphrases of lines, 152
Parker, Floyd (character),
  46-47, 52; letters con-
  cerning, 180, 203, 208,
  216, 217
Parker, Katie (character),
  46; letters concerning,
  203, 206, 208, 216, 217
participant observation, 20-
  33
Peacock, James, 15, 238, 245
Perkurny, Robert, 89, 91, 245
performers, 122, 123, 135-36,
  230, 231; appearance, 133-
  34; casting, 88; cameras
  and, 154-55; character
  identification, 148-52;
  commercials, appearances
  in, 78; contract guarantees, 128; day players,
  130-31; directors and,
  140-43; extras, 27, 125,
  130; firing, 134; future
  story and, 156; letters
  concerning, 188, 194, 196,
  232; letters to 188; noncontract, 125, 130-31;
  personal lives and script
  changes, 128; publicity,
  95-97; ratings, 184;
  rewards for, 145; sala-
  ries, 26, 64; standardization and, 84; tardiness,
  27; under-fives, 125, 130;
  writers and, 125, 129-30
personal care products, commercials for, 73
Peterson, Richard, 245

Phillip (character), see
  Spaulding, Philip
Phillips, Irna, 83, 124, 238
photographic techniques, 61
photograph requests, 221-22
Pickett, Cindy, 216
pick up edits, 144, 171
Pingree, Suzanne, 35, 238,
  240
plot: characters and, 101;
  complications of, 60-61;
  emphasis on, 85;
  repetition, 92-93
Porter, Dennis, 34, 50, 77-
  78, 226, 245
power, protrayal of, 32
preemption of program, 217-19
pregnancy, 110
premarital sex, 109-10, 211-
  14
press interview, 23
prime time programming: plot
  emphasis on, 101; risks
  of, 63, 65
Pringle's (potato chips), 74
printed word, role of, 11-12
procedures of author, 21-33
Procter and Gamble, 30, 26,
  62, 63, 66, 69-70;
  audience desired by, 72;
  audience research, 94,
  232; CBS and, 81, 226,
  227, 228; commercials, 64,
  79; corporate image, 102,
  103; expectations of, 184;
  hour programs and, 159;
  leasing by, 67; letters
  answered by, 188; ownership of shows, 66-67, 69-
  70, 83, 228; prime time
  shows, 64; production
  process and, 122-24;
  programing control, 66-67,
  69-70, 83, 126, 127, 135;
  publicity, 95-97; staff, 92
Procter and Gamble Productions, Incorporated, 67,
  135

producers, 25, 131; executive, 122-24, 126, 132-34, 135; line, see line producers; supervising, 122-24, 126, 132-34, 135
production assistant, 23
production costs, 27, 63, 109, 135-37; budgets, see budgets; lengthening program, 159; location shooting, see location shooting; performers and, 155-56
production process, 121-45; casting, 130-33; shooting, 135-36, 138, 161-64, 171, 182, 231; table of organization, 123
production schedules, 23-24, 27-28, 30
production staff, 122, 126
production studies, 7-11
profanity, 212
professionalism, 27, 155-56, 177
professions, 99-100
programming: CBS, 229; commercials and, 76-77; types of, 4-5
promotional patterns, 145
propaganda, 15
prop persons, 25
props, 25, 121, 123, 125
public affairs programs, 30
public television, 30
punishment of evil characters, 109, 207-08, 213, 224, 230

Quint (character), see McCord, Quint

Raiders of the Lost Ark, 51
rape, 97, 98, 99, 106, 192-93
Rather, Dan, 217, 218
ratings, 27, 68, 86, 88-89, 103, 182, 184-87, 188, 224-25, 230, 231; corporate timidity and, 103; sweeps, 89, 186
Reardon, Bea (character), 46, 47, 209, 220
Reardon, Maureen (character), 46, 57
Reardon, Nola (character), 46, 47, 52; letters concerning, 189-91, 195, 200-03, 207-09, 215, 217, 219-21
Reardon, Tony (character), 46, 47, 220
recapitulations, 153, 159, 174
recasting, 134
rehearsals, 24, 27, 64, 138, 170, 171; dress, 138
religious faith, portrayal of, 34
Renfield, Mrs. (character), 47
retribution, 109, 207-08, 213, 224, 230
Ricoeur, Paul, 11-12
Riley, Linda, 52, 246
risk reduction, 102-16, 230
Rita (character), see Bauer, Rita
Roger (character), see Thorpe, Roger
romance elements in plot, 92-93
Rose, Brian, 246
Ross (character), see Marler, Ross
Roussel, Elvera, 198, 199
Ruby, Jay, 6, 20, 246
Ruffles (potato chips), 76
Ryan's Hope, 66, 69

salaries of performers, 64
Sara (character), see McIntyre, Sara
scenes, number of, 159, 231
Schechner, Richard, 3, 246
schedules, shooting, 135-38

Schiller, Dan, 73, 239, 246
Schipp, John, 180, 189
Schlesinger, Philip, 237, 246
Schnitman, J., 244
school year, scripts affected by, 88
Schroeder, Fred, 158, 246
Schudson, Michael, 8, 10, 241
scripts, 84; availability, 145, 182; changes in, 122, 127, 135; conventions in, 84, 158; future, 22, 27, 156
Search for Tomorrow, 26, 66, 168
Secret (deodorant), 75
secretiveness, 22; budgets and, 22, 25-27, 28; story and, 22, 27
self-understanding, 6, 7
sets, 123, 125 126, 135, 228, 232; moving, 137; shooting use of, 165, 167
settings, socioeconomic, 36-38
sex: crimes involving, 86, 97-99, 106, 192-193, 233; illicit, 86, 211-14, 233; programming and, 4
Shirley, 66
"show business," glamor of, 21, 29
Simon, Peter, 75, 79
situation comedies, 4, 15, 63
Skill, Thomas, 233, 237, 241, 246
Smith, Jackie, 68
Smythe, Dallas, 80, 246
soap companies, 62-63
Soap Opera Digest, The, 238
soap operas: choice of as dissertation topic, 20-22; comprehension of, 29; economic importance, 6, 13; history, 81; opinions of, 5-6; prime-time, 65

social classes: characters of, 38-39, 41, 47, 48, 61; sets and, 36-37
social messages, avoidance of, 102
society: defining, 4; soap opera reflecting, 1-7, 233; symbolic forms and, 238
sociovidistic studies, 8
Spaulding, Alan (character), 39, 52, 55-56; letters concerning, 198-99, 202, 205, 206, 208, 211, 212, 216, 217
Spaulding, Hope Bauer (character), 40, 55, 56; letters concerning, 198-99, 204-06, 208
Spaulding, Philip (character), 39, 48, 206
spinoffs, 93
sponsors, 62, 63
spot commercials, 67-68, 228
Springfield, U.S.A., 36
staff reactions to show, 184
Stafford, Chet (character), 43
Stafford family, 217
Stahl, Leslie, 217
standardization of narrative, 82-84, 91, 95; cost factors, 84
star system, 90
start-up costs, 159
statutory rape,, 110
steady cam, 169
Stedman, Raymond, 51, 246
Steinberg, Cobbett, 6, 63, 65, 246
Steve (character), see Jackson, Steve
story, 82, 227, 229-31; future projections, 22, 27; letters concerning, 188, 195, 211-23; music and, 177-79; number of, 228

story conferences, 126-27
strikes, writers, 28, 148
Studio One, 170
suspense, 52, 54, 223
sweeps, 89, 186
symbolic forms, 16; Peacock
on, 238
symbols, 1, 2, 235, 236, 238
syndication, 65

tag lines, 152
take notes, 178
Tally's Corner (book), 28
Tannenbaum, Percy H., 246
taping, 135-36, 138, 161-64,
171, 182, 231
Taylor, Elizabeth, 90
technical staff, 24-26, 123,
135, 138, 227;
camerapersons, 24, 25,
138, 155, 164-65
teenagers: alcoholism, 99;
attracting, 70, 228, 232
telephone conversations, 159
teleprompters, 154-55
television, movies compared
with, 77
Television Production Handbook, 171
Texas, 26, 66, 90, 92, 182-
83, 215
textbooks, 6, 234
Theragram (vitamins), 75
Thomas, Sari, 10, 246
Thorpe, Adam (character), 44,
216, 217
Thorpe, Barbara (character),
45, 48; letters concerning,
206, 216, 217
Thorpe, Roger (character),
95, 129; letters concern-
ing, 199, 200, 210, 213,
216
Thurber, James, 80-81, 247
Tim (character), see Werner,
Tim
Timberg, Bernard, 164, 247

time condensation in scripts,
160
Tony (character), see Reardon, Tony
topicality, 50, 97
Total (cereal), 76
Tracey, Michael, 237, 247
Trish (character), see Lewis,
Trish
Tuchman, Gaye, 21, 90, 237,
247; camera conventions,
on, 165-67; news, on,
98-99, 184
Turner, Victor, 3, 8, 247
Tylo, Michael, 189
typology of mass communication, 17-18

uncertainty, reduction of,
89-102, 230
under-fives, 125, 130
unpleasant letters, 188

values, 16, 17, 226, 230,
233, 234-35; characters in
soaps, 49, 53-55, 61; letters concerning, 188, 196,
204-05, 207, 211-14
Vanessa (character), see
Chamberlain, Vanessa
videotape characteristics,
163
violence, programming and, 4
visual conventions, 161-73,
227
voice-overs, 174

Welby, Marcus (character), 79
Werner, Tim (character), 45,
203, 206, 215, 217, 219
westerns, 4
Wexler, Lucille (character),
43, 207, 216
wife beating, 86, 233
Wilhoit, G. Cleveland, 247
Williams, Raymond, 2, 3, 8-9,
20, 82, 237, 247; audience,

on, 66; scriptwriting, on, 83

Williams, Tennessee, 149, 220

women:  abuse of, 86, 233; changing roles portrayed, 35, 48; primary audience, as, 31, 62–63, 65, 69

women's rights, 115

Woodward, Joan, 121, 248

work, unimportance in lives of characters, 49

Worth, Sol, 8, 248

writers:  dialogue, 123, 125; directors and, 126, 141–42; future story and, 135; headwriters, 25, 122–33, 148–52, 158–60, 229; letters to, 195; performers and, 128–32; ratings, 184; strike by, 28, 148

Wyatt, Detective (character), 47

Young, Robert, 79

Young and the Restless, The, 66, 69, 70, 71

youth market, 70, 228, 232

Zaslow, Michael, 129, 200

Zettl, Herbert, 171, 248

Zillmann, Dolf, 223, 248

zoom lens, 170–71

# About the Author

Michael J. Intintoli is an associate professor of anthropology and sociology at Burlington County College, New Jersey, where he has taught since 1970.

Dr. Intintoli has published studies in visual anthropology, mass media, and popular culture.

Dr. Intintoli holds a B.A. from Columbia College, an M.A. from Teachers College, Columbia University, and a Ph.D. from Temple University, Philadelphia, Pennsylvania.

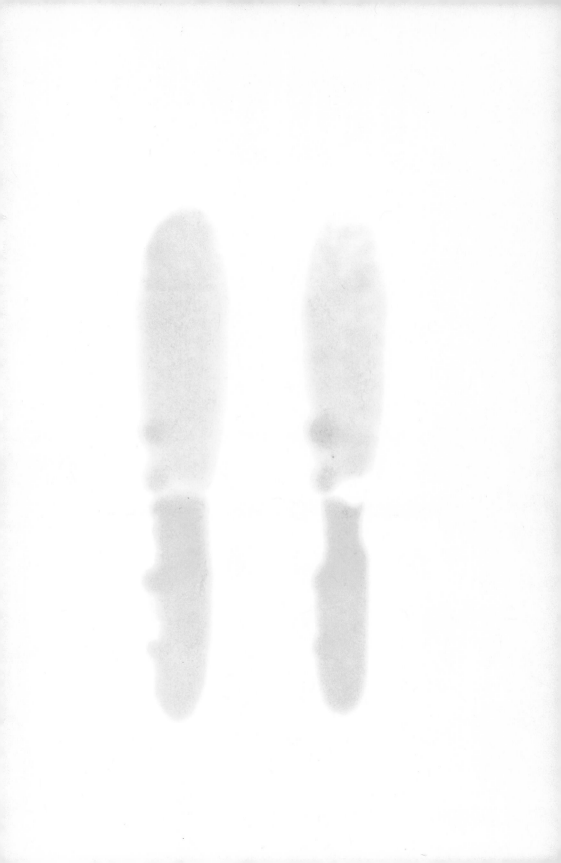

96903

PN
1992.77
.G83
I57
1984

INTINTOLI, MICHAEL
    TAKING SOAPS SERIOUSLY.